# Top Accounting Issues for 2007 CPE Course

CCH Editorial Staff Publication

.CCH
a Wolters Kluwer business

## Contributors

Editor.................................................. Colleen Neuharth McClain, CPA
Contributing Editors........................................... Julia K. Brazelton, Ph.D.
Joseph V. Carcello, Ph.D., CPA CMA, CIA
Steven C. Fustolo, CPA
Jan R. Williams , Ph.D., CPA
Production Coordinator ............................................. Gabriel E. Santana
Cover Design ........................................................Craig Arritola
Layout & Design................................................................Laila Gaidulis
Heather Jonas

This publication is designed to provide accurate and authoritative information in regard to the subject matter covered. It is sold with the understanding that the publisher is not engaged in rendering legal, accounting, or other professional service. If legal advice or other expert assistance is required, the services of a competent professional person should be sought.

ISBN 0-8080-1537-0
ISBN 978-0-8080-1537-6

No claim is made to original government works; however, within this Product or Publication, the following are subject to CCH's copyright: (1) the gathering, compilation, and arrangement of such government materials; (2) the magnetic translation and digital conversion of data, if applicable; (3) the historical, statutory and other notes and references; and (4) the commentary and other materials.

Printed in the United States of America

TOP ACCOUNTING ISSUES FOR 2007 CPE COURSE

# Introduction

CCH's Top Accounting Issues for 2007 Course helps CPAs stay abreast of the most significant new standards and important projects. It does so by identifying the events of the past year that have developed into hot issues and reviewing the opportunities and pitfalls presented by the changes. The topics reviewed were selected because of their impact on financial reporting and because of the role they play in understanding the accounting landscape in the year ahead. The topics examined in Top Accounting Issues for 2006 are:

- Leases
- Business Combinations
- Intangible Assets
- Balance Sheet Classifications
- Accounting and Financial Reporting: Current Developments
- FASB 123R: Share-Based Compensation

Throughout the course you will find Study Questions to help you test your knowledge. Examples are located throughout to assist you with comprehension of the course material.

This course is divided into three Modules. Take your time and review all course Modules. When you feel confident that you thoroughly understand the material, turn to the CPE Quizzer. Complete one, two or all Module Quizzers for continuing professional education credit. Further information is provided in the Quizzer instructions on page 279.

September 2006

## COURSE OBJECTIVES

This course was prepared to provide the participant with an overview of important developments affecting accounting. At the completion of the course, you will be able to:

- Be familiar with accounting and reporting by lessees, including capital leases and operating leases and the financial statement disclosure guidelines for each
- Prepare journal entries for a business combination
- Summarize the impairment rules regarding intangible assets
- Define basic concepts and terms associated with balance sheet classification
- Understand the selected Emerging Issues Task Force (EITF) consensus opinions discussed in the chapter, namely:
  - EITF Issue No. 04-5
  - EITF Issue No. 04-8
  - EITF Issue No. 04-10
  - EITF Issue No. 04-12
  - EITF Issue No. 05-2
  - EITF Issue No. 05-5
  - EITF Issue No. 05-6
  - EITF Issue No. 05-7
  - EITF Issue No. 05-8
- Identify the types of plans subject to FASB No. 123R

## CCH'S PLEDGE TO QUALITY

Thank you for choosing this CCH Continuing Education product. We will continue to produce high quality products that challenge your intellect and give you the best option for your Continuing Education requirements. Should you have a concern about this or any other CCH CPE product, please call our Customer Service Department at 1-800-248-3248.

---

**NEW ONLINE GRADING** gives you immediate 24/7 grading with instant results and no Express Grading Fee.

The **CCH Testing Center** website gives you and others in your firm easy, free access to CCH print Courses and allows you to complete your CPE Quizzers online for immediate results. Plus, the **My Courses** feature provides convenient storage for your CPE Course Certificates and completed Quizzers.

Go to **www.cchtestingcenter.com** to complete your Quizzer online.

---

One **complimentary copy** of this Course is provided with copies of selected CCH Accounting titles. Additional copies of this Course may be ordered for $27.50 each by calling 1-800-248-3248 (ask for product 0-0996-200).

TOP ACCOUNTING ISSUES FOR 2007 CPE COURSE

# Contents

## 4  Balance Sheet Classifications

## MODULE 3

## 5  Accounting and Financial Reporting: Current Developments

# 6 FASB 123R: Share-Based Compensation

MODULE 1 – CHAPTER 1

# Leases

## LEARNING OBJECTIVES

> Upon completion of this chapter, the practitioners should:
> - Understand the terminology of leasing
> - Be familiar with accounting and reporting by lessees, including capital leases and operating leases and the financial statement disclosure guidelines for each
> - Be familiar with accounting and reporting by lessors, including capital leases, operating leases, lease sale or assignment to third parties, and financial statement disclosures for capital and operating leases
> - Become familiar with the accounting procedures for leases involving real estate, including land, buildings and equipment

## OVERVIEW

A lease is an agreement that conveys the right to use property, usually for a specified period. Leases typically involve two parties: the owner of the property (lessor) and the party contracting to use the property (lessee). Because of certain tax, cash flow, and other advantages, leases have become an important alternative to the outright purchase of property by which companies (lessees) acquire the resources needed to operate.

Leases include agreements that, while not nominally referred to as leases, have the characteristic of transferring the right to use property (e.g., heat supply contracts), and agreements that transfer the right to use property even though the contractor may be required to provide substantial services in connection with the operation or maintenance of the assets (FAS-13, par. 1).

The term *lease*, as used in promulgated GAAP, does not include the following (FAS-13, par. 1):
- Agreements that are contracts for services that do not transfer the right to use property from one contracting party to another
- Agreements that concern the right to explore for or exploit natural resources such as oil, gas, minerals, and timber
- Agreements that represent licensing agreements for items such as motion picture films, plays, manuscripts, patents, and copyrights

A central accounting issue associated with leases is the identification of those leases that are treated appropriately as sales of the property by lessors and as purchases of the **property by lessees** (*capital leases*). Those leases that are not identified as capital leases are called *operating leases* and are not treated as sales by lessors and as purchases by lessees. Rather, they are treated on a prospective basis as a series of cash flows from the lessee to the lessor.

GAAP for leases include the largest number of authoritative accounting pronouncements of any single subject in accounting literature. Pronouncements that follow FAS-13 (Accounting for Leases) explain, interpret, or amend that pronouncement in a variety of ways; many of them arose as a result of attempts to implement FAS-13. Following are pronouncements that collectively establish promulgated GAAP for lease accounting:

FAS-13   *Accounting for Leases*
FAS-22   *Changes in the Provisions of Lease Agreements Resulting from Refundings of Tax-Exempt Debt*
FAS-23   *Inception of the Lease*
FAS-27   *Classification of Renewals or Extensions of Existing Sales-Type or Direct Financing Leases*
FAS-28   *Accounting for Sales with Leasebacks*
FAS-29   *Determining Contingent Rentals*
FAS-91   *Accounting for Nonrefundable Fees and Costs Associated with Originating or Acquiring Loans and Initial Direct Costs of Leases*
FAS-98   *Accounting for Leases:*
　　　　　— Sale-Leaseback Transactions Involving Real Estate
　　　　　— Sales-Type Leases of Real Estate
　　　　　— Definition of the Lease Term
　　　　　— Initial Direct Costs of Direct Financing Leases
FAS-145 *Rescission of FASB Statements No. 4, 44, and 64, Amendment of FASB Statement No. 13, and Technical Corrections*
FIN-19   *Lessee Guarantee of the Residual Value of Leased Property*
FIN-21   *Accounting for Leases in a Business Combination*
FIN-23   *Leases of Certain Property Owned by a Governmental Unit or Authority*
FIN-24   *Leases Involving Only Part of a Building*
FIN-26   *Accounting for Purchase of a Leased Asset by the Lessee during the Term of the Lease*
FIN-27   *Accounting for a Loss on a Sublease*

Following is a brief overview of the nine Statements of Financial Accounting Standards included in the promulgated GAAP for leases.

**FAS-13** defines a lease as an agreement that conveys the right to use assets (tangible or intangible) for a stated period. A lease that transfers substantially all the benefits and risks inherent in the ownership of property is called a *capital lease.* Such a lease is accounted for by the lessee as the acquisition of an asset and the incurrence of a liability. The lessor accounts for such a lease as a sale (sales-type lease) or financing (direct financing lease). All other leases are referred to as *operating leases.*

**FAS-22** addresses an inconsistency between FAS-13 and APB-26 (Early Extinguishment of Debt) arising from refundings of tax-exempt debt, including advance refundings that are accounted for as early extinguishments of debt. FAS-22 is covered in more detail later in this chapter.

**FAS-23** amends FAS-13 to specify that, if the leased property is yet to be constructed or acquired by the lessor at the inception of the lease, the lessor's criterion pertaining to "no important uncertainties of unreimbursable costs yet to be incurred by the lessor" is applied at the date that construction of the property is completed or the property is acquired. FAS-23 amends FAS-13 to specify that any increases in the minimum lease payments that have occurred during the preacquisition or preconstruction period as a result of an escalation clause are to be considered in determining the fair value of the leased property at the inception of the lease. FAS-23 also amends FAS-13 to limit the amount that can be recorded by the lessor for the residual value of leased property to an amount not greater than the estimate as of the inception of the lease. FAS-23 is discussed more fully throughout this chapter.

**FAS-27** modifies FAS-13 to require a lessor to classify a renewal or an extension of a sales-type or direct financing lease as a sales-type lease if the lease would otherwise qualify as a sales-type lease and the renewal or extension occurs at or near the end of the lease term. Otherwise, FAS-13 prohibits the classification of a renewal or extension of a sales-type or direct financing lease as a sales-type lease at any other time during the lease term.

**FAS-28** amends FAS-13 to specify the appropriate accounting for sale-leaseback transactions depending on the percentage amount of the property that the seller-lessee leases back (substantially all of the property, a minor portion of the property, or more than a minor portion of the property but less than substantially all) and whether the lease is classified as a capital lease or an operating lease.

**FAS-29** amends FAS-13 to provide a new definition for *contingent rentals* as those that cannot be determined at the inception of the lease because they depend on future factors or events. Rental payments based on future sales volume, future machine hours, future interest rates, and future price indexes are examples of contingent rentals. Contingent rentals can either increase or decrease lease payments.

**FAS-91** establishes accounting and reporting standards for nonrefundable fees and costs associated with lending, committing to lend, or purchasing a loan or group of loans. Under FAS-91, direct loan origination fees and costs, including initial direct costs incurred by a lessor in negotiating and consummating a lease, are offset against each other and the net amount is deferred and recognized over the life of the loan as an adjustment to the yield on the loan. The provisions of FAS-91 apply to all types of loans, including debt securities, and to all types of lenders, including banks, thrift institutions, insurance companies, mortgage bankers, and other financial and nonfinancial institutions. However, FAS-91 does not apply to nonrefundable fees and costs that are associated with originating or acquiring loans which are carried at market value.

**FAS-98** amends FAS-13 to establish a new definition of *penalty* and *lease term* for all leasing transactions. FAS-98 specifies the appropriate accounting for a seller-lessee in a sale-leaseback transaction involving real estate, including real estate with equipment, such as manufacturing facilities, power plants, furnished office buildings, etc. FAS-98 establishes the appropriate accounting for a sale-leaseback transaction in which property improvements or integral equipment is sold to a purchaser-lessor and leased back by the seller-lessee who retains the ownership of the underlying land. FAS-98 also provides the appropriate accounting for sale-leaseback transactions involving real estate with equipment that include separate sale and leaseback agreements for the real estate and the equipment (a) with the same entity or related parties and (b) that are consummated at or near the same time, suggesting that they were negotiated as a package.

**FAS-145** amends FAS-13 to eliminate certain inconsistencies between how sale-leaseback transactions are accounted for under FAS-98 or FAS-28 and how certain lease modifications, where the modification results in the lease transaction being similar to a sale-leaseback, have been accounted for under FAS-13.

## BACKGROUND

Some lease agreements are such that an asset and a related liability should be reported on the balance sheet of the lessee enterprise. The distinction is one of *substance over form* when the transaction actually *transfers substantially all the benefits and risks inherent in the ownership of the property.*

Established in GAAP are criteria to determine whether a lease transaction is in substance a transfer of the incidents of ownership. If, *at its inception*, a lease meets one or more of the following four criteria, the lease is classified as a capital lease (FAS-13, par. 7):

1. By the end of the lease term, ownership of the leased property is transferred to the lessee.
2. The lease contains a bargain purchase option.
3. The lease term is substantially (75% or more) equal to the estimated useful life of the leased property.
4. At the inception of the lease, the present value of the minimum lease payments, with certain adjustments, is 90% or more of the fair value of the leased property.

## TERMINOLOGY

The authoritative literature includes many terms that are important for an understanding of lease accounting. Several of these terms are explained below.

**Capital lease.** A capital lease transfers the benefits and risks inherent in the ownership of the property to the lessee, who accounts for the lease as an acquisition of an asset and the incurrence of a liability (FAS-13, par. 6a).

**Sales-type lease.** A sales-type lease is a type of capital lease that results in a manufacturer's or dealer's profit or loss to the lessor and transfers substantially all the benefits and risks inherent in the ownership of the leased property to the lessee; in addition, (a) the minimum lease payments are reasonably predictable of collection and (b) no important uncertainties exist regarding costs to be incurred by the lessor under the terms of the lease (FAS-13, par. 6b).

In a sales-type lease, the *fair value* of the leased property at the inception of the lease differs from the cost or carrying amount because a manufacturer's or dealer's profit or loss exists. Fair value usually is the *normal selling price* of the property.

**Direct financing lease.** A direct financing lease is a type of capital lease that does *not* result in a manufacturer's or dealer's profit or loss to the lessor, but does transfer substantially all the benefits and risks inherent in the owner-ship of the leased property to the lessee; in addition, (a) the minimum lease payments are reasonably predictable of collection and (b) no important uncertainties exist regarding costs to be incurred by the lessor under the terms of the lease (FAS-13, par. 6b).

Separately identifying sales-type and direct financing leases is an accounting issue for the lessor only, who accounts for the two types of capital leases differ-ently, as described later in this chapter. Both types of leases transfer substantially all the benefits and risks inherent in the ownership of the leased property to the lessee, who records the transaction as a *capital lease*.

**Fair value.** Fair value is the price for which the leased property could be sold between unrelated parties in an arm's-length transaction (FAS-13, par. 5c). For the manufacturer or dealer, fair value usually is the normal selling price less trade or volume discounts. Fair value may be less than the normal selling price, however, and sometimes less than the cost of the property.
For others, fair value usually is cost less trade or volume discounts. Fair value may be less than cost, however, especially in circumstances in which a long period elapses between the acquisition of the property by the lessor and the inception of a lease.

**Fair rental.** Fair rental is the rental rate for similar property under similar lease terms and conditions.

**Related parties.** Related parties are one or more entities subject to the significant influence over the operating and financial policies of another entity (FAS-13, par. 5a).

**Executory costs.** Executory costs are items such as insurance, maintenance, and taxes paid in connection with the leased property (FAS-13, par. 7d).

**Bargain purchase option.** A bargain purchase option is a lessee's option to purchase the leased property at a sufficiently low price that makes the exercise of the option relatively certain (FAS-13, par. 5d).

**Bargain renewal option.** A bargain renewal option is a lessee's option to renew the lease at a sufficiently low rental that makes the exercise of the option relatively certain (FAS-13, par. 5e).

**Estimated economic life.** Estimated economic life is the estimated remaining useful life of the property for the purpose for which it was intended, regardless of the term of the lease (FAS-13, par. 5g).

**Estimated residual value.** Estimated residual value is the estimated fair value of the leased property at the end of the lease term. The estimated residual value shall not exceed the amount estimated at the inception of the lease except for the effect of any increases that result during the construction or preacquisition period, because of escalation provisions in the lease (FAS-13, par. 5h).

**Unguaranteed residual value.** Unguaranteed residual value is the estimated fair value of the leased property at the end of the lease term that is not guaranteed by either the lessee or a third party unrelated to the lessor. A guarantee by a third party related to the lessee is considered a lessee guarantee (FAS-13, par. 5i).

**Lessee's incremental borrowing rate.** The lessee's incremental borrowing rate is the rate of interest that the lessee would have had to pay at the inception of the lease to borrow the funds, on similar terms, to purchase the leased property (FAS-13, par. 5l).

**Inception of lease.** The inception of the lease is the date of the lease agreement or the date of a written commitment signed by the parties involved that sets forth the principal provisions of the lease transaction. A written commitment that does not contain all of the principal provisions of the lease transaction does not establish the inception date (FAS-23, par. 6).

**Interest rate implicit in the lease.** The interest rate implicit in the lease is the rate that, when applied to certain items (enumerated below), results in an aggregate present value equal to the fair value of the leased property at the beginning of the lease term, less any investment credit expected to be realized and retained by the lessor. The discount rate is applied to (a) the minimum lease payments, excluding executory costs such as insurance, maintenance, and taxes (including any profit thereon) that are paid by the lessor and (b) the estimated fair value of the property at the end of the lease term, exclusive of any portion guaranteed by either the lessee or a third party unrelated to the lessor (unguaranteed residual value) (FAS-13, par. 5k).

**Initial direct costs.** The definition of *initial direct costs* is as follows (FAS-91, par. 24):

> Initial direct costs (Initial direct cost shall be offset by nonrefundable fees that are yield adjustments as prescribed in FAS-91). Only those costs incurred by the lessor that are (a) costs to originate a lease incurred in transactions with independent third parties that (i) result directly from and are essential to acquire that lease and (ii) would not have been incurred had that leasing transaction not occurred and (b) certain costs directly related to specified activities performed by the lessor for that lease. Those activities are: evaluating the prospective lessee's financial condition; evaluating and recording guarantees, collateral, and other security arrangements; negotiating lease terms; preparing and processing lease documents; and closing the transaction. The costs directly related to those activities shall include only that portion of the employees' total compensation and payroll-related fringe benefits directly related to time spent performing those activities for that lease and other costs related to those activities that would not have been incurred but for that lease. Initial direct costs shall not include costs related to activities performed by the lessor for advertising, soliciting potential lessees, servicing existing leases, and other ancillary activities related to establishing and monitoring credit policies, supervision, and administration. Initial direct costs shall not include administrative costs, rent, depreciation, any other occupancy and equipment costs, and employees' compensation and fringe benefits related to activities described in the previous sentence, unsuccessful origination efforts, and idle time.

In determining the net amount of initial direct costs in a leasing transaction under FAS-13, a lessor shall apply the provisions of FAS-91 relating to loan origination fees, commitment fees, and direct loan origination costs of completed loans. Initial direct costs are accounted for by lessors as part of the investment in a direct financing lease.

**OBSERVATION**

The recognition of a portion of the unearned income at the inception of a lease transaction to offset initial direct costs is not permitted (FAS-91, par. 23).

**Contingent rentals.** Contingent rentals are those that cannot be determined at the inception of the lease because they depend on future factors or events. Rental payments based on future sales volume, future machine hours, future interest rates, and future price indexes are examples of contingent rentals. Contingent rentals can either increase or decrease lease payments (FAS-29, par. 11).

Increases in minimum lease payments that occur during the preacquisition or construction period as a result of an escalation clause in the lease are not considered contingent rentals (FAS-29, par. 11).

**Lease term.** The lease term includes all of the following (FAS-98, par. 22a):
- Any fixed noncancelable term
- Any period covered by a bargain renewal option
- Any period in which penalties are imposed in an amount that at the inception of the lease reasonably assures the renewal of the lease by the lessee
- Any period covered by ordinary renewal options during which a guarantee by the lessee of the lessor's debt that is directly or indirectly related to the leased property is expected to be in effect or a loan from the lessee to the lessor that is directly or indirectly related to the leased property is expected to be outstanding

> **NOTE**
>
> The phrase *indirectly related to the leased property* is used to cover situations that in substance are guarantees of the lessor's debt or loans to the lessor by the lessee that are related to the leased property, but are structured in such a manner that they do not represent a direct guarantee or loan.

- Any period covered by ordinary renewal options preceding the date on which a bargain purchase option is exercisable
- Any period representing renewals or extensions of the lease at the lessor's option. A lease term does not extend beyond the date a bargain purchase option becomes exercisable.

**Noncancelable lease term.** A noncancelable lease term is a provision in a lease agreement that specifies that the lease may be canceled only (a) on some remote contingency, (b) with permission of the lessor, or (c) if the lessee enters into a new lease with the same lessor (FAS-98, par. 22a).

**Penalty.** The term *penalty* refers to any outside factor or provision of the lease agreement that does or can impose on the lessee the requirement to disburse cash, incur or assume a liability, perform services, surrender or transfer an asset or rights to an asset or otherwise forego an economic benefit, or suffer an economic detriment (FAS-98, par. 22b).

## Minimum Lease Payments

Normal minimum lease payments for the lessee include (FAS-13, par. 5j):

- The minimum rent called for during the lease term
- Any payment or guarantee that the lessee must make or is required to make concerning the leased property at the end of the lease term (residual value), including:
  - Any amount stated to purchase the leased property
  - Any amount stated to make up any deficiency from a specified minimum
  - Any amount payable for failure to renew or extend the lease at the expiration of the lease term

When a lease contains a bargain purchase option, the minimum lease payments include only (a) the minimum rental payments over the lease term and (b) the payment required to exercise the bargain purchase option.

The following are excluded in determining minimum lease payments (FAS-13, par. 5j):

- A guarantee by the lessee to pay the lessor's debt on the leased property
- The lessee's obligation (separate from the rental payments) to pay executory costs (insurance, taxes, etc.) in connection with the leased property
- Contingent rentals (FAS-29, par. 10)

### OBSERVATION

FIN-19 (Lessee Guarantee of the Residual Value of Leased Property) clarifies certain guarantees of the residual value of leased property made by a lessee, as follows:

- A guarantee by a lessee to make up a residual value deficiency caused by damage, extraordinary wear and tear, or excessive usage is similar to a contingent rental, since the amount is not determinable at the inception of the lease. Therefore, this type of lessee guarantee does not constitute a lessee guarantee of residual value for purposes of computing the lessee's minimum lease payments (FIN-19, par. 3).

- A lessee's guarantee to make up a residual value deficiency at the end of a lease term is limited to the specified maximum deficiency called for by the lease (FIN-19, par. 4).

- Unless the lessor explicitly releases the lessee, a guarantee of residual value by an unrelated third party for the benefit of the lessor does not release the obligation of the lessee. Therefore, such a guarantee by an unrelated third party shall not be used to reduce the lessee's minimum lease payments. Costs incurred in connection with a guarantee by an unrelated third party are considered executory costs and are not included in computing the lessee's minimum lease payments (FIN-19, par. 5).

The minimum lease payments to a lessor are the sum of (FAS-13, par. 5j):

- The minimum lease payments under the lease terms
- Any guarantee by a third party, unrelated to the lessee and lessor, of the residual value or rental payments beyond the lease term, providing such guarantor is financially capable of discharging the potential obligation

### Lease Classification

**Lessees.** If one or more of the following four criteria is present at the inception of a lease, it is classified as a capital lease by the lessee (FAS-13, par. 7):

1. Ownership of the property is transferred to the lessee by the end of the lease term.
2. The lease contains a bargain purchase option.
3. The lease term, at inception, is substantially (75% or more) equal to the estimated economic life of the leased property, including earlier years of use. (**Exception:** This criterion cannot be used for a lease that begins within the last 25% of the original estimated economic life of the leased property. **Example:** A jet aircraft that has an estimated economic life of 25 years is leased for five successive five-year leases. If the first four five-year leases were classified as operating leases, the last five-year lease cannot be classified as a capital lease, because the lease would commence within the last 25% of the estimated economic life of the property and would fall under this exception.)
4. The present value of the minimum lease payments at the beginning of the lease term, excluding executory costs and profits thereon to be paid by the lessor, is 90% or more of the fair value of the property at the inception of the lease, less any investment tax credit retained and expected to be realized by the lessor. (**Exception:** This criterion cannot be used for a lease that begins within the last 25% of the original estimated economic life of the leased property.)

A lessee's incremental borrowing rate is used to determine the present value of the minimum lease payments, except that the lessor's implicit rate of interest is used if it is known and it is lower (FAS-13, par. 7d).

**PRACTICE POINTER**

While the criteria for identifying a capital lease appear very specific, significant professional judgment must be exercised in implementing them. For example:

- Except in the simplest cases, determining the lease term may involve judgment.

- Several of the criteria include terms that require judgment when they are applied to a specific lease. These include "bargain purchase option," "estimated useful life of the property," and "fair value of the property."

- The lease term and the present value of minimum lease payments criteria are not available for leases that begin within the last 25% of the asset's estimated useful life, which is subject to judgment.

- Determining the minimum lease payments for the lessee may require use of that party's incremental borrowing rate, which may involve judgment.

**Lessors.** If, at inception, a lease meets any one (or more) of the four criteria indicating that substantially all the benefits and risks of ownership have been transferred to the lessee, and it meets both the following conditions, the lease is classified by the lessor as a sales-type or direct financing lease, whichever is appropriate:

- *Collection of the minimum lease payments is reasonably predictable.* A receivable resulting from a lease subject to an estimate of uncollectibility based on experience is not precluded from being classified as either a sales-type or a direct financing lease (FAS-98, par. 22f).

- *No important uncertainties exist for unreimbursable costs yet to be incurred by the lessor under the lease.* Important uncertainties include extensive warranties and material commitments beyond normal practice. *Executory costs*, such as insurance, maintenance, and taxes, are not considered important uncertainties (FAS-13, par. 8b).

**NOTE**

In the event the leased property is not acquired or constructed before the inception of the lease, this condition is not applied until such time as the leased property is acquired or constructed by the lessor (FAS-23, par. 7).

In applying the fourth basic capitalization criterion—the present value of the lease equals or exceeds 90% of the fair value of the property—a *lessor* computes the present value of the minimum lease payments, using the interest rate *implicit in the lease* (FAS-13, par. 7d).

A lease involving real estate is not classified by the lessor as a sales-type lease unless the title to the leased property is transferred to the lessee at or shortly after the end of the lease term (FAS-98, par. 22c).

Classification of a lease as a capital or operating lease is summarized in Figure 1 below.

**Figure 1: Classification of a Lease as a Capital or Operating Lease**

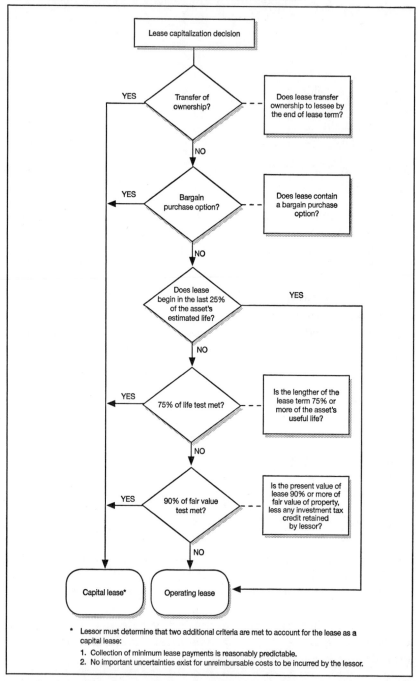

### Changing a Provision of a Lease

If a change in a provision of a lease results in a different lease classification at the inception of the lease because it meets different criteria, a new lease agreement is created that must be reclassified according to its different criteria. Renewal, extension, or a new lease under which the lessee continues to use the same property is not considered a change in a lease provision (FAS-13, par. 9).

Any action that extends the lease term, except to void a residual guarantee, or a penalty for failure to renew the lease at the end of the lease term, is considered a new lease agreement that is classified according to the different criteria (FAS-13, par. 9).

Changes in estimates or circumstances do not cause a reclassification.

**Refunding of tax-exempt debt.** If a change in a lease occurs as a result of a refunding by the lessor of tax-exempt debt and (a) the lessee receives the economic advantages of the refunding, and (b) the revised lease qualifies and is classified either as a capital lease by the lessee or as a direct financing lease by the lessor, the change in the lease shall be accounted for on the basis of whether or not an extinguishment of debt has occurred, as follows (FAS-22, par. 12):

- Accounted for as an extinguishment of debt:
  - The lessee adjusts the lease obligation to the present value of the future minimum lease payments under the revised agreement, using the effective interest rate of the new lease agreement. Any gain or loss is treated as a gain or loss on an early extinguishment of debt.
  - The lessor adjusts the balance of the minimum lease payments receivable and the gross investment in the lease (if affected) for the difference between the present values of the old and new or revised agreement. Any gain or loss is recognized in the current period.
- Not accounted for as an extinguishment of debt:
  - The lessee accrues any costs connected with the refunding that are obligated to be reimbursed to the lessor. The interest method is used to amortize the costs over the period from the date of the refunding to the call date of the debt to be refunded.
  - The lessor recognizes as revenue any reimbursements to be received from the lessee for costs paid related to the debt to be refunded over the period from the date of the refunding to the call date of the debt to be refunded.

## STUDY QUESTIONS

**1.** Which of the following is *not* one of the criteria for a capital lease?

   **a.** At the inception of the lease, the present value of the minimum lease payments, with certain adjustments, is 75% of more of the fair value of the leased property.

   **b.** The lease contains a bargain purchase option.

   **c.** The lease is substantially (75% or more) equal to the estimated useful life of the leased property.

   **d.** By the end of the lease term, ownership of the lease property is transferred to the lessee.

**2.** Which of the following is true?

   **a.** The inception of the lease may be the date of the lease agreement only.

   **b.** The inception date of the lease may only be the date of a written commitment signed by the parties involved that sets forth the major provisions of the lease.

   **c.** A written commitment that is missing some of the principal provisions of the lease transaction still establishes the inception date of the lease.

   **d.** The inception of the lease is either the date of the lease agreement or the date of a written commitment signed by the parties that sets forth the principle provisions of the lease transaction.

**3.** Which of the following is an example of an initial direct cost?

   **a.** Cost related to soliciting potential lessees

   **b.** Ancillary activities related to establishing and monitoring credit policies, supervision and administration

   **c.** Preparing and processing lease documents

   **d.** Activities performed by the lessor for advertising

**4.** Which of the following is excluded in determining minimum lease payments?

   **a.** Any amount stated to make up any deficiency from a specified minimum

   **b.** A guarantee by the lessee to pay the lessor's debt on a leased property

   **c.** The minimum rent called for during the lease term

   **d.** Any amount stated to purchase the leased property

**5.** Rental payments based on future sales volume, future interest rates, or future machine hours are examples of _____.

   **a.** Accelerated rentals

   **b.** Avoidable obligations

   **c.** Deferred commitments

   **d.** Contingent rentals

**NOTE**

Answers to Study Questions, with feedback to both the correct and incorrect responses, are provided in a special section beginning on page **237**.

## ACCOUNTING AND REPORTING BY LESSEES

### Capital Leases

**Initial recording.** The lessee records a capital lease as an asset and a corresponding liability. The initial recording value of a lease is the lesser of the fair value of the leased property or the present value of the minimum lease payments, excluding any portion representing executory costs and profit thereon to be paid by the lessor. Fair value is determined as of the inception of the lease, and the present value of the minimum lease payments is computed at the beginning of the lease term. The inception of the lease and the beginning of the lease term are not necessarily the same dates (FAS-13, par. 10).

Because the lessee's minimum lease payments exclude a lessee's obligation to pay executory costs, executory costs paid by the lessee are expensed as paid or appropriately accrued. If such costs are included in the rental payments and are not identified separately (which is the most likely case), an estimate of the amount is necessary (FAS-13, par. 10).

A lessee's incremental borrowing rate is used to determine the present value of the minimum lease payments unless the lessor's implicit rate of interest is known and is lower (FAS-13, par. 7d).

**Leases with escalation clauses.** In lease agreements or written commitments in which the leased property is to be acquired or constructed by the lessor, there may be a provision for the escalation of the minimum lease payments during the construction or preacquisition period. Usually, the escalation is based on increased costs of acquisition or construction of the leased property. A provision to escalate the minimum lease payments during the construction or preacquisition period can also be based on other measures of cost or value, including general price-level changes or changes in the consumer price index.

The relationship between the total amount of minimum lease payments and the fair value of a lease is such that when one increases so does the other. For example, assume that the total minimum lease payments of a particular lease are $100,000 payable in five equal annual installments, and the fair value of the same lease is $350,000. If the minimum lease payments are increased 20% to $120,000, it is likely that the fair value of the lease will increase correspondingly, because the lease is then worth more to an investor.

FAS-23 requires that increases in the minimum lease payments that occur during the preacquisition or construction period as a result of an escalation clause be considered in determining the fair value of the leased property at the inception of the lease for the purposes of the initial recording of the lease transaction by the lessee, or where fair value is used as a basis of allocation (FAS-23, par. 8).

The initial recording value of a lease transaction by the lessee, which is required by FAS-13, is the lesser of the fair value of the leased property or the present value of the minimum lease payments. FAS-23 changes the lessee's determination of fair value for leases that contain escalation clauses from the fair value on the inception date to a fair value amount that includes the effect of any increases which have occurred as a result of the escalation clause. The changes embodied in FAS-23 are intended to create lease classifications that more closely reflect the substance of a lease transaction.

### OBSERVATION

The question arises as to when leases of this type should be recorded on the books of the lessee. FAS-23 appears to indicate that the initial recording should be made only after the effects of the escalation clause on the fair value of the leased property are determined. Otherwise, FAS-23 is silent in all respects as to when the lease transaction should be recorded. In the case of significant amounts of leases, it appears illogical to wait several years to record the transaction. If this is the only viable alternative, however, full disclosure of all pertinent facts pertaining to the lease agreement or commitment should be made in a prominent footnote.

The other alternative is to record these types of lease transactions immediately at the inception of the lease, utilizing whatever information is available and subsequently adjusting the recorded amounts when the effects of the escalation clauses are known. This alternative does not appear to be viable because of the difficulties mentioned in the following paragraphs.

The last-enumerated criterion in FAS-13 for capitalizing a lease is when the present value of the minimum lease payments is 90% or more of the fair value of the leased property at the inception of the lease. When this criterion is considered for capitalizing a lease in conjunction with the alternative of recording lease transactions covered by FAS-23 at the inception of the lease and then subsequently adjusting the recorded amounts when the effects of the escalation clauses become known, the following problems arise, which are not addressed by either FAS-13 or FAS-23.

■ If we assume that FAS-23 requires that the fair value of leases with escalation clauses be determined at a future date, what fair value should be used to determine whether the lease is or is not a capital lease in accordance with the criterion of whether the present value of the minimum lease payments is 90% or more of the fair value of the leased property at the inception of the lease?

■ What if a lease of this type is capitalized in accordance with the criterion that the present value of the minimum lease payments is 90% or more of the fair value at inception of the lease, and subsequently, as a result of the escalation clause, the present value becomes less than 90% of the fair value, so that the lease should not have been capitalized?

- Suppose a lease with an escalation clause is properly classified as an operating lease at inception of the lease and subsequently, as a result of the escalation clause, the lease qualifies as a capital lease.

The above are just a few of the complications that could arise in applying the provisions of FAS-23 to lease transactions.

FAS-23 also permits increases in the estimated residual value (see definition) that occur as a result of escalation provisions in leases in which the leased property is to be acquired or constructed by the lessor. For example, if the estimated residual value is 10% of the fair value at the inception of a lease and during the construction or preacquisition period of the leased property the effects of the escalation clause increase the fair value, then the estimated residual value also is allowed to increase above the amount that was estimated at the date of the inception of the lease (FAS-23, par. 9).

### Amortization

The asset recorded under a capital lease is amortized in a manner consistent with the lessee's normal depreciation policy for other owned assets. The period for amortization is either (a) the estimated economic life or (b) the lease term, depending on which criterion was used to classify the lease. If the criterion used is either of the first two criteria (ownership of the property is transferred to the lessee by the end of the lease term or the lease contains a bargain purchase option), the asset is amortized over its estimated economic life. In all other cases, the asset is amortized over the lease term. Any estimated residual value is deducted from the asset to determine the amortizable base (FAS-13, par. 11).

**PRACTICE POINTER**

Determining the appropriate amortization period for capital leases is an important issue where the lease term is significantly less than the expected useful life of the asset. A simple rule of thumb is simply to determine which party to the lease is expected to have use of the property during the period between the end of the lease period and the end of the expected life of the asset. If the lease is capitalized by the first or second capitalization criteria (transfer of title and bargain purchase option), the underlying assumption is that the lessee will become the legal owner of the asset by the end of the lease term and will have use of it for the remainder of the asset's expected life. Thus, the estimated life of the asset is the logical period of amortization. On the other hand, an assumption of the transfer of legal title does not underlie the lease if it is capitalized because of the third or fourth criteria (lease term and the present value of minimum lease payments). In either of these circumstances, the lease term is the logical period for amortization of the leased asset. Generally, if the same lease satisfies one or both of the first two criteria and one or both of the second criteria, use the expected life of the asset as the period of amortization.

**Interest Expense: Interest Method.** The interest method, sometimes referred to as the effective interest method, is used to produce a constant rate of interest on the remaining lease liability. A portion of each minimum lease payment is allocated to interest expense and/or amortization, and the balance is applied to reduce the lease liability. Any residual guarantee(s) by the lessee or penalty payments are automatically taken into consideration by using the interest method and will result in a balance at the end of the lease term equal to the amount of the guarantee or penalty payments at that date (FAS-13, par. 12).

### Illustration of Interest Method

Jones Company leases a tractor-trailer for $8,000 per year on a noncancelable five-year lease. The yearly lease payment is due at the beginning of the year. Jones guarantees to the lessor that the tractor-trailer will have a residual value of at least $5,000 at the end of the lease term.

Assume that a 12% interest rate is used.

| | | |
|---|---|---|
| Present value of $8,000 payments for five years at 12% | = | $32,299* |
| Present value of $5,000 guaranteed residual value in five years at 12% | = | 2,837** |
| Total asset and lease obligation | | $35,136 |

\* $8,000 x 4.03735    \*\* $5,000 x .56713

A schedule of interest expense, amortization, and reduction of the lease obligation of $35,136 to the $5,000 residual guarantee using the interest method follows:

| Book Value Lease Obligation Beginning of Year | Rental Payment/ Reduction in Lease Obligation | Outstanding Balance During Year | Interest@ 12% | Book Value Lease Obligation End of Year |
|---|---|---|---|---|
| $ 35,136 | $ 8,000 | $ 27,136 | $ 3,256 | $ 30,392 |
| 30,392 | 8,000 | 22,392 | 2,687 | 25,079 |
| 25,079 | 8,000 | 17,079 | 2,049 | 19,129 |
| 19,129 | 8,000 | 11,129 | 1,335 | 12,464 |
| 12,464 | 8,000 | 4,464 | 536 | 5,000 |

**Change in Lease Terms.** If a guarantee or penalty is rendered inoperative because of a renewal or other extension of the *lease term*, or if a new lease is consummated in which the lessee continues to lease the same property, an adjustment must be made to the asset and lease obligation for the difference between the present values of the old and the revised agreements. In these cases, the present value of the future minimum lease payments under the new or revised agreement is computed using the original rate of interest on the initial lease (FAS-13, par. 12).

Other lease changes are accounted for as follows (FAS-13, par. 14):

■ If a lease change results in revised minimum lease payments, but also is classified as a capital lease, an adjustment is made to the asset and lease obligation for the difference between the present values of the old and the new or revised agreement. The present value of the future minimum lease payments under the new or revised agreement is computed using the original rate of interest used on the initial lease.

■ A capital lease may be modified in such a way that the new lease agreement is treated as an operating lease. FAS-13 required that the lease asset and obligation (liability) be removed from the accounts and any resulting gain or loss be recognized in determining current period income. The new lease agreement was accounted for as an operating lease (FAS-13, par. 14a).

FASB concluded that the economic effects of the above transaction are similar to those of a sale-leaseback. However, FAS-13 does not require sale-leaseback accounting. FAS-145 requires sale-leaseback accounting, under the provisions of FAS-98 or FAS-28, when a capital lease is modified such that the revised lease agreement is classified as an operating lease. FAS-98 (Accounting for Leases: Sale-Leaseback Transactions Involving Real Estate; Sales-Type Leases of Real Estate; Definition of the Lease Term; Initial Direct Costs of Direct Financing Leases) provides guidance on sale-leaseback transactions involving real estate; FAS-28 (Accounting for Sales with Leasebacks) provides guidance on all other types of sale-leaseback transactions (FAS-145, par. 8).

■ A renewal, extension, or new lease under which the lessee continues to use the same property, except when a guarantee or penalty is rendered inoperative (see above), is accounted for as follows:

  — *Renewal or extension classified as a capital lease:* An adjustment is made for the difference between the original and revised present values, using the original discount rate.

  — *Renewal or extension classified as an operating lease:* The existing lease continues to be accounted for as a capital lease to the end of its lease term, and the renewal or extension is accounted for as an operating lease.

When leased property under a capital lease is purchased by the lessee, it is accounted for as a renewal or extension of a capital lease. Thus, any difference between the carrying amount and the purchase price on the date of purchase is treated as an adjustment of the carrying amount of the property (FIN-26, par. 5).

**Termination of a lease.** Gain or loss, if any, is recognized on the termination of a capital lease, and the asset and lease liability is removed from the books (FAS-13, par. 14).

### Illustration of Capital Lease (Lessee)

Paine Corporation leases a computer under a noncancelable five-year lease for annual rental payments of $10,000. The yearly lease payment is due at the beginning of the year. The fair value of the computer at the inception of the lease is $40,373, and the incremental borrowing rate of Paine is 10%. There are no executory costs. The annual rent of $10,000 is considered a fair rental as opposed to a bargain rental. The estimated economic life of the computer is ten years.

### Classification of Lease

A review is made of the criteria involved in the provisions of the lease to determine its classification.

- **Criterion (1)** is not met, because there is no transfer of the ownership of the leased property before the end of the lease term.
- **Criterion (2)** is not met, because the lease does not contain a bargain purchase option.
- **Criterion (3)** is not met, because the lease term (five years) is not equal to 75% or more of the estimated economic life (10 years) of the leased property. [**Note:** There are no other provisions affecting the lease term other than the five-year noncancelable term.]
- **Criterion (4)** is met, because the present value ($41,699) of the minimum lease payments, excluding executory costs and profits thereon paid by the lessor, is 90% or more of the fair value ($40,373 * .9 = $36,336) of the leased property. [**Note:** The present value of the lease is $41,699, computed as follows: $10,000 x 4.16987, the present value factor for an annuity due, 5 periods, 10%.]

Paine Corporation should record the transaction as a capital lease.

### Accounting for the Lease

The initial recording value of the leased property, at the beginning of the lease term, is the lesser of the fair value of the leased property or the present value of the minimum lease payments, excluding any portion that represents executory costs and profit thereon to be paid by the lessor.

The discount rate used by the lessee to find the present value of the minimum lease payments is its incremental borrowing rate of 10%, unless the lessee has knowledge of the lessor's implicit interest rate in the lease, and that rate is lower.

The lessor's interest rate implicit in the lease in this example is 12%. As a rule, the interest rate implicit in the lease is equal to the discount rate that, when applied to the minimum lease payments of $10,000 per year for five years and, if any, the unguaranteed residual value of the leased property, results in a present value equal to the fair value of the leased property at the inception of the lease.

(For simplicity, this definition excludes any unusual factors that a lessor might recognize in determining its rate of return.)

This means that Paine must use its incremental borrowing rate of 10% to discount the minimum lease payments to their present value, which is $41,699.

The initial recording value of the leased property is the lesser of the fair value of the leased property at inception or the present value of the minimum lease payments using the lower interest rate. Therefore, the $40,373 fair value is less than the minimum lease payments of $41,699 (computed by using the lower incremental borrowing rate) and is used to initially record the lease, as follows:

| | |
|---|---|
| Lease property, capital leases | $40,373 |
| Obligations, capital leases | $40,373 |

### Amortization by Lessee

The asset(s) recorded under a capital lease is amortized in a manner consistent with the lessee's normal depreciation policy for other owned assets. The period for amortization is either (a) the estimated economic life or (b) the lease term, depending on which criterion was used to classify the lease. If the criterion used to classify the lease as a capital lease was either criterion (1) (ownership of the property is transferred to the lessee by the end of the lease term) or criterion (2) (lease contains a bargain purchase option), the asset is amortized over its economic life. In all other cases, the asset is amortized over the lease term. Any residual value is deducted from the asset to determine the amortizable base.

Because the Paine Corporation's lease qualified under criterion (4) (present value of the minimum lease payments, excluding executory costs and profit thereon paid by the lessor, is 90% or more of the fair value of the leased property), the amortization period is over the lease term.

A schedule of amortization, interest expense, and lease obligation payments for Paine Corporation's computer lease, using the interest method, follows:

| Book Value Lease Obligation Beginning of Year | Rental Payment/ Reduction in Lease Obligation | Outstanding Balance During Year | Interest@ 12% | Book Value Lease Obligation End of Year |
|---|---|---|---|---|
| $ 40,373 | $ 10,000 | $ 30,373 | $ 3,645 | $ 34,018 |
| 34,018 | 10,000 | 24,018 | 2,882 | 26,900 |
| 26,900 | 10,000 | 16,900 | 2,028 | 18,928 |
| 18,928 | 10,000 | 8,928 | 1,072 | 10,000 |
| 10,000 | 10,000 | -0- | -0- | -0- |

**NOTE**

The interest rate used is 12%, which is the interest rate implicit in the lease.

## Operating Leases

Leases that do not qualify as capital leases in accordance with the provisions of FAS-13 are classified as operating leases. The cost of property covering an operating lease is included in the lessor's balance sheet as property, plant, and equipment. FAS-13 requires that rental income and expense relating to an operating lease be recognized over the periods in which the lessee derives benefit from the physical usage of the leased property. Thus, rental expense is recognized over the lease term on a straight-line basis, unless some other systematic and rational basis is more representative of the time pattern in which the benefits of the leased property are derived by the lessee (FAS-13, par. 15).

### PRACTICE POINTER

Use care when implementing accounting standards for sales-type leases involving real estate. FAS-98 amended FAS-13 to require that the lessor shall not classify a lease involving real estate as a sales-type lease unless title to the leased property is transferred to the lessee at or shortly after the end of the lease term. As a result, a lessor may be required to classify a lease involving real estate as an operating lease, instead of a sales-type lease, because the lease agreement does not provide for the transfer of the leased property to the lessee by the end of the lease term. In this event, the lessor must recognize a loss at the inception of an operating lease involving real estate if the fair value of the leased property is less than its cost or carrying amount, whichever is applicable. The amount of loss is equal to the difference between the fair value of the leased property and its cost or carrying amount at the inception of the lease.

**Contingent rental expense.** Some operating lease agreements provide for rental increases or decreases based on one or more future conditions, such as future sales volume, future machine hours, future interest rates, or future price indexes. These types of rental increases or decreases are classified as contingent rentals. Contingent rentals are defined as those that cannot be determined at the inception of the lease because they depend on future conditions or events. A lessee's contingent rental payments are deducted as an expense in the period in which they arise (FAS-29, par. 11).

**Scheduled rent increases or decreases.** To accommodate the lessee, a lessor may structure an operating lease agreement to provide for smaller rental payments in the early years of the lease and higher rental payments toward the end of the lease. Example: A six-year operating lease agreement may provide for rental payments of $1,000 per month for the first two years; $1,500 per month for the next two years; and $2,000 per month for the last two years; for a total rental payment of $108,000 for the six years. Under this circumstance, FAS-13 requires that the $108,000 total rental payments be amortized over the six-year lease term on a straight-line basis.

The monthly amortization for the first two years of the lease term is $1,500, even though only $1,000 per month is paid by the lessee under the terms of the lease (FAS-13, par. 15).

> **OBSERVATION**
>
> A reasonable argument can be made that in the early years of the above type of lease agreement, the lessee receives not only the use of the leased property, but also the temporary use of cash, equal to the excess of the fair rental value of the leased property over the actual rental payments. Theoretically, to recognize the economic substance of this lease transaction, both the lessee and the lessor should record imputed interest on the difference between the actual amount of rental payments and the computed amount of level rental payments. FAS-13, however, precludes the use of the time value of money as a factor in recognizing rentals under operating leases.

### Financial Statement Disclosure

**General disclosure.** A general description of the lessee's leasing arrangements, including (a) basis of contingent rental payments; (b) terms of renewals, purchase options, and escalation clauses; and (c) restrictions imposed by lease agreements, such as additional debt, dividends, and leasing limitations, must be disclosed (FAS-13, par. 16).

**Capital leases.** Assets, accumulated amortization, and liabilities from capital leases are reported separately in the balance sheet and classified as current or noncurrent in the same manner as other assets and liabilities (FAS-13, par. 13).

Current amortization charges to income must be disclosed clearly, along with additional information (FAS-13, par. 16):

- **Gross assets:** as of each balance sheet date presented, in aggregate and by major property categories (this information may be combined with comparable owned assets)
- **Minimum future lease payments:** in total and for each of the next five years, showing deductions for executory costs, including any profit thereon, and the amount of imputed interest to reduce the net minimum lease payments to present values
- **Minimum sublease income:** due in future periods under noncancelable subleases
- **Total contingent rentals:** actually incurred for each period for which an income statement is presented

**Operating Leases.** The following financial statement disclosure is required for all operating leases of lessees having noncancelable lease terms in excess of one year (FAS-13, par. 16):

- **Minimum future rental payments:** in total and for each of the next five years
- **Minimum sublease income:** due in future periods under noncancelable subleases
- **Schedule of total rental expense:** showing the composition by minimum rentals, contingent rentals, and sublease income (excluding leases with terms of a month or less that were not renewed)

Following is an illustration of a lessee's financial statement disclosure (using assumed numbers).

### Illustration of Lessee's Financial Statement Disclosure

*Lessee's Balance Sheet (in thousands)*

|  | December 31 | |
|---|---|---|
|  | **20X6** | **20X5** |
| *Assets:* | | |
| Leased property: | | |
| Capital leases, less accumulated amortization | $ 2,200 | $ 1,600 |
| *Liabilities:* | | |
| Current: | | |
| Obligations under capital leases | $ 365 | $ 340 |
| Noncurrent: | | |
| Obligations under capital leases | $ 1,368 | $ 1,260 |

*Capital Leases Gross Assets and Accumulated Amortization (in thousands)*

|  | December 31 | |
|---|---|---|
|  | **20X6** | **20X5** |
| *Type of Property:* | | |
| Manufacturing plants | $ 1,500 | $ 1,100 |
| Retail stores | 1,200 | 840 |
| Other | 300 | 210 |
| Total | $ 3,000 | $ 2,150 |
| Less: Accumulated amortization | 800 | 550 |
| Capital Leases, net | $ 2,200 | $ 1,600 |

*Capital Leases Minimum Future Lease Payments and*
*Present Values of the Net Minimum Lease Payments (in thousands)*

| Year Ended December 31 | |
|---|---:|
| 20X7 | $ 406 |
| 20X8 | 1,232 |
| 20X9 | 160 |
| 20Y0 | 125 |
| 20Y1 | 100 |
| After 20Y1 | 450 |
| Total minimum lease payments | $2,473 |
| Less: Executory costs (estimated) | 250 |
| Net minimum lease payments | $2,223 |
| Less: Imputed interest | 490 |
| Present value of net minimum lease payments | $1,733 |

In addition to the foregoing statements and schedules, footnotes describing minimum sublease income and contingent rentals should be included, if required.

*Operating Leases Schedule of Minimum Future Rental Payments (in thousands)*

| Year Ended December 31 | |
|---|---:|
| 20X7 | $ 815 |
| 20X8 | 2,400 |
| 20X9 | 320 |
| 20Y0 | 250 |
| 20Y1 | 200 |
| After 20Y1 | 900 |
| Total minimum future rental payments | $ 4,885 |

In addition to the above information on operating leases, a note should be included describing minimum sublease income due in the future under noncancelable subleases.

*Operating Leases Composition of Total Rental Expense (in thousands)*

|  | December 31 | |
|---|---|---|
|  | **20X6** | **20X5** |
| Minimum rentals | $ 1,100 | $ 1,050 |
| Contingent rentals | 100 | 125 |
| Less: Sublease rental income | (200) | (150) |
| Total rental expense, net | $ 1,000 | $ 1,025 |

---

**NOTE**

The above schedule of total rental expense excludes leases with terms of one month or less that were not renewed.

---

In addition to the foregoing information on capital and operating leases, a footnote describing the general disclosure policy for the lessee's leases should be included, containing (a) general leasing arrangements, (b) basis of contingent rental payments, (c) terms of renewals, purchase options, and escalation clauses, and (d) restrictions imposed by lease agreements, such as additional debt, dividends, and leasing limitations.

## ACCOUNTING AND REPORTING BY LESSORS

Leases are classified for the lessor as either (a) sales-type, (b) direct financing, or (c) operating. Both sales-type and direct financing are forms of capital leases.

Sales-type leases usually are used by sellers of property to increase the marketability of expensive assets. The occurrence of a manufacturer's or dealer's profit or loss generally is present in a sales-type lease.

Direct financing leases do not give rise to a manufacturer's or dealer's profit or loss, and the fair value usually is the cost or the carrying amount of the property.

### Capital Leases

**Recording sales-type leases.** The lessor's *gross investment* in the lease is the sum of (a) the minimum lease payments to be received less any executory costs and profit thereon to be paid by the lessor and (b) any unguaranteed residual value accruing to the benefit of the lessor (this is the estimated fair value of the leased property at the end of the lease term, which is not guaranteed). (**Note:** If the residual value is guaranteed, it is included in the minimum lease payments) (FAS-13, par. 17a).

The estimated residual value used to compute the unguaranteed residual value accruing to the benefit of the lessor shall not exceed the amount estimated at the inception of the lease (FAS-13, par. 17d).

Using the interest rate implicit in the lease, the lessor's gross investment in the lease is discounted to its present value. The present value of the lessor's gross investment in the lease represents the sales price of the property that is included in income for the period. (**Note:** When using the interest rate implicit in the lease, the present value will always be equal to the fair value) (FAS-13, par. 17c).

The cost or carrying amount of the property sold plus any initial direct costs (costs incurred by the lessor to negotiate and consummate the lease, such as legal fees and commissions), less the present value of the unguaranteed residual value (if any) accruing to the benefit of the lessor is charged against income in the period in which the corresponding sale is recorded (FAS-13, par. 17c).

The difference between the lessor's gross investment in the lease and the sales price of the property is recorded as unearned income, which is amortized to income over the lease term by the interest method. The unearned income is included in the balance sheet as a deduction from the related gross investment, which results in the net investment in the lease (FAS-13, par. 17b).

A lease involving real estate is not classified by the lessor as a sales-type lease unless the title to the leased property is transferred to the lessee at or shortly after the end of the lease term (FAS-98, par. 22c).

**Recording direct financing leases.** The lessor's gross investment in the lease is computed, which is equal to the sum of (a) the minimum lease payments to be received by the lessor, less any executory costs and profit thereon to be paid by the lessor, and (b) any unguaranteed residual value accruing to the benefit of the lessor (this is the estimated fair value of the lease property at the end of the lease term, which is not guaranteed). If the residual value is guaranteed, it is included in the minimum lease payments (FAS-98, par. 22h).

Under FAS-91, loan origination fees and direct loan origination costs, including initial direct costs incurred by the lessor in negotiating and consummating the lease, are offset against each other and the resulting net amount is deferred and recognized over the life of the loan as an adjustment to the yield on the loan (FAS-91, par. 5).

The difference between the lessor's gross investment in the lease and the cost or carrying amount of the leased property, if different, is recorded as unearned income, which is amortized to income over the lease term by the interest method. The unearned income is included in the balance sheet as a deduction from the related gross investment, which results in the net investment in the lease (FAS-98, par. 22i).

**OBSERVATION**

The practice of recognizing a portion of the unearned income at the inception of the lease to offset initial direct costs is no longer acceptable (FAS-91, par 5).

**Balance sheet cassification.** The resulting net investment in both sales-type and direct financing leases is subject to the same treatment as other assets in classifying as current or noncurrent (FAS-98, par. 22i).

**Annual review of residual values.** The unguaranteed residual values of both sales-type and direct financing leases should be reviewed at least annually to determine whether a decline, other than temporary, has occurred in their estimated values. If a decline is not temporary, the accounting for the transaction should be revised using the new estimate, and the resulting loss should be recognized in the period that the change is made. Upward adjustments are not allowed (FAS-13, pars. 17d and 18d).

**Accounting for lease changes.** The definition of lease term includes any periods in which penalties are imposed in an amount that reasonably assures the renewal of the lease by the lessee. The definition of minimum lease payments includes any payments or guarantees that the lessee is required to make concerning the leased property, including any amount (a) to purchase the leased property, (b) to make up any deficiency from a specified minimum, and (c) for failure to renew or extend the lease at the expiration of the lease term. Guarantees and penalties such as these usually are canceled and become inoperative in the event the lease is renewed or extended or a new lease for the same property is consummated.

If a sales-type or direct financing lease contains a residual guarantee or a penalty for failure to renew and is rendered inoperative as a result of a lease renewal or other extension of the lease term, or if a new lease is consummated in which the lessee continues to lease the same property, an adjustment must be made to the unearned income account for the difference between the present values of the old and the revised agreements. The present value of the future minimum lease payments under the new agreement is computed by using the original rate of interest used for the initial lease (FAS-13, par. 17e).

In sales-type and direct financing leases that do not contain residual guarantees or penalties for failure to renew, an adjustment is made to account for lease changes, renewals, or other extensions, including a new lease in which the lessee continues to lease the same property. If the classification of the lease remains unchanged or is classified as a direct financing lease and the amount of the remaining minimum lease payments is changed, an adjustment is made to unearned income to account for the difference between the present values of the old and the new agreements (FAS-13, par. 17f). If a new classification results in a sales-type lease, it is classified and treated as a direct financing lease, unless the transaction occurs within the last few months of the original lease, in which case it is classified as a sales-type lease (FAS-27, par. 6).

If the classification of a lease is changed to an operating lease, the accounting treatment depends upon whether the operating lease starts immediately or at the end of the existing lease. If the operating lease starts immediately, the remaining net investment is eliminated from the accounts and the leased property is recorded as an asset using the lower of (a) original cost, (b) present fair value, or (c) present carrying amount. The difference between the remaining net investment and the new recorded value of the asset is charged to income in the period of change (FAS-13, par. 17f).

If the operating lease starts at the end of the existing lease, the existing lease continues to be accounted for as a sales-type or direct financing lease until the new operating lease commences, at which time the accounting treatment is the same as if the operating lease started immediately. Renewals and extensions usually commence at the end of the original sales-type or direct financing lease. Under these circumstances there should not be any remaining investment to eliminate from the books and the leased property is not recorded as an asset (FAS-13, par. 17f).

**Termination of a lease.** Termination of a lease is recognized in the income of the period in which the termination occurs by the following journal entries (FAS-13, par. 17f):
- The remaining net investment is eliminated from the accounts.
- The leased property is recorded as an asset using the lower of the (a) original cost, (b) present fair value, or (c) present carrying amount.

### Operating Leases

Leases that do not qualify as capital leases in accordance with the provisions of FAS-13 are classified as operating leases. The cost of the property leased to the lessee is included in the lessor's balance sheet as property, plant, and equipment. The lessor's income statement will normally include the expenses of the leased property (unless it is a net lease), such as depreciation, maintenance, taxes, insurance, and other related items. Material initial direct costs (those directly related to the negotiation and consummation of the lease) are deferred and allocated to income over the lease term (FAS-13, pars. 19a and 19c).

FAS-13 requires that rental income from an operating lease be amortized over the periods in which the lessor's benefits in the leased property are depleted. Thus, rental income is amortized over the lease term on a straight-line basis, unless some other systematic and rational basis is more representative of the time pattern in which the benefits of the leased property are depleted (FAS-13, par. 19b).

FAS-98 amended FAS-13 to require that a lease involving real estate not be classified by the lessor as a sales-type lease unless title to the leased property is transferred to the lessee at or shortly after the end of the lease term. As a result, an enterprise may be required to classify a lease involving real estate as an operating lease, instead of a sales-type lease, because the lease agreement does not provide for the transfer of the leased property to the lessee by the end of the lease term. In this event, the lessor recognizes a loss at the inception of an operating lease involving real estate if the fair value of the leased property is less than its cost or carrying amount, whichever is applicable. The amount of loss is equal to the difference between the fair value of the leased property and its cost or carrying amount at the inception of the lease (FAS-98, par. 22c).

**Contingent rental income.** Contingent rental income is defined as that which cannot be determined at the inception of the lease because it depends on future conditions or events. A lessor's contingent rental income is accrued in the period in which it arises (FAS-29, par. 13).

### Lease Sale or Assignment to Third Parties

Sale or assignment of a sales-type or a direct financing lease does not negate the original accounting treatment. The transfer of minimum lease payments under a sales-type or direct financing lease are accounted for in accordance with FAS-140 (Accounting for Transfers and Servicing of Financial Assets and Extinguishments of Liabilities). The accounting for transfers of residual values depends on whether the residual value is guaranteed. If the residual value is guaranteed, its transfer is accounted for in accordance with FAS-140. Transfers of unguaranteed residual values are not subject to the guidance in FAS-140 (FAS-140, par. 352).

Frequently, a sale of property *subject to an operating lease* is complicated by some type of indemnification agreement by the seller. The seller may guarantee that the property will remain leased or may agree to reacquire the property if the tenant does not pay the specified rent. These types of transactions cannot be accounted for as a sale because of the substantial risk assumed by the seller. The principle of *substance over form* must be applied to such situations and treated accordingly. Examples of *substantial risk* on the part of the seller are (FAS-13, par. 21):

- Agreements to reacquire the property or lease
- Agreements to substitute another existing lease
- Agreements to use "best efforts" to secure a replacement buyer or lessee

Examples of nonsubstantial risk situations on the part of the seller are (FAS-13, par. 21):

- Execution of a remarketing agreement that includes a fee for the seller
- Situations in which the seller does not give priority to the releasing or other disposition of the property owned by a third party

If a sale to a third-party purchaser is not recorded as a sale because of the substantial risk factor assumed by the seller, it is accounted for as a borrowing. The proceeds from the "sale" are recorded as an obligation on the books of the seller. Rental payments made by the lessee under the operating lease are recorded as revenue to the seller, even if the rentals are paid to the third party. Each rental payment shall consist of imputed interest, and the balance of the payment shall be applied as a reduction of the obligation. Any sale or assignment of lease payments under an operating lease is accounted for as a borrowing (FAS-13, par. 22).

### Financial Statement Disclosure

The following financial statement disclosure is required by lessors whose significant business activity is leasing (not including leveraged leasing):

**General disclosures.** General disclosures for leases of lessors: a general description of the lessor's leasing arrangements (FAS-13, par. 23c).

**Capital leases.** *For sales-type and direct financing leases* (FAS-13, par. 23a and FAS-91, par. 25d):

- A schedule of the components of the net investment in leases, as of each balance sheet date, including:
  - Future minimum lease payments, with separate deductions for executory costs and the allowance for uncollectibles
  - Unguaranteed residual values accruing to the benefit of the lessor
  - Initial direct costs (direct financing leases only)
  - Unearned income
- A schedule of the minimum lease payments, in total and for the next five years
- Contingent rentals included in income

**Operating leases.** For operating leases (FAS-13, par. 23b):

- A schedule of the investment in property on operating leases, and property held for lease, by major categories, less accumulated depreciation, as of each balance sheet presented
- A schedule of future minimum rentals on noncancelable operating leases, in total and for each of the next five years

- The amount of contingent rentals included in each income statement presented

Following is an illustration of a lessor's disclosure (using assumed numbers).

## Illustration of a Lessor's Financial Statement Disclosure
*Lessor's Balance Sheet (in thousands)*

|  | December 31 | |
|---|---|---|
|  | **20X6** | **20X5** |
| *Assets:* | | |
| Current assets: | | |
| Net investment in sales-type and direct financing leases | $ 208 | $ 200 |
| Noncurrent assets: | | |
| Net investment in sales-type and direct financing leases | $ 972 | $ 830 |
| Property on operating leases and property held for leases (net of accumulated depreciation of $450 and $400 for 20X4 and 20X3, respectively) | $ 1,800 | $ 1,600 |

*Schedule of Components—Net Investment in Leases Sales-Type and Direct Financing*

|  | **20X6** | **20X5** |
|---|---|---|
| Total minimum lease payments receivable | $ 1,450 | $ 1,250 |
| Less: Estimated executory costs, including profit thereon | 150 | 125 |
| Minimum lease payments | $ 1,300 | $ 1,125 |
| Less: Allowance for uncollectibles | 65 | 60 |
| Net minimum lease payments receivable | $ 1,235 | $ 1,065 |
| Add: Estimated unguaranteed residual values of leased properties | 240 | 215 |
|  | $ 1,475 | $ 1,280 |
| Less: Unearned income | 295 | 250 |
| Net investment in sales-type and direct financing leases | $ 1,180 | $ 1,030 |

A footnote should be included for contingent rentals.

**Schedule of Minimum Lease Payments (in thousands)**

| Year Ended December 31 | |
|---|---:|
| 20X7 | $ 260 |
| 20X8 | 195 |
| 20X9 | 156 |
| 20Y0 | 132 |
| 20Y1 | 125 |
| After 20Y1 | 432 |
| Total minimum lease payments receivable, net of executory costs | $ 1,300 |

**Schedule of Investment in Property on Operating Leases and Property Held for Lease (by Major Class Categories) (in thousands)**

| | |
|---|---:|
| Data-processing equipment | $ 900 |
| Transportation equipment | 700 |
| Construction equipment | 400 |
| Other | 200 |
| Total | $ 2,200 |
| Less: Accumulated deprecation | 400 |
| Net investment | $ 1,800 |

**Schedule of Future Minimum Rentals on Noncancelable Operating Leases (in thousands)**

| Year Ended December 31 | |
|---|---:|
| 20X7 | $ 200 |
| 20X8 | 175 |
| 20X9 | 165 |
| 20Y0 | 125 |
| 20Y1 | 110 |
| After 20Y1 | 200 |
| Total future minimum rentals | $ 975 |

A footnote should be included for contingent rentals.

## STUDY QUESTIONS

**6.** Which of the following is true?

    **a.** Direct financing is not a form of capital leases.

    **b.** Direct financing leases do not create a manufacturer's or dealer's profit or loss.

    **c.** Sales-type leases are not a form of capital leases.

    **d.** The occurrence of a manufacturer's or dealer's profit or loss is generally not present in a sales-type lease.

**7.** In a direct financing lease, the lessor's _____ in the lease is equal to the sum of (a) the minimum lease payments to be received by the lessor, less any executory costs and profit thereon to be paid to the lessor and (b) any unguaranteed residual value accruing to the benefit of the lessor.

    **a.** purported investment

    **b.** net investment

    **c.** gross investment

    **d.** contingent investment

**8.** Which of the following statements is false regarding review of residual values?

    **a.** Upward annual adjustments are allowed.

    **b.** The unguaranteed residual values of both sales-type and direct financing leases should be reviewed at least annually.

    **c.** If a decline in estimated value is not temporary, the accounting for the transaction should be revised using the new estimate.

    **d.** If a decline is not temporary, the resulting loss should be recognized in the period that the change is made.

**9.** The practice of recognizing a portion of the unearned income at lease inception to offset initial direct costs was ruled unacceptable by _____.

    **a.** FAS-98

    **b.** FAS-91

    **c.** FAS-23

    **d.** FAS-28

**10.** Which of the following statements is true when a sales-type or direct financing lease is sold or assigned to a third party?

    **a.** If the residual value is guaranteed, its transfer is not subject to the guidance of FAS-140.

    **b.** The original accounting treatment is negated.

    **c.** Transfers of unguaranteed residual values are subject to the guidance of FAS-140.

    **d.** The transfer of minimum-lease payments under a sales-type or direct financing lease are accounted for in accordance with FAS-140.

## LEASES INVOLVING REAL ESTATE

### Overview

Leases involving real estate are categorized as follows (FAS-13, par. 24):

- Land only
- Land and building(s)
- Land, building(s), and equipment
- Only part of a building(s)

### Review of Classification of Leases by Lessees

A review of the classifications of leases by lessees is necessary because accounting for leases involving real estate depends primarily on the criteria for classifying leases.

If one or more of the following four criteria are present at the inception of a lease, it is classified as a capital lease by the lessee:

- **Criteria 1.** Ownership of the property is transferred to the lessee by the end of the lease term.
- **Criteria 2.** The lease contains a bargain purchase option.
- **Criteria 3.** The lease term, at inception, is substantially (75% or more) equal to the estimated economic life of the leased property, including earlier years of use. (**Exception:** This criterion cannot be used for a lease that begins within the last 25% of the original estimated economic life of the leased property.)
- **Criteria 4.** The present value of the minimum lease payments at the beginning of the lease term, excluding executory costs and profits thereon to be paid by the lessor, is 90% or more of the fair value of the property at the inception of the lease, less any investment tax credit retained and expected to be realized by the lessor. (**Exception:** This criterion cannot be used for a lease that begins within the last 25% of the original estimated economic life of the leased property.)

These criteria are referred to by number in the following discussion.

### Leases Involving Land Only

A *lessee* accounts for a lease involving land only as a capital lease if either criterion (1) or criterion (2) is met. All other leases involving land only are classified as operating leases by the lessee.

A lessor classifies a lease involving land only as a sales-type lease and accounts for the transaction as a sale under the provisions of FAS-66, if the lease gives rise to a manufacturer's or dealer's profit (or loss) and criterion (1) is met. A lessor classifies a lease involving land only as a direct financing lease or a leveraged lease, whichever is applicable, if the lease does not give rise to a manufacturer's or dealer's profit (or loss), criterion (1) is met, and (a) the collection of the minimum lease payments is reasonably predictable and (b) no important uncertainties exist regarding costs yet to be incurred by the lessor under the lease. A lessor classifies a lease involving land only as a direct financing lease, a leveraged lease, or an operating lease, whichever is applicable, if criterion (2) is met, and (a) the collection of the minimum lease payments is reasonably predictable and (b) no important uncertainties exist regarding costs yet to be incurred by the lessor under the lease. All other leases involving land only are classified as operating leases by the lessor (FAS-98, par. 22k).

---

**PRACTICE POINTER**

The criteria for recognition of a sale under FAS-66 are quite similar to the additional criteria that must be met by lessors under FAS-13 in order for the lease to qualify as a capital lease. That is, under FAS-66, two criteria must be met in order for profit to be recognized in full at the time of the sale: (1) the sales price is reasonably predictable of collection and (2) the lessor of the land is not obligated to perform significant activities under the terms of the lease (FAS-66, par. 3). Collectibility is assessed by evaluating the adequacy of the lessee's initial and continuing investment (FAS-66, par. 4). For land to be developed within (after) two years of the sale, the lessee's initial investment should be at least 20% (25%) of the land's sales value (FAS-66, par. 54). The lessee's continuing investment must be at least an amount equal to the level annual payment required to liquidate the unpaid balance (both interest and principal) over no more than 20 years for a lease involving land (FAS-66, par. 12).

---

### Leases Involving Land and Building(s)

Leases involving land and building(s) may be categorized as follows:
- Leases that meet criterion (1) or criterion (2)
- Leases in which the fair value of the land is less than 25% of the total fair value of the leased property at the inception of the lease
- Leases in which the fair value of the land is 25% or more of the total fair value of the leased property at the inception of the lease

**Leases That Meet Criterion (1) or Criterion (2).** Leases that meet either criterion (1) or criterion (2) are accounted for as follows:

The present value of the minimum lease payments, less executory costs and profits thereon (to be paid by the lessor), is allocated between the land and building(s) in proportion to their fair value at the inception of the lease. The present value assigned to the building(s) is amortized in accordance with the lessee's normal depreciation policy (FAS-13, par. 26a).

If a lease gives rise to a manufacturer's or dealer's profit (or loss) and criterion (1) is met, a lessor classifies a lease involving land and building(s) as a sales-type lease and accounts for the transaction as a sale under the provisions of FAS-66.

If a lease does not give rise to a manufacturer's or dealer's profit (or loss) and criterion (1) is met, a lessor classifies a lease involving land and building(s) as a direct financing lease or a leveraged lease, whichever is applicable, providing that (a) collection of the minimum lease payments are reasonably predictable and (b) no important uncertainties exist regarding costs yet to be incurred by the lessor under the lease (FAS-98, par. 22l).

If a lease gives rise to a manufacturer's or dealer's profit (or loss) and criterion (2) is met, a lessor classifies a lease involving land and building(s) as an operating lease. If the lease does not give rise to a manufacturer's or dealer's profit (or loss) and criterion (2) is met, a lessor classifies a lease involving land and building(s) as a direct financing lease or a leveraged lease, whichever is applicable, providing that (a) collection of the minimum lease payments is reasonably predictable and (b) no important uncertainties exist regarding costs yet to be incurred by the lessor under the lease (FAS-98, par. 22l).

All other leases involving land and building(s) are classified as operating leases by the lessor.

**Fair Value of the Land Is Less Than 25% of the Total Fair Value of the Leased Property at the Inception of the Lease.** When applying criteria (3) and (4), both the lessee and the lessor consider the land and building(s) as a single unit, and the estimated economic life of the building(s) is the estimated economic life of the single unit. This type of lease is accounted for as follows:

- **Lessee.** The land and building(s) are accounted for as a single capitalized asset and amortized in accordance with the lessee's normal depreciation policy over the lease term if either criterion (3) or criterion (4) is met (FAS-13, par. 26b).

- **Lessor.** If a lease gives rise to a manufacturer's or dealer's profit (or loss) and criterion (3) or criterion (4) is met, a lessor classifies a lease involving land and building(s), in which the fair value of the land is less than 25% of the total fair value of the leased property at the inception of the lease as an operating lease. If the lease does not give rise to a manufacturer's or dealer's profit (or loss) and criterion (3) or criterion (4) is met, a lessor classifies a lease involving land and building(s) in which the fair value of the land is less than 25% of the total fair value of the leased property at the inception of the lease as a direct financing lease or a leveraged lease, whichever is applicable, providing that (a) collection of the minimum lease payments is reasonably predictable and (b) no important uncertainties exist regarding costs yet to be incurred by the lessor under the lease. All other leases involving land and building(s) are classified as operating leases by the lessor (FAS-98, par. 22m).

**Fair Value of the Land Is 25% or More of the Total Fair Value of the Leased Property at the Inception of the Lease.** When applying criteria (3) and (4), both the lessee and the lessor shall consider the land and building(s) separately. To determine the separate values of the land and building(s), the lessee's incremental borrowing rate is applied to the fair value of the land to determine the annual minimum lease payments applicable to the land. The balance of the minimum lease payments remaining is attributed to the building(s). This type of lease is accounted for as follows (FAS-13, par. 26b):

- **Lessee.** The building(s) portion is accounted for as a capital lease and amortized in accordance with the lessee's normal depreciation policy over the lease term if the building(s) portion meets either criterion (3) or criterion (4). The land portion is accounted for separately as an operating lease.
- **Lessor.** If a lease gives rise to a manufacturer's or dealer's profit (or loss) and criterion (3) or criterion (4) is met, a lessor classifies a lease involving land and building(s) in which the fair value of the land is 25% or more of the total fair value of the leased property at the inception of the lease as an operating lease. If the lease does not give rise to a manufacturer's or dealer's profit (or loss) and criterion (3) or (4) is met, a lessor shall classify the building(s) portion of a lease in which the fair value of the land is 25% or more of the total fair value of the leased property at the inception of the lease as a direct financing lease or a leveraged lease, whichever is applicable, providing that (a) collection of the minimum lease payments is reasonably predictable and (b) no important uncertainties exist regarding costs yet to be incurred by the lessor under the lease. The land portion is accounted for separately as an operating lease.

All other leases involving land and building(s) are classified as operating leases by the lessor.

**Leases Involving Land, Buildings and Equipment.** Equipment values, if material, should not be commingled with real estate values in leases. The minimum lease payments attributed to the equipment shall, if necessary, be estimated appropriately and stated separately. The criteria for the classification of leases are applied separately to the equipment to determine proper accountability (FAS-13, par. 27).

**Leases Involving Only Part of a Building(s).** If the cost and fair value of a lease involving only part of a building(s) can be determined objectively, the lease classification and accounting are the same as for any other land and building(s) lease. An independent appraisal of the leased property or replacement cost can be made as a basis for the objective determination of fair value (FIN-24, par. 6). In the event that cost and fair value cannot be determined objectively, leases involving only part of a building(s) are classified and accounted for as follows (FAS-13, par. 28):

■ **Lessee.** The lessee classifies the lease only in accordance with criterion (3) as follows: The lease term, at inception, is substantially (75% or more) equal to the estimated economic life of the leased property, including earlier years of use. (**Exception:** This particular criterion cannot be used for a lease that begins within the last 25% of the original estimated economic life of the leased property.)

In applying the above criterion, the estimated economic life of the building(s) in which the leased premises are located is used.

In the event the above criterion is met, the leased property is capitalized as a single unit and amortized in accordance with the lessee's normal depreciation policy over the lease term. In all other cases, the lease is classified as an operating lease.

■ **Lessor.** In all cases in which the cost and fair value are indeterminable, the lessor accounts for the lease as an operating lease.

## Sale-Leaseback Transactions

A sale-leaseback is a transaction in which an owner sells property and then leases back part or all of the same property. Such an owner is referred to as the seller-lessee. The purchaser-lessor is the party who purchases the property and leases back the same property to the seller-lessee. Sale-leaseback transactions involving real estate are addressed in FAS-98. All other sale-leaseback transactions are covered by FAS-28.

**Non-Real Estate.** Profit or loss on the sale is the amount that would have been recognized on the sale by the seller-lessee, assuming there was no leaseback (FAS-28, par. 3).

Recognition of profit or loss from the sale-leaseback by the seller-lessee is determined by the degree of rights in the remaining use of the property the seller-lessee retains, as follows:
■ Substantially all
■ Minor
■ More than minor but less than substantially all

*Substantially All or Minor.* Under the terms of the lease, the seller-lessee may have a minor portion or substantially all of the rights to the remaining use of the property. This is determined by the present value of a total reasonable rental for the rights to the remaining use of the property retained by the seller-lessee. The seller-lessee has transferred substantially all of the rights to the remaining use of the property to the purchaser-lessor i lessee has transferred a minor portion of the remaining rights to the purchaser-lessor if the terms of the leaseback include the entire property sold and qualify as a capital lease under FAS-13 (FAS-28, par. 3a).

> **OBSERVATION**
>
> FAS-28 does not define reasonable rental or fair value. FAS-13, however, defines fair value as the price the leased property could be sold for between unrelated parties in an arm's length transaction. FAS-13 defines fair rental as the rental rate for similar property under similar lease terms and conditions.

Whether the lease is recorded as a capital lease or an operating lease, any profit or loss on the sale by the seller-lessee must be deferred and amortized as follows:

- **Capital lease.** For a capital lease, the deferred profit or loss on the sale is amortized in proportion to the amortization of the leased property.
- **Operating lease.** For an operating lease, the deferred profit or loss on the sale is amortized in proportion to the gross rental charged to expense over the lease term.

Whether a capital lease or an operating lease, if the leased asset is land only, the amortization of the deferred profit or loss on the sale must be on a straight-line basis over the lease term.

If the seller-lessee retains the rights to a minor portion of the remaining use in the property, the seller-lessee accounts for the sale and leaseback as two independent transactions based on their separate terms. The lease must provide for a reasonable amount of rent, however, considering prevailing market conditions at the inception of the lease. The seller-lessee must increase or decrease the profit or loss on the sale by an amount, if any, which brings the total rental for the leased property to a reasonable amount. Any amount created by this adjustment is amortized, as follows:

- **Capital lease.** For a capital lease, the deferred or accrued amount is amortized in proportion to the amortization of the leased property.
- **Operating lease.** For an operating lease, the deferred or accrued amount is amortized in proportion to the gross rental charged to expense over the lease term.

Whether a capital lease or an operating lease, if the leased asset is land only, the amortization of the deferred or accrued amount must be on a straight-line basis over the lease term.

### PRACTICE POINTER

If the total rental on the lease is less than a reasonable amount compared to prevailing market conditions at the inception of the lease, increase a profit on the sale and decrease a loss on the sale.

For an operating lease, the journal entry is a debit to prepaid rent and a credit to profit or loss. Amortize the prepaid rent in an amount that increases the periodic rental expense over the lease term to a reasonable amount. Conversely, if the total rental on the lease is more than a reasonable amount compared to prevailing market conditions at the inception of the lease, decrease a profit on the sale and increase a loss on the sale. The journal entry is a debit to profit or loss and a credit to deferred rent. Amortize the deferred rent in an amount that decreases the periodic rental expense over the lease term to a reasonable amount.

For a capital lease, make no debit to prepaid rent or credit to deferred rent. Instead, the debit or credit increases or decreases the amount that is recorded for the leased property. Then, amortize the leased property in the usual manner.

*More than minor but less than substantially all.* If the seller-lessee retains the rights to more than minor but less than substantially all of the remaining use in the property, the seller-lessee shall recognize any excess profit (not losses) determined at the date of sale as follows (FAS-28, par. 3b):

- **Capital lease.** The excess profit (if any) on a sale-leaseback transaction is equal to the amount of profit that exceeds the seller-lessee's recorded amount of the property as determined under the provisions of FAS-13 (the lesser of the fair value of the leased property or the present value of the minimum lease payments). For example, if the seller-lessee's recorded amount of the sale-leaseback property is $100,000 as determined under the provisions of FAS-13, and the amount of profit on the sale-leaseback transaction is $120,000, the excess profit that is recognized by the seller-lessee is $20,000. The balance of the profit ($100,000) is deferred and amortized in proportion to the amortization of the leased property.

- **Operating lease.** The excess profit (if any) on a sale-leaseback transaction is equal to the amount of profit that exceeds the present value of the minimum lease payments over the term of the lease. The amount of profit on the sale-leaseback transaction that is not recognized at the date of the sale is deferred and amortized over the lease term in proportion to the gross rentals charged to expense.

Whether a capital lease or an operating lease, if the leased property is land only, the amortization of the deferred profit (if any) must be on a straight-line basis over the lease term.

**Real estate.** Under the provisions of FAS-98, the definition of sale-leaseback accounting is analogous to the definition of the full accrual method of accounting. Under sale-leaseback accounting, the sale portion of a sale-leaseback transaction is recorded as a sale by the seller-lessee, the property sold and all of its related liabilities are eliminated from the seller-lessee's balance sheet, gain or loss on the sale portion of the sale-leaseback transaction is recognized by the seller-lessee in accordance with the provisions of FAS-13 (as amended by FAS-28, FAS-66, and FAS-98), and the lease portion of the sale-leaseback transaction is accounted for in accordance with the provisions of FAS-13 (as amended by FAS-28).

Under FAS-98, a seller-lessee applies sale-leaseback accounting only to those sale-leaseback transactions that include payment terms and provisions that provide for (a) a normal leaseback (as defined by FAS-98), (b) an adequate initial and continuing investment by the purchaser-lessor (as defined by FAS-66), (c) the transfer of all of the other risks and rewards of ownership to the purchaser-lessor, and (d) no other continued involvement by the seller-lessee, other than the continued involvement represented by the lease portion of the sale-leaseback transaction (FAS-98, par. 7).

*Normal leaseback.* Under FAS-98, a normal leaseback is one in which the seller-lessee actively uses substantially all of the leased property in its trade or business during the lease term. The seller-lessee may sublease a minor portion of the leased property, equal to 10% or less of the reasonable rental value for the entire leased property, and the lease will still qualify as a normal leaseback. Thus, to qualify as a normal leaseback, the seller-lessee must actively use substantially all of the leased property in its trade or business in consideration for rent payments, which may include contingent rentals that are based on the seller-lessee's future operations (FAS-98, par. 8).

If occupancy by the seller-lessee's customers is transient or short-term, the seller-lessee may provide ancillary services, such as housekeeping, inventory control, entertainment, bookkeeping, and food service. Thus, active use by a seller-lessee in its trade or business includes the use of the leased property as a hotel, bonded warehouse, parking lot, or some other similar business.

*Adequate initial and continuing investment by the purchaser-lessor.* To qualify for sale-leaseback accounting under FAS-98, the purchaser-lessor's initial and continuing investment in the property must be adequate as prescribed by FAS-66 (Accounting for Sales of Real Estate) (FAS-98, par. 10). Under FAS-66, the purchaser's minimum initial investment must be made at or before the time of sale in cash or cash equivalents. A purchaser's note does not qualify for the minimum initial investment unless payment of the note is unconditionally guaranteed by an irrevocable letter of credit from an established unrelated lending institution. A permanent loan commitment by an independent third party to replace a loan made by the seller shall not be included in the purchaser's initial investment. Any funds that have been loaned or will be loaned, directly or indirectly, to the purchaser by the seller must be deducted from the purchaser's initial investment to determine whether the required minimum has been met. For the purposes of this provision, the seller must be exposed to a potential loss as a result of the funds loaned to the purchaser. For example, if a purchaser made an initial cash investment of $200,000 in a real estate transaction, $25,000 of which was a loan from the seller, the purchaser's minimum initial investment would be $175,000. If an unrelated banking institution unconditionally guaranteed the timely repayment of the $25,000 to the seller, however, the entire $200,000 would be eligible as the purchaser's initial investment.

**Accounting for certain losses on sale-leasebacks.** Under any circumstances, if the fair value of the property at the time of the sale-leaseback is less than its undepreciated cost, the seller-lessee recognizes immediately a loss in an amount not to exceed the difference between the fair value and the undepreciated cost of the property sold (FAS-28, par. 3c).

### Lease Modifications

Under the provisions of FAS-13, a capital lease may be modified in such a way that the new lease agreement is treated as an operating lease. FAS-13 requires that the lease asset and obligation (liability) be removed from the accounts and any resulting gain or loss be recognized in determining current period income. The new lease agreement is accounted for as an operating lease.

The FASB concluded that the economic effects of the above transaction are similar to those of a sale-leaseback accounting, under the provisions of FAS-98 or FAS-28, when a capital lease is modified such that the revised lease agreement is classified as an operating lease. FAS-98 (Accounting for Leases: Sale-Leaseback Transactions Involving Real Estate; Sales-Type Leases of Real Estate; Definition of the Lease Term; Initial Direct Costs of Direct Financing Leases) provides guidance on sale-leaseback transactions involving real estate; FAS-28 (Accounting for Sales with Leasebacks) provides guidance on all other types of sale-leaseback transactions.

### Other Lease Accounting Issues

**Wrap lease transactions.** In a wrap lease transaction, a lessor leases equipment to a lessee and obtains nonrecourse financing from a financial institution using the lease receivable and the asset as collateral. The lessor sells the asset subject to the lease and the nonrecourse financing to a third-party investor and then leases the asset back. Thus, the original lessor remains the principal lessor, who continues to service the lease. The transaction with the third-party investor may or may not occur at the same time that the original lease is executed with the original equipment user. As a matter of fact, it is not unusual in a wrap lease transaction for the subsequent nonrecourse financing or sale to a third party to occur up to six months after the original lease agreement is executed.

In exchange for the sale of the asset to a third-party investor, the lessor may receive a combination of cash, a note, an interest in the residual value of the leased asset, and certain other rights or contingent rights, such as the right to remarket the asset at the end of the lease term. Depending on the terms of the specific transaction, (a) the lessor may or may not be liable for the leaseback payments if the primary lessee defaults, (b) the lessor may or may not receive a fee for servicing the lease, (c) payments under the leaseback may or may not approximate collections under the note, and (d) the terms of the leaseback may or may not correspond with the terms of the original equipment lease.

A wrap lease transaction consists primarily of a sale-leaseback of property and is accounted for as such under FAS-13 or FAS-98, whichever is applicable. If the property involved in a wrap lease transaction is other than real estate, the provisions of FAS-13, as amended by FAS-28, must be followed. On the other hand, if the property involved is real estate, the provisions of FAS-98 must be observed in accounting for the sale-leaseback transaction.

Under sale-leaseback accounting, the sale portion of a sale-leaseback transaction is recorded as a sale by the seller-lessee. The property sold and all of its related liabilities are eliminated from the seller-lessee's balance sheet. Gain or loss on the sale portion of the sale-leaseback transaction is recognized by the seller-lessee in accordance with paragraph 33 of FAS-13, as amended by FAS-28. The lease portion of the sale-leaseback transaction should be classified as a capital lease or an operating lease in accordance with paragraph 6 of FAS-13 and accounted for by the seller-lessee in accordance with paragraph 33 of FAS-13 (FAS-28, par. 3).

The purchaser-lessor records a sale-leaseback transaction as a purchase and a direct financing lease if the lease portion of the sale-leaseback meets the criteria of a capital lease under FAS-13. Otherwise, the purchaser-lessor records the transaction as a purchase and an operating lease (FAS-13, par. 34).

The main difference in accounting for a sale-leaseback under FAS-13 and FAS-98 is that under the provisions of FAS-98, the sale portion of the sale-leaseback must meet all of the criteria for sales recognition under the provisions of FAS-66. FAS-98 prohibits a lease involving real estate from being classified as a sales-type lease unless the lease agreement provides for the title of the leased property to be transferred to the lessee at or shortly after the end of the lease term.

In reporting a wrap lease transaction, an enterprise's statement of financial position should include (a) the amount of the retained residual interest in the leased property, (b) the amount of the gross sublease receivable, (c) the amount of the nonrecourse third-party debt, (d) the amount of the leaseback obligation, and (e) the amount of the note receivable from the investor.

## Illustration of Wrap Lease Transactions

Assume that a lessor leases an asset with an undepreciated cost of $1,000 to a lessee for five years at $19.12 a month. The residual value of the leased asset at the end of the lease term is estimated to be $164.53 and the interest rate implicit in the lease is 10%. The lessor would classify the lease as a direct financing lease under the provisions of FAS-13 and record the following journal entry:

| | | |
|---|---|---|
| Lease receivable (60 x $19.12) | $ 1,147.20 | |
| Residual value of leased asset | 164.53 | |
| Asset | | $ 1,000.00 |
| Unearned income—lease receivable | | 247.20 |
| Unearned income—residual | | 64.53 |

> **NOTE**
>
> For financial reporting purposes, FAS-13 requires that the lease receivable and residual value of the leased asset be combined and reported as the gross investment in the lease. In addition, the unearned income amounts must also be combined.

Using the lease receivable and the asset as collateral, the lessor enters into a nonrecourse financing arrangement with a financial institution for $900.00 (the present value of the $19.12 monthly lease payment for 60 months discounted at 10%) at a rate of 10%. The lessor would record the following journal entry to reflect the liability for the nonrecourse debt:

| | | |
|---|---|---|
| Cash | $ 900.00 | |
| Nonrecourse debt | | $ 900.00 |

The lessor then sells the asset subject to the lease and the nonrecourse debt to a group of equity partners and leases the asset back for five years at $19.12 a month (for simplicity, assume that the lease, the nonrecourse financing, and the sale to the equity partners occur at the same time). The lessor is now the lessee-sublessor and remains the obligor with the financial institution that financed the nonrecourse debt. In return for the asset, the lessor receives the following:

- Cash of $50, representing the sale of 50% of the residual value of the leased asset
- An additional $103.66 in cash, representing the transfer of tax benefits
- A note receivable for $900.00 bearing interest at 10% with 60 monthly payments of $19.12 (60 payments at $19.12 represent a gross note of $1,147.20 and unearned income of $247.20)

- The right to receive a fee of $82.27 for remarketing the asset at the end of the initial lease term (the present value of an $82.27 payment 60 months in the future discounted at 10% equals $50.00)
- In addition, the lessor retains a 50% interest in the proceeds of the residual value of the leased asset at the end of the lease term

**Subleases and Similar Transactions.** Unless the original lease agreement is replaced by a new agreement, the original lessor continues to account for the lease as before (FAS-13, par. 36).

A termination of a lease is recognized by a lessor in the income of the period in which termination occurs, as follows (FAS-13, par. 37):

- The remaining net investment is eliminated from the accounts.
- The leased property is recorded as an asset using the lower of the (a) original cost, (b) present value at termination, or (c) present carrying amount at termination.

When an original lessee subleases property, the new lessee is either (1) substituted under the *original* lease agreement (paragraph 35b of FAS-13) or (2) substituted through a new lease agreement (paragraph 35c of FAS-13). In either case, the original lessee is relieved of the primary obligation under the original lease. FAS-145, through its replacement of paragraph 38 of FAS-13, indicates that the accounting for the termination of the original lease agreement depends on whether the original lease was for property other than real estate or whether it was for real estate.

If the original lease was a capital lease for property other than real estate, the termination of the lease agreement is accounted for as follows (FAS-145, par. 9c[a]):

- Remove the asset and liability pertaining to the capital lease from the books.
- Recognize a gain or loss for the difference between the lease asset and lease liability, and consider any consideration received or paid upon lease termination in computing the gain or loss.
- If the original lessee remains secondarily liable, recognize this guarantee obligation under the provisions specified in FAS-140 (Accounting for Transfers and Servicing of Financial Assets and Extinguishments of Liabilities).

If the original lease was a capital lease for real estate, the termination of the lease agreement is accounted for as follows (FAS-145, par. 9c[b]):

- The lease asset and liability are to be removed from the books if the FAS-66 (Accounting for Sales of Real Estate) criteria for sale recognition are met.
- If the FAS-66 sales criteria are met, treatment of (1) the lease asset and liability, (2) any consideration received or paid, and (3) any guarantees are all accounted for as immediately above (the same as if the original lease was a capital lease for property other than real estate).

- Any gain should be recognized by the full accrual method if the FAS-66 criteria for the use of this method are met; otherwise, gain should be recognized using one of the other revenue recognition methods discussed in FAS-66 (installment, cost recovery, deposit, or reduced-profit methods).
- Any loss is recognized immediately.

Finally, the original lessee is to recognize its guarantee obligation (per FAS-140) if it remains secondarily liable on a lease that was originally classified as an operating lease (FAS-145, par. 9c[c]).

When a lessee subleases leased property, the original lease continues and a simultaneous new lease is created in which the lessee becomes a sublessor. The results are that the original lessee is both a lessee in the original lease and, at the same time, a sublessor in the new lease. In situations like this, the original lease continues to be accounted for as if nothing happened, but the new lease is classified and accounted for separately.

If an original lessee is not relieved of the primary obligation under an original lease, the transaction is accounted for by the original lessee-sublessor as follows (FAS-13, par. 39):

- If the criterion for the original lease was criterion (1) (ownership of the property is transferred before the end of the lease term) or (2) (lease contains a bargain purchase option), the new lease is classified based on its own new criteria. If the new lease qualifies for capitalization, it is accounted for as a sales-type or a direct financing lease, whichever is appropriate, and the unamortized balance of the asset under the original lease is treated as the cost of the leased property to the sublessor (original lessee).

   In the event that the new lease does not qualify for capitalization, it is treated as an operating lease.

- If the criterion for the original lease was criterion (3) (lease term is substantially—75% or more—equal to the estimated economic life of the leased property at the inception of the lease) or (4) (present value of the minimum lease payments—excluding executory costs—is 90% or more of the fair value at inception), the new lease is capitalized only if it meets criterion (3) and (a) the collection of the minimum lease payments is reasonably predictable and (b) no important uncertainties exist regarding costs yet to be incurred by the lessor under the lease. If the new lease meets the criteria above, it is accounted for as a direct financing lease, with the amortized balance of the asset under the original lease as the cost of the leased property.

   If the new lease does not meet the specific conditions above, it is accounted for as an operating lease.

*In any event, if the original lease is an operating lease, the sublease also is accounted for as an operating lease (FAS-13, par. 39c).*

Even though the sublessor (original lessee) remains primarily obligated under an original lease, a loss may be recognized on a sublease. The loss is measured as the difference between the unamortized cost of the leased property (net carrying amount) and the present value of the minimum lease payments which will be received under the terms of the sublease (FIN-27, par. 2).

---

**OBSERVATION**

FIN-27 (Accounting for a Loss on a Sublease) is silent as to recognition of any gain on subleases in which the sublessor (original lessee) remains primarily obligated under the original lease. FAS-13, paragraph 39, however, implies that both gain and loss may be recognized on sales-type and direct financing leases.

FAS-144 supersedes the discussion in APB-30 and FIN-27 on the accounting treatment of long-term leases (including related sublease revenue) terminated as part of the disposal of a component of a business entity. FAS-144 requires that the assets in the component of the business entity being disposed of be carried at the lower of the asset's carrying amount or fair value less cost to sell. Although explicit guidance on this topic no longer appears in the literature, the authors believe that the fair value of the component of the business entity to be disposed of will be (implicitly) reduced by the present value of future rental receipts to be paid on the original lease in excess of the present value of future rental receipts that will be collected on the operating sublease.

---

**Leases Involving Governmental Units.** Leases with governmental units usually lack fair values, have indeterminable economic lives, and cannot provide for transfer of ownership. These special provisions usually prevent their classification as any other than operating leases (FAS-13, par. 28).

Leases involving governmental units, however, are subject to the same criteria as any other lease unless all of the following conditions exist; and in that event, these leases are classified as operating leases (FIN-23, par. 8):

- A governmental unit or authority owns the leased property.
- The leased property is operated by or on behalf of a governmental unit or authority and is part of a larger facility, such as an airport.
- The leased property cannot be moved to another location because it is a permanent structure or part of a permanent structure.
- Any governmental unit or authority can terminate the lease agreement at any time under the terms of the lease agreement, existing statutes, or regulations.
- Ownership is not transferred to the lessee and the lessee cannot purchase the leased property.
- Equivalent property in the same area as the leased property cannot be purchased or leased from anyone else.

**Related Party Leases.** Except in cases in which the substance of a lease transaction indicates clearly that the terms and conditions have been significantly influenced by the related parties, related party leases are classified and accounted for as if the parties were unrelated (FAS-13, par. 29).

It is important to note that, generally, a subsidiary whose principal business activity is leasing property to its parent must be consolidated with the parent's financial statements (FAS-13, par. 31).

---

**OBSERVATION**

Specific financial statement disclosures pertaining to related parties are required by FAS-57 (Related Party Disclosures).

---

**Leveraged Leases.** A lessee classifies and accounts for leveraged leases in the same manner as nonleveraged leases. Only a lessor must classify and account for leveraged leases in the specific manner prescribed herein (FAS-13, par. 41).

FAS-13 defines a leveraged lease as a lease having all the following characteristics (FAS-13, par. 42):

- A leveraged lease meets the definition of a direct financing lease as follows:
  - A direct financing lease is a lease that does not result in a manufacturer's or dealer's profit or loss because the fair value of the leased property at the inception of the lease is the same as the cost or carrying amount. In a direct financing lease, substantially all the benefits and risks inherent in the ownership of the leased property are transferred to the lessee. In addition, the following requirements must be met:
    - The minimum lease payments are reasonably predictable of collection.
    - No important uncertainties exist regarding costs to be incurred by the lessor under the terms of the lease.
- It involves at least three parties: (a) a lessee, (b) a lessor, and (c) a long-term creditor. (**Note:** The lessor is sometimes referred to as the equity participant.)
- The financing is sufficient to provide the lessor with substantial leverage in the transaction and is nonrecourse as to the general credit of the lessor.
- Once the lessor's net investment is completed, it declines in the early years and rises in later years before being liquidated. These fluctuations in the lessor's net investment can occur more than once in the lease term.

**PRACTICE POINTER**

Leveraged leases are complex contracts that meet very specific criteria. Accounting for leveraged leases is unique in certain ways (e.g., offsetting assets and liabilities) and, therefore, determining whether a given lease is a leveraged lease is particularly important. A lease must meet all of the following specific criteria (taken from the definition of a leveraged lease) to be accounted for as a leveraged lease:

1. The lease is a direct financing lease.
2. The lease involves three parties rather than the normal two.
3. The lease provides the lessor with substantial leverage.
4. The pattern of the lessor's investment declines then rises.

Only when all four of these conditions are met is the lease subject to leveraged lease accounting. If the investment tax credit is accounted for as provided herein and a lease meets the preceding definition, it is classified and accounted for as a leveraged lease (FAS-13, par. 42).

The initial and continuing investment of the lessor in a leveraged lease is recorded net of the nonrecourse debt, as follows (FAS-13, par. 43):

- Rentals receivable, net of that portion applicable to principal and interest on the nonrecourse debt
- A receivable for the amount of the investment tax credit to be realized on the transaction
- The estimated residual value of the leased property
- Unearned and deferred income consisting of (a) the estimated pretax lease income or loss, after deducting initial direct costs of negotiating and consummating the lease transaction, that remains to be allocated to income over the lease term and (b) the investment tax credit that remains to be allocated to income over the lease term

The investment in a leveraged lease, less applicable deferred taxes, represents the lessor's net investment for purposes of computing periodic net income from the leveraged lease (FAS-13, par. 43). The following method is used to compute periodic net income (FAS-13, par. 44):

1. A projected cash flow analysis is prepared for the lease term.
2. The rate of return on net investment in the years it is positive is computed (usually by trial and error).
3. Every year the net investment is increased or decreased by the difference between the net cash flow and the amount of income recognized, if any.

The amount of net income that is recognized each year consists of (FAS-13, par. 44):

- Pretax lease income or loss (allocated from the unearned income portion of the net investment)
- Investment tax credit (allocated from the deferred income portion of the net investment)
- The tax effect of the pretax lease income or loss recognized (which is reflected in tax expense for the year)

Any tax effect on the difference between pretax accounting income or loss and taxable income or loss is charged or credited to deferred taxes.

All the important assumptions affecting the estimated net income from the leveraged lease, including any estimated residual values, should be reviewed at least annually.

If, at the inception or at any time during the lease, the projected net cash receipts over the initial or remaining lease term are less than the lessor's initial or current investment, the resulting loss is immediately recognized (FAS-13, par. 45).

Upward adjustments of the estimated residual value are not permitted (FAS-13, par. 46).

The lessor's financial statement disclosure for leveraged leases shall include the amount of deferred taxes stated separately. When leveraged leasing is a significant part of the lessor's business activity, a schedule of the components of the net investment in leveraged leases shall be disclosed fully in the footnotes to the financial statements (FAS-13, par. 47).

***Lessor's Existing Asset in a Leveraged Lease.*** Only a direct financing lease may qualify as a leveraged lease (FAS-13, par. 42a). One of the requirements of a direct financing lease is that it may not result in a manufacturer's or dealer's profit or loss. It is difficult for an existing asset of a lessor to qualify for leveraged lease accounting because the carrying amount (cost less accumulated depreciation) of an asset previously placed in service is not likely to be the same as its fair value. An existing asset of a lessor may qualify for leveraged lease accounting, however, if its carrying amount is equal to its fair value, without any write-down or other adjustment to its fair value.

**Business Combinations.** A business combination, in itself (FIN-21, pars. 13–14), does not affect the classification of a lease. If as a result of a business combination, however, a lease is revised or modified to the extent that under FAS-13 it is considered a new agreement, it is reclassified based on its revision or modification. Ordinarily, a lease retains its previous classification under FAS-13 and is accounted for in the same manner as it was prior to the combination.

The acquiring company in a business combination accounts for a leveraged lease by assigning a fair value (present value, net of tax) to the net investment in a leveraged lease based on the remaining future cash flows with appropriate recognition for any future estimated tax effects. After the fair value (present value, net of tax) of the net investment is determined, it is allocated to net rentals receivable, estimated residual value, and unearned income. Thereafter, a company accounts for the leveraged lease by allocating the periodic cash flow between the net investment and the lease income (FIN-21, par. 16).

In a business combination in which an acquired lease has not been conformed to FAS-13, the acquiring company classifies such a lease to conform retroactively to FAS-13 (FIN-21, par. 17).

**Recent Developments.** The FASB currently has two projects on its agenda that would affect the accounting for lease transactions by both lessees and lessors. Those projects involve the following topics:

- The effect of a change in the timing of income tax benefits on a lessor's accounting for leveraged leases; and
- Lessee accounting for rent expense recognized during the construction of improvements.

In addition to these projects, the FASB Exposure Draft (ED), Business Combinations, would modify the accounting for leases acquired in a business combination, but only slightly.

The summary that follows reflects the actions taken by the FASB through September 28, 2005. The FASB continues to deliberate these matters and accountants should be alert to further actions or changes.

***Leveraged Leases.*** The FASB issued an ED of proposed FASB Staff Position (FSP) FAS 13-a, "Accounting for a Change or Projected Change in the Timing of Cash Flows Relating to Income Taxes Generated by a Leveraged Lease Transaction," on July 14, 2005. The proposed FSP would amend paragraph 46 of Statement 13 to require that a change in the timing of income tax benefits be treated as a change in an important assumption. Paragraph 46 of Statement 13 states, in part:

> If during the lease term . . . the revision of another important assumption changes the estimated total net income from the lease, the rate of return and the allocation of income to positive investment years shall be recalculated from the inception of the lease following the method described in paragraph 44 and using the revised assumption. The accounts constituting the net investment balance shall be adjusted to conform to the recalculated balances, and the change in the net investment shall be recognized as a gain or loss in the year in which the assumption is changed.

Because the timing of tax deductions may have a significant effect on the periods in which the lessor recognizes the income from the leveraged lease, the FASB concluded that a change in the timing should be reflected in the income recognition pattern, even when the change has no effect on the estimated total net income from the lease. Proposed FSP FAS 13-a would establish the appropriate accounting when changes in the timing of cash flows from the leveraged lease are the result of the following circumstances:

- An interpretation of the tax law;
- Changes in the lessor's assessment of the likelihood of prevailing if challenged by the taxing authorities; and
- Changes in the lessor's intent to settle with taxing authorities that will change the timing of the tax benefits from the leveraged lease.

The proposed FSP indicates that assessments of the likelihood that the lessor would prevail if challenged by the taxing authorities should consider the guidance in the ED of proposed FASB Interpretation (FIN), *Accounting for Uncertain Tax Positions.*

Changes in the timing or expected timing of cash flows that are not directly related to the leveraged lease transaction are not subject to the guidance in proposed FSP FAS 13-a. For example, the proposed FSP would not apply when the timing of tax deductions changes as a result of: (a) an alternative minimum tax (AMT) credit or (b) the lessor not having sufficient taxable income to absorb the deductions generated by the lease. (However, if the AMT credit or insufficient taxable income changes the estimated total net income from the leveraged lease, the existing guidance in paragraph 46 of Statement 13 applies and an entity would be required to recalculate the rate of return from the lease.)

Proposed FSP FAS 13-a would also require the lessor to reconsider whether the change in the timing of the cash flows from the leveraged lease would have caused the lease to not meet the conditions in paragraph 42 to be classified as a leveraged lease, in particular the criterion requiring the lessor's net investment to decline, rise, and decline again before the final elimination of that investment. A lease that no longer met all of the criteria of paragraph 42 would be classified as a direct financing lease. The components of the net investment (the direct financing lease, the nonrecourse debt, and the deferred taxes related to the lease) would be recorded separately on the lessor's balance sheet.

The proposed FSP is scheduled to be effective as of the end of the first fiscal year ending after December 15, 2005 (for calendar-year companies, December 31, 2005).

**Rental Costs Incurred During Construction.** The FASB issued an ED of proposed FSP FAS 13-b, "Accounting for Rental Costs Incurred during a Construction Period," on July 19, 2005, to clarify a lessee's accounting for rent expense recognized on leased property during a construction period. An example of the arrangement that would be addressed by the proposed FSP follows:

> Retailer enters into a lease of unfinished space from Developer on January 1, 20X1. The lease expires on January 1, 20X6. The lease agreement states that the lease term commences March 1, 20X1, and requires Retailer to begin making scheduled monthly rent payments at that time. During January and February 20X1, Retailer constructs tenant improvements it requires to be able to operate its store. Retailer completes the installation of improvements on February 28, 20X1, and opens the store for business on March 1, 20X1.

Paragraph 15 of Statement 13 requires a lessee to recognize rent expense on a straight-line basis over the term of an operating lease. The FASB addressed the time pattern of the physical use of leased property in paragraph 2 of FASB Technical Bulletin (FTB) 88-1, Issues Relating to Accounting for Leases, and concluded, in part:

> If rents escalate in contemplation of the lessee's physical use of leased property, including equipment, but the lessee takes possession of or controls the physical use of the property at the beginning of the lease term, all rental payments, including the escalated rents, should be recognized as rental expense or rental revenue on a straight-line basis in accordance with paragraph 15 of Statement 13 and Technical Bulletin 85-3 starting with the beginning of the lease term.

Proposed FSP FAS 13-b notes that even though the leased asset is undergoing construction, the lessee does control the physical use of that asset and therefore is required to begin recognizing rent expense on a straight-line basis over a period that includes the period during which the lessee is making the improvements.

The lack of guidance on the accounting for rental expense recognized during the period when the lessee is constructing the improvements led to diversity in practice, with some lessees capitalizing the rent expense recognized during the construction period as part of the cost of the leasehold improvements and other lessees not capitalizing the rent expense.

The FASB concluded that rental expense associated with operating leases of land or buildings that are recognized during a construction period should not be recognized as part of the cost of the asset being constructed.

**Business combinations.** The FASB issued an ED on accounting for business combinations on June 30, 2005. The most significant change proposed in the ED is to clarify that the guidance in FIN No. 26, *Accounting for Purchase of a Leased Asset by the Lessee during the Term of the Lease,* does not apply when the leased asset is acquired as part of a business combination. In that circumstance, the guidance on terminations of executory contracts would be applicable. In addition, the FASB has proposed amending FIN No. 21, *Accounting for Leases in a Business Combination,* to clarify that the accounting for modifications made subsequent to the acquisition date is subject to Statement 13, even if the modifications were contemplated at the acquisition date.

The ED confirms the following:

- Unless the terms of the lease are modified such that a new lease would result under paragraph 9 of Statement 13, the acquirer should not change the classification of the acquired leases.
- If the acquiree is a lessee under an operating lease, the acquirer should not recognize an asset and a liability associated with the right to use the leased asset and the obligation to pay for that right.
- If the acquiree is a lessee under a capital lease, the acquirer should separately recognize an asset and a related liability for the right to use the leased asset and the obligation to pay for that right. The asset and related liability would be recorded at the acquisition-date fair value.
- If the acquiree is a lessor under an operating lease, the acquirer should recognize the asset subject to the lease at its acquisition-date fair value.
- If the acquiree's operating leases are not at market terms, the acquirer should record an intangible asset (if the terms of the lease are favorable relative to market terms) or a liability (if the terms of the lease are unfavorable relative to market terms).

**Leasehold improvements.** The EITF was asked to address whether the consensus on EITF Issue No. 05-6, "Determining the Amortization Period for Leasehold Improvements Purchased after Lease Inception or Acquired in a Business Combination," could be used to support reevaluating the amortization period for preexisting leasehold improvements when new, previously uncontemplated leasehold improvements are placed into service after lease inception. The EITF modified the consensus on Issue 05-6 to clarify that the guidance in Issue 05-6 should not be used as a basis to support a change in the amortization period for preexisting leasehold improvements. The EITF noted that if the lessee does reevaluate the amortization period for those leasehold improvements, that reevaluation should be based on other appropriate literature.

## STUDY QUESTIONS

**11.** A lessor classifies a lease involving land only as a sales-type lease and accounts for the transaction as a sale under the provisions of _____ ___ if the lease gives rise to a manufacturer's or dealer's profit/loss and ownership of the property is transferred to the lessee by the end of the lease term.

   **a.** FAS-94

   **b.** FAS-29

   **c.** FAS-145

   **d.** FAS-66

**12.** One of the criteria for a capital lease is that the present value of the minimum lease payments at the beginning of the lease term, excluding executory costs and profits thereon to be paid by the lessor, is ___ or more of the fair value of the property at lease inception, less any investment tax credit retained and expected to be realized by the lessor.

   **a.** 99%

   **b.** 80%

   **c.** 95%

   **d.** 90%

**13.** Leases involving land and buildings fall into different categories and are handled differently if the fair value of the land is either less or more than _____ of the total fair value of the leased property at the inception of the lease.

   **a.** 10%

   **b.** 25%

   **c.** 50%

   **d.** 75%

**14.** Which one of the following statements is true?

   **a.** Equipment values, if material, can be commingled with real estate values in leases.

   **b.** Minimum lease payments attributable to equipment should not be estimated appropriately and stated separately.

   **c.** Equipment values, if material, should not be commingled with real estate values in leases.

   **d.** FAS-13 does not address the issue of the criteria for the classification of leases being applied separately to the equipment to determine proper accountability.

**15.** Which one of the following statements is false regarding sale-lease-back?

**a.** Under FAS-66, the purchaser's minimum initial investment does not have to be made at or before time of sale.

**b.** A purchaser's note does not qualify for the minimum initial investment unless payment of the note is unconditionally guaranteed by an irrevocable letter of credit from an established unrelated lending institution.

**c.** Any funds that have been loaned to the purchaser by the seller must be deducted from the purchaser's initial investment in determining whether the required minimum has been met.

**d.** To qualify for sale-leaseback accounting under FAS-98, the purchaser-lessor's initial and continuing investment in the property must be adequate as prescribed by FAS-66.

MODULE 1 – CHAPTER 2
# Business Combinations

## LEARNING OBJECTIVES

This chapter is designed to provide you with an overview on financial accounting issues as they pertain to business combinations.

Upon successful completion of this course, you will be able to:

- Identify the rules relating to business combinations
- Understand the determination of goodwill
- Comprehend the deferred tax assets and liabilities
- Prepare journal entries for a business combination
- Acquire an understanding of the changes being discussed to the business combination rules

## INTRODUCTION

This course contains information about accounting for business combinations:

- The implementation of SFAS No. 141 is addressed, which eliminates pooling of interests.
- Various definitions related to combinations are explored, including the parties involved, the date of acquisition, and the fair market value of the consideration.
- The proper procedures for allocating the purchase price to net assets unfold.
- Issues related to allocation methods is the treatment of goodwill.
- Resulting deferred tax assets and liabilities are explained.
- Brief treatments of preacquisition contingencies, special banking rules, consolidated statements, and disclosure requirements are presented.

## GETTING STARTED

In June 2001, the Financial Accounting Standards Board (FASB) issued SFAS No. 141 in response to concerns aired by constituents regarding the pooling method.

This Statement (No. 141) indicates that the pooling-of-interest method of accounting for business combinations is no longer an acceptable accounting method. For all business combinations initiated after June 30, 2001, transactions are accounted for using the purchase method.

The purchase method uses rules formerly proscribed by APB Opinion No. 16. SFAS No. 141 supersedes APB Opinion No. 16, among others.

Accountants, both internal and external to a company, must understand the different accounting environment for business combinations. There are also many implications regarding financial reporting requirements.

FASB indicates that Statement No. 141 improves the transparency of accounting and reporting for business combinations. Because all combinations are accounted for identically under the amended provisions, comparability across companies and combinations is enhanced.

However, FASB has been working with several Boards on a project named Business Combinations: Purchase Method Procedures (Including Combinations Between Mutual Enterprises) and Certain Issues Related to the Accounting for and Reporting of Noncontrolling (Minority) Interests. The objective of this project is to replace FASB Statement 141 with a new statement that will:

- Require the use of the acquisition method to account for business combinations
- Develop a single high-quality standard for accounting for business combinations that can be used for both domestic and cross-border financial reporting
- Provide more consistency in accounting for combinations in which no cash or other assets are exchanged as consideration
- Provide clarity in the accounting for combinations that appear to be similar to the pooling of interests method—a method now prohibited for business enterprises

Under the acquisition method, the acquiring entity would be required to recognize the acquiree, including all of its assets and liabilities, at their fair value as of the date of acquisition.

FASB is reconsidering the existing guidance for applying the purchase method of accounting for business combinations (now called the acquisition method) that IFRS 3, Business Combinations, and FASB Statement No. 141, Business Combinations, carried forward without reconsideration. The purpose is to develop guidance for applying the acquisition method of accounting that will improve the completeness, relevance, and comparability of financial information about business combinations that is reported in financial statements by:

- Eliminating existing inconsistencies in the guidance for measuring assets acquired and liabilities assumed in a business combination
- Developing guidance for identifying the assets and liabilities that should be recognized in a business combination
- Determining whether a transaction or event other than a purchase of net assets or equity interests that results in a reporting entity obtaining control over a business should be accounted for by the acquisition method

The following fundamental principles are recognized for all business combinations:

- Business combinations are exchange transactions in which knowledgeable, unrelated willing parties are presumed to exchange equal values.
- The acquirer obtains control of the acquiree at the acquisition date and, therefore, becomes responsible and accountable for all of the acquiree's assets, liabilities, and activities, regardless of the percentage of its ownership of the acquiree.
- The total amount to be recognized for the acquiree should be the fair value of the acquiree as a whole.
- The identifiable assets acquired and liabilities assumed in a business combination should be recognized at their fair values on the date control is obtained.

FASB has also been working since 1999 on guidance that would apply to all not-for-profit (NFP) business combinations excluded from the scope of Statement 141. Currently, Statement 141 applies to acquisitions of NFPs by business enterprises, but not to other combinations involving NFPs.

Potential changes being discussed with the issuance of this new statement will be noted in text boxes throughout the rest of the course. This new statement is expected to be released by the beginning of 2007.

## STUDY QUESTIONS

**1.** What is the effective date of the SFAS No. 141 rules for business combinations?

  **a.** June 1, 2001

  **b.** June 30, 2001

  **c.** December 31, 2001

  **d.** January 1, 2001

**2.** What is the primary reason SFAS No. 141 was adopted?

  **a.** The purchase method is superior.

  **b.** The pooling method is superior.

  **c.** The method improves comparability.

  **d.** More accurately reflects actual effects of business combination.

> **NOTE**
>
> Answers to Study Questions, with feedback to both the correct and incorrect responses, are provided in a special section beginning on page **237**.

## DEFINITIONS RELATED TO BUSINESS COMBINATIONS

### Acquired and Acquiring Entities

A business combination occurs when two (or more) entities combine to become one entity. In business combinations, the company buying another is referred to as the acquiring company and the company being purchased or absorbed is the acquired company. A business combination meets one of two criteria:

- An enterprise acquires the net assets of a business or
- An enterprise acquires an equity interest in one or more entities and then controls the acquired entities.

A controlling equity interest exists when the acquiring company owns, either directly or indirectly, 50 percent of the outstanding voting stock of the target companies.

- Examples of qualifying business combinations:
  - Combination of companies
  - Exchange of a business for a business
  - Merger of one or more companies
  - Transaction that results in subsidiaries
  - Transfer of net assets or equity interest to another company
- Examples of transactions not qualifying as business combinations:
  - Control of other entities obtained by other than transfer of net assets or equity interest
  - Combinations involving not-for-profit enterprises
  - Acquisition by a not-for-profits entity of a profit enterprise
- Examples of transactions that are not business combinations but require SFAS No. 141 treatment:
  - Acquisition of minority (noncontrolling) interest of a subsidiary
  - Transfer of equity interest or net assets between entities under common control
  - Formation of a joint venture

**NOTE**

In a major change from Statement 141, the FASB is considering expanding the definition of a business to include more entities than the definition in EITF Issue No. 98-3, "Determining Whether a Nonmonetary Transaction Involves Receipt of Productive Assets or of a Business." The broader definition would include more development stage entities and reflect other changes designed to make both the definition and its application guidance more applicable to variable interest entities (VIEs), a term or concept arising from the issuance of FASB Interpretation (FIN) No. 46, Consolidation of Variable Interest Entities, which was revised in December 2003 (FIN 46R). These changes would clarify that the assessment of whether a set of assets or activities is a business should be made in terms of a hypothetical potential acquirer, rather than only the specific acquirer. If incorporated into the final standard, the definitional changes would nullify Issue 98-3 and supersede Appendix C to FIN 46R.

A purchase business combination involves one company buying out another. It is necessary to determine the acquiring company in all business combinations because this enterprise must record the acquired assets, etc.

When a combination involves cash payments, the company issuing the payment is typically the acquiring company.

Determination of the acquiring company often becomes more difficult with other forms of payment. Generally, the firm issuing an equity interest is also the acquiring company; however, the company receiving an equity interest is sometimes the acquiring company.

**EXAMPLES**

Com Corporation directly owns 50 percent of Minisoft Corporation and 20 percent of Pewter Corporation. Minisoft directly owns 60 percent of Pewter. Com owns 50 percent of Pewter (i.e., 20% directly and 50% of 60% indirectly).

Parent Corporation purchased 20 percent of Target, Inc.'s stock four years ago. Parent acquires an additional 70 percent of Target's stock during the current year in exchange for its own stock. Parent is the acquiring company in this business combination, controlling 50 percent or more of Target's equity.

> **NOTE**
>
> The definition of a business combination is expected to also be broadened beyond the one in Statement 141 under the new proposed standard. The new definition would include events and circumstances in which an entity obtains control over a business through means other than a transaction involving an acquisition of the net assets or equity interests in that business. Examples include joint venture formations and variable interest entities (VIEs) subject to FIN 46R. As a result of these definitional changes, some newly consolidated VIEs could become subject to the initial measurement requirements of Statement 141 in the future.

## STUDY QUESTIONS

**3.** B-Flat Music Company and F-Sharp Music, Inc. transfer all of the company assets to a new business, Chord Corporation. This transfer qualifies as a business combination. *True or False?*

**4.** Trek Corporation transfers assets to a new corporation, Star, in exchange for all of Star's voting stock. This transfer qualifies as a business combination. *True or False?*

**5.** The American Red Cross (a not-for-profit entity) pays cash for all of the stock of a for-profit entity, Blue X Corporation. This transfer qualifies as a business combination. *True or False?*

**6.** Hole Donut Corporation directly owns 10 percent of Bagel Holes, Inc. after acquiring its stock with cash. This transfer qualifies as a business combination. *True or False?*

**7.** Which of the following require SFAS No. 141 treatment even though it is a non-qualifying business?

    **a.** Control of other entities obtained by other than transfer of net assets or equity interest

    **b.** Combinations involving not-for-profit enterprises

    **c.** Acquisition by a not-for profits entity of a profit enterprise

    **d.** Acquisition of minority (non-controlling) interest of a subsidiary

### Date of Acquisition

The assets acquired in a combination are recorded at cost, where cost is the fair market value of the consideration given on the date of the acquisition.

**The date of the acquisition** is the date that the transaction is consummated; however, the parties may designate another date if the end of the accounting period falls between the initiation and consummation dates. Some adjustments to income may be required if the end of the accounting period is used as the date of acquisition.

## STUDY QUESTIONS

8. Two calendar-year entities, Alpha Company and Omega Company, enter into an arrangement on December 1, 20X3 for Alpha to purchase the net assets of Omega on January 1, 20X4. What is the only date that does *not* qualify as an acquisition date?

   a. December 1, 20X3
   b. December 31, 20X3
   c. January 1, 20X4

9. The assets and liabilities, including goodwill, are assigned to a reporting unit on:

   a. The date of acquisition
   b. The end of the current accounting period
   c. The day their value is measurable.

### Fair Value of Consideration

The fair market value of the business combination is the quoted market price of the common stock issued in the combination. As an alternative, consideration received by the acquiring company may be used.

Consideration received is measured as the fair market value of the net assets including goodwill. Direct costs incurred in the combination are included in the acquisition cost, while indirect costs are current period expenses. The costs associated with the issuance of securities, such as registration fees and costs of preparing the registration statement, reduce the contributed capital.

Under paragraph 24 of IFRS 3, the cost of acquisition should be measured at the fair value of the compensation surrendered.

**EXAMPLE**

Assume Company X acquires an interest in Company Y. Company Y is not listed on a stock exchange. As part of the consideration for the interest in Company Y, Company X transfers certain "know-how." Know-how represents engineering services and was valued at U.S. dollars (USD) 18 million. The direct cost of know-how to Company X was USD 5 million, representing primarily the wages of specialists and travel and accommodation expenses.

Because the value of the Company Y shares being purchased cannot be objectively measured, the value of the services may be a better indication of the fair value. The services should be measured at their fair value. Fair value would usually include the cost to provide such services, added to a normal margin realized by the company on similar activities. In other words, the amount that Company X would normally charge a customer for the same project (USD 18 million in this example) would be an indication of the fair value of the engineering services and should be included in the cost of acquisition.

**NOTE**

The working principle for future business combinations would be similar to the one underlying Statement 141 (i.e., the total amount to be recognized by the acquirer in a business combination should be the fair value of the business acquired) under the proposed new standard. This value could be determined by the consideration paid or by direct measurement of the business acquired. In choosing between two methods, companies should select the one that provides the clearest evidence of the fair value of the business acquired. Absent any evidence to the contrary, consideration in the form of financial assets (e.g., cash and marketable securities) would be deemed to provide the clearest evidence. The consideration paid would encompass only consideration paid to the prior owners of the acquired enterprise. Direct transaction costs would not be part of the consideration paid and would be charged to expense as incurred.

**NOTE**

Other areas of possible change include the areas singled out for specific guidance as part of the FASB's deliberations on two questions that often arise in applying the purchase method:

**1.** How to identify the assets and liabilities that should be considered part of the business combination

**2.** How to determine the fair values of specific types of acquired assets

The key points:

■ **Excludable transactions.** As a general rule, the acquirer should recognize the assets acquired and liabilities assumed as part of the combination at their fair values at the acquisition date. However, transactions arranged to achieve an accounting result favorable to the acquirer should be excluded from the accounting for the combination. The FASB is planning to provide guidance on the factors to consider in determining whether a transaction was structured to achieve a favorable accounting result. Such factors might include the timing of and reasons for transactions, as well as the identity of the most significant beneficiary of the arrangement (i.e., the combined entity vs. the acquiree or its owners).

■ **Stock options.** Specific guidance would apply to replaced equity-based awards and outstanding awards issued by an acquiree, such as stock options. These awards are treated as a separate compensation arrangement of the acquirer, unless the acquirer has an obligation as part of the business combination to replace outstanding equity-based awards issued by the acquiree. When such an obligation exists, the replacement awards would be considered part of the consideration paid for the business combination. The amount of the consideration that would be allocated to the purchase price would take into account such factors as the percentage of requisite service rendered at the date of the acquisition.

■ **Receivables and loans.** Receivables and loans held by the acquiree are recorded at fair value, which includes consideration of credit issues. Accordingly, no allowance for doubtful accounts should be recorded with respect to acquired receivables and loans.

■ **Restructuring costs.** Specific guidance would apply to costs of selling and exiting activities, such as the costs that may be incurred under a plan to exit an activity of an acquired entity, involuntarily terminate employees of an acquired entity, or relocate employees of an acquired entity. The FASB's current thinking is that if these costs are appropriately reflected as a liability on the books of the acquiree and the liability will be assumed by the acquiring entity, then the acquirer should treat the costs as an assumed liability at the acquisition date. This will have the effect of increasing goodwill. Conversely, if the costs are not appropriately reflected as a liability on the books of the acquiree, then the restructuring costs are considered costs of the acquirer and are accounted for in accordance with FASB Statement No. 146, Accounting for Costs Associated with Exit or Disposal Activities, that is, as charges to expense. Presumably, the guidance in EITF Issue No. 95-3, "Recognition of Liabilities in Connection with a Purchase Business Combination," will be superseded.

■ **Pension and other postretirement benefits.** FASB Statements No. 87, Employers' Accounting for Pensions, and No. 106, Employers' Accounting for Postretirement Benefits Other Than Pensions, would be revised to indicate that any amendments an acquirer expects to make to an acquiree's retirement benefit plans would no longer be part of the assumed benefit plan liabilities in a business combination. Instead, the amendments would be treated the same as any other amendment made by the acquirer as unrecognized prior service cost.

■ **In-process research and development costs.** The FASB is considering a change under which acquired in-process research and development (IPR&D) assets would be recognized as intangible assets. This would replace the current requirement to expense these costs under FIN No. 4, Applicability of FASB Statement No. 2 to Business Combinations Accounted for by the Purchase Method. The FASB's tentative thinking is that these assets would be considered indefinite-lived until the completion or abandonment of the associated research and development (R&D) efforts, with the result that they would not be amortized and would be subject to the impairment and testing provisions for indefinite-lived intangible assets. Under this approach, subsequent R&D expenditures associated with the acquired IPR&D would not be capitalized and would be charged to expense as incurred, as required by FASB Statement No. 2, Accounting for Research and Development Costs.

■ **Accounting for income taxes.** FASB Statement No. 109, Accounting for Income Taxes, would be amended so that deferred tax benefits recognized subsequent to the acquisition could be reported as a reduction of income tax expense. There would be a rebuttable presumption that acquired deferred tax benefits recognized within one year following the acquisition date should be reported as an adjustment to goodwill, rather than as a reduction of income tax expense. If that presumption is overcome, the deferred tax benefit would be reported as a reduction of income tax expense for that period and disclosures would be required of the events or change in circumstances that resulted in the subsequent recognition of deferred tax benefits.

In addition, as part of the business combinations project, the FASB also agreed on a hierarchy for estimating fair value. The decisions made in this area will be released separately as part of a project on fair value measurement.

## STUDY QUESTION

**10.** Bee Company acquires the net assets of Birds, Inc., in exchange for 10,000 shares of Bee's $12 market price voting stock. Bird's assets including goodwill have a fair market value of $1,100,000, and its liabilities total $200,000. What is the fair value of consideration in the business combination?

    **a.** $900,000

    **b.** $1,100,000

    **c.** $1,000,000

## ALLOCATION OF COST TO NET ASSETS

### Goodwill

Goodwill is the excess of the total acquisition cost over the fair value of the assets acquired, less the liabilities assumed. The amount of goodwill purchased is no longer amortized; instead, it is tested for impairment according to the provisions of SFAS No. 142.

### EXAMPLE

ACO acquires the net assets of ASUB by purchasing all of its 100,000 shares of common stock at a price of $10 per share. Assume that there is no difference between the book and tax basis of the assets and liabilities acquired, nor is there a preacquisition contingency. On the acquisition date, ASUB's partial summary balance sheet, at fair market value, is as follows:

| | |
|---|---|
| Current assets (including receivables at present value) | $200,000 |
| Long-term investments at realizable value | $100,000 |
| Property, plant, and equipment | $550,000 |
| Intangibles | $350,000 |
| Current liabilities (at present value) | $150,000 |
| Long-term debt (at present value) | $200,000 |
| Residual value | $150,000 |

The difference between the purchase price ($1,000,000) and the cost of the net assets ($850,000) represents goodwill. Assigning the residual value to goodwill, the summary entry for ACO's acquisition of ASUB is:

| | | |
|---|---|---|
| Current assets | 200,000 | |
| Long-term investments | 100,000 | |
| Property, plant, and equipment | 550,000 | |
| Intangible assets | 350,000 | |
| Goodwill | 150,000 | |
| Current liabilities | | 150,000 |
| Long-term debt | | 200,000 |
| Cash (100,000 shares x $10 per share) | | 1,000,000 |

> **NOTE**
>
> In recording the transaction, business enterprises compare the consideration paid with the fair value of the recognized assets acquired and liabilities assumed. Any excess consideration would be recognized as goodwill. Any excess fair value (negative goodwill) would be recognized as a gain in the income statement. In a departure from current practice, the new treatment would not provide for allocations to certain acquired assets prior to recognizing the excess negative goodwill as a gain. This course will discuss negative goodwill next.

## STUDY QUESTIONS

**11.** How is goodwill accounted for when it occurs in an acquisition?

   **a.** It is capitalized and amortized over 40 years.

   **b.** It is expensed in the first year of acquisition.

   **c.** It is tested for impairment according to the provisions of SFAS No. 142.

**12.** If the acquiring company pays $600,000 for the net assets of the acquired company, which have a fair market value of $500,000 and a book value of $600,000, what is the amount of goodwill recognized by the acquiring company?

   **a.** $100,000

   **b.** $-100,000

   **c.** $0

**13.** If the acquiring company pays $5 per share for 100,000 shares of acquired company voting stock in exchange for assets with a fair value of $500,000 and liabilities at a fair value of $25,000, what is the amount of goodwill recognized by the acquiring company?

   **a.** $500,000

   **b.** $475,000

   **c.** $25,000

   **d.** $0

### Negative Goodwill

Negative goodwill occurs when the fair value of the acquired assets exceeds the acquisition cost. This difference between the cost and fair value is allocated pro rata to all acquired assets except:

- Financial assets
- Assets subject to sale
- Pension or postretirement prepaid assets
- Deferred tax assets
- Other current assets

Once all acquired assets have been reduced to zero, an extraordinary gain is reported to the remaining excess.

### EXAMPLE

Slide Corporation paid $500,000 cash for Rule Company's net assets, which have a fair value of $600,000. This business combination results in negative goodwill since the purchase price is less than the fair value of the net assets. A summary, partial fair value balance sheet for Rule is:

| | |
|---|---:|
| Financial assets | $200,000 |
| Property, Plant & Equipment (PPE) | $300,000 |
| Patent | $250,000 |
| Liabilities | $150,000 |
| Net assets | $600,000 |

The $500,000 purchase price is allocated to the assets and liabilities as follows:

| | |
|---|---:|
| Financial assets, at fair value | $200,000 |
| Liabilities, at present value | ($150,000) |
| PPE, allocate remaining basis based on relative FMVs | $245, 455 |
| (300,000/550,000 x (500,000 - 200,000 + 150,000)) | |
| Patent, allocate based on relative FMV | $204,545 |
| (250,000/550,000 x (500,000 – 200,000 + 150,000)) | |
| Total cost assigned to assets and liabilities | $500,000 |

Then, Slide records the acquisition of Rule's assets in this summary journal entry:

| | | |
|---|---:|---:|
| Current assets | 200,000 | |
| PPE | 245,455 | |
| Patent | 204,545 | |
| Liabilities | | 150,000 |
| Cash | | 500,000 |

As an alternative, the $100,000 negative goodwill is computed and then allocated to the assets as follows:

| | |
|---|---|
| **PPE:** | $300,000 |
| | -54,545 ($100,000 x $300,000/$550,000) |
| | $245,455 |
| | |
| **Patent:** | $250,000 |
| | -45,455 ($100,000 x $250,000/$550,000) |
| | $204,545 |

## STUDY QUESTIONS

**14.** What amount of negative goodwill is allocated to PPE in the following situation? The company acquired $160,000 of negative goodwill when purchasing:

Current Assets, fair value - $400,000
PPE, fair value - $900,000
Franchises, fair value - $300,000

**a.** $160,000
**b.** $0
**c.** $120,000
**d.** $90,000

**15.** Negative goodwill results when the fair value of the acquired assets exceeds the acquisition cost. The difference between the cost and fair value is prorated to which of the following?

**a.** Property, plant, & equipment and pension prepaid assets
**b.** Patent and other current assets
**c.** Liabilities and deferred tax assets
**d.** Property plant & equipment & patents

**16.** What is the amount of the negative goodwill when an acquiring company pays $800,000 for net assets worth $950,000 and with a book value of $750,000?

**a.** $0
**b.** $150,000
**c.** $50,000

### Difference Between Book and Tax Bases of Acquired Company

If there is a difference between the book and tax bases of an acquired company, a variance may result. A variance is often created attributable to the difference between the book and tax bases of assets and liabilities acquired in the purchase combination.

When the acquired company assets and liabilities are revalued in accordance with SFAS No. 141, a difference frequently results. This difference is a temporary or timing difference, and a deferred tax asset or liability is recognized. Deferred taxes should not include differences attributable to goodwill, negative goodwill, leveraged leases, and other similar items (e.g., see SFAS No. 109, paragraph 30).

**EXAMPLE**

Adele, Inc. acquires the net assets of Line Corporation by purchasing all of its 100,000 shares of common stock at a price of $20 per share. Assume that there is no difference between the book and tax bases of the assets and liabilities acquired except for property, plant, and equipment with a tax basis of $500,000, and there is no preacquisition contingency. On the acquisition date, Line's partial summary balance sheet, at fair market value, is as follows:

| | |
|---|---|
| Current assets (including receivables at present value) | $400,000 |
| Long-term investments at realizable value | $200,000 |
| Property, plant, and equipment | $1,100,000 |
| Intangibles | $700,000 |
| Total assets | $2,400,000 |
| Current liabilities (at present value) | $300,000 |
| Long-term debt (at present value) | $400,000 |
| Residual value | $300,000 |

Since the book basis of the assets exceeds the tax basis, a deferred tax liability is reported. The deferred tax liability is computed as follows (assuming a 35-percent corporate income tax rate):

| | |
|---|---|
| Book basis of PPE | $1,100,000 |
| Tax basis of PPE | $500,000 |
| Temporary difference | $600,000 |
| Tax rate | x 35% |
| Deferred tax liability | $210,000 |

Since the $210,000 deferred tax liability is included as a liability in the acquisition, goodwill is increased by that amount. Goodwill is computed as follows:

| | | |
|---|---|---|
| Purchase price (100,000 shares x $20 per share) | | $2,000,000 |
| Less: Fair value of net assets | | |
| Assets | $2,400,000 | |
| Less: Current liabilities | 300,000 | |
| Long-term liabilities | 400,000 | |
| Deferred tax liability | 210,000 | $1,490,000 |
| Goodwill | | $510,000 |

The journal entry to record the acquisition on Adele, the acquiring company, books is:

| | |
|---|---:|
| Current assets | 400,000 |
| Long-term investments | 200,000 |
| Property, plant, and equipment | 1,100,000 |
| Intangible assets | 700,000 |
| Goodwill | 510,000 |
| Current liabilities | 300,000 |
| Long-term debt | 400,000 |
| Deferred tax liability | 210,000 |
| Cash | 2,000,000 |

## STUDY QUESTIONS

**17.** If the acquiring company determines that a $500,000 difference exists between the book and tax bases (book basis > tax basis) and the company's tax rate is 40 percent, what is the amount of the deferred tax liability?

**a.** A deferred tax asset of $200,000 results

**b.** None, a deferred tax item only results when there is a difference between fair value and tax basis

**c.** A deferred tax liability amounting to $200,000

**18.** When there is a difference between the book and tax basis of an acquired company, the difference is:

**a.** A permanent difference

**b.** Is usually immaterial and not recognized

**c.** Is a temporary difference

**d.** Written off as an expense

**19.** Assume a 35% corporate tax rate. If the book basis of the assets exceeds the tax basis by $500,000, a deferred tax liability is reported. If the deferred tax liability is included as a liability in the acquisition, what is the amount of goodwill reported when the fair value of other net assets is $700,000 and the purchase price is $1 million?

**a.** $175,000

**b.** $300,000

**c.** $475,000

**d.** $500,000

## Preacquisition Contingencies

It is common for business combinations to have certain uncertainties in the financial condition of one of the companies involved. These uncertainties are preacquisition contingencies.

A preacquisition contingency is a contingency of an acquired company that existed prior to the consummation of a purchase business combination. Contingencies that develop in the process of a business combination are associated with the purchasing company and do not constitute a preacquisition contingency. A contingent liability is an example of a preacquisition contingency.

The contingency should be included at its fair value.

**EXAMPLE**

Abacus acquires the net assets of Ledger by purchasing all of its 100,000 shares of common stock at a price of $7 per share. Assume that there is no difference between the book and tax bases of the assets and liabilities acquired. On the acquisition date, Ledger's partial summary balance sheet, at fair market value, is as follows:

| | |
|---|---|
| Current assets (including receivables at present value) | $200,000 |
| Long-term investments at realizable value | $100,000 |
| Property, plant, and equipment | $550,000 |
| Intangibles | $350,000 |
| Current liabilities (at present value) | $150,000 |
| Long-term debt (at present value) | $200,000 |
| Contingent liabilities (at present value) | $150,000 |

The summary entry for the acquisition of Ledger by Abacus is:

| | | |
|---|---|---|
| Current assets | 200,000 | |
| Long-term investments | 100,000 | |
| Property, plant, and equipment | 550,000 | |
| Intangible assets | 350,000 | |
| Current liabilities | | 150,000 |
| Long-term debt | | 200,000 |
| Contingent liabilities | | 150,000 |
| Cash (100,000 shares x $7 per share) | | 700,000 |

Similar to the treatment for accounting for other contingent liabilities, the less likely and reliable the estimate, the less likely the liability is recorded in the financial statements. If the fair value of the preacquisition contingency cannot be determined during the allocation period, the contingency is ignored during the allocation process. The allocation period is defined as the time period necessary to determine and quantify the assets and liabilities involved in a business combination accounted for as a purchase.

Two conditions are required before the contingency can be included in the allocation process:

- Before the end of the allocation period, the entity has information indicating that the contingency is probable
- The enterprise can estimate the amount of the contingency. Following the allocation period, any adjustments related to preacquisition contingencies are included in income.

Another major change to Statement 141 would require initial recognition at fair value of preacquisition contingencies and could also require subsequent remeasurements of these values. A preacquisition contingency of an acquired entity is defined in Statement 141 as a contingent asset, contingent liability, or contingent impairment of an asset in existence before the combination is consummated. Statement 141 provides an option for situations in which the fair value is not readily determinable. Under this option, the value of the contingency does not need to be recognized unless: (a) it is probable that an asset existed, a liability had been incurred, or an asset had been impaired when the business combination was consummated, and (b) the amount of the asset or liability can be reasonably estimated. This option would be eliminated, and preacquisition contingencies would be recorded at fair value whether or not fair value is readily determinable.

Following initial recognition, subsequent changes in value would be recognized in the income statement using these guidelines:

- **Contingent assets.** Contingent assets acquired in a business combination that are financial instruments would be accounted for in accordance with the applicable accounting guidance for financial instruments. Other contingent assets acquired would continue to be accounted for as intangible assets under Statement 142.
- **Contingent liabilities.** Contingent liabilities assumed in a business combination that are financial instruments would be accounted for in accordance with the applicable accounting guidance for financial instruments. Other contingent liabilities assumed in a business combination would be measured on a fair value (fresh-start) basis.

Initial recognition at fair value would also be required for contingent consideration provided in exchange for the business acquired. Contingent consideration is defined as an obligation of the acquirer (at the acquisition date) to deliver assets or equity instruments in the future if one or more specified events occurs or fails to occur. Subsequent remeasurements could also be required. The tentative decisions about contingent consideration and the exchange transaction are as follows:

- **Contingent consideration.** In a major change from current practice, contingent consideration would be recognized as part of the purchase price and measured at its fair value on the date of the acquisition. The requirements for subsequent measurement (after the acquisition date) would depend on whether the obligation under the contingent consideration is classified as a liability or equity. If classified as a liability, the contingent consideration would be measured on a fair value (fresh-start) basis, and changes in value due to subsequent remeasurement would be recognized as a component of earnings. If classified in equity, the contingent consideration would be recorded at the acquisition date at fair value and would not be subsequently remeasured.

- **Acquisition-related costs.** In another major change from current practice, acquisition-related costs (e.g., finder's fees, advisory fees, legal fees, accounting fees, and other professional fees) would be expensed as incurred. Currently, under Statement 141, these costs are capitalized as part of the fair value of the consideration paid in a business combination.

- **Stock issued as part of purchase price.** Equity securities issued as consideration in a business combination would be measured at their fair value on the acquisition date. The description of the acquisition date in Statement 141 would be modified to clarify that the acquisition date is the date the acquirer gains control over the target entity, rather than the "substantive agreement" date currently used.

## STUDY QUESTIONS

---

**20.** What is the appropriate response to an indeterminate, uncertain, pre-acquisition contingency?

  **a.** Estimate the amount of the contingency as closely as feasible.
  **b.** Include the contingency on the balance sheet as a liability.
  **c.** Ignore the contingency.

**21.** At what value should an accountant record a preacquisition contingency?

  **a.** Fair value
  **b.** Cost
  **c.** Tax basis
  **d.** Present value

---

## SPECIAL CIRCUMSTANCES FOR
## BANKING AND THRIFT ENTERPRISES

There are certain exceptions to the general rule that goodwill constitutes the excess of purchase price over the fair value of identifiable net assets acquired. One exception is accounting for identifiable intangible assets related to loans and deposits, in which the fair value is determined using the expected benefit existing on the date the entity is acquired.

An example of this type of asset in the banking industry includes existing deposits and loan accounts with the ability to generate new bank business, which is an identifiable intangible asset.

An unidentifiable intangible asset may also result in a business combination involving a bank or thrift. If low-yield assets are acquired in a combination during periods with high interest rates, the resulting asset values may be less than the market value of the liabilities assumed.

In this case, an intangible asset that cannot be identified is established and periodically charged to expense using the modified interest method. The amortization period is the lesser of (1) 40 years or (2) a period of time not exceeding the remaining useful life of the interest-bearing noncurrent assets acquired.

### CONSOLIDATED FINANCIAL STATEMENTS

ARB No. 51 and SFAS No. 94 specify the accounting and reporting requirements for consolidated financial statements.

Although this particular course is not designed to brief consolidation procedures, one main item has relevance to the topic covered.

Unless the control is temporary, the financial statements of all majority-owned subsidiaries are consolidated with the financial statements of the parent company.

Consolidation involves elimination of all intercompany transactions since the financial statements now involve a single reporting entity.

### DISCLOSURE REQUIREMENTS

The required disclosures for material business combinations differ from those for immaterial combinations that are material in total. The following chart summarizes the accounting distinctions between the two types of combinations.

| Factor | Material Combination | Immaterial Combination |
|---|---|---|
| Name of acquired company | Yes, with description and percentage ownership | No, but description |
| Goodwill | Describe factors affecting<br><br>Disclose amounts for each segment | Same |
| Income from acquired entity | Indicate time period in which income included | |
| Cost of entity acquired | Disclose with information on valuation | Disclose with information on shares issued to effect combination |
| Acquired entity financial statements | Provide balance sheet on acquisition date with allocations<br><br>Consolidation method<br><br>Disclose contingent liabilities<br><br>Income statement R&D write-offs Contingencies disclosed | |
| Intangibles | Assigned amounts Amortization information | Same |

## SUMMARY

For all business combinations initiated after June 30, 2001, transactions are accounted for using the purchase method, similar to many of the former rules. The acquiring company must properly account for the business combination. A controlling equity interest exists when the acquiring company owns, either directly or indirectly, 50 percent of the outstanding voting stock of the target companies.

The date of the acquisition is the date that the transaction is consummated; however, the parties may designate another date if the end of the accounting period falls between the initiation and consummation date. The fair market value of the business combination is the quoted market price of the voting stock issued or the consideration received by the acquiring company.

After determining the cost of the acquired company, the cost is allocated to the identifiable assets and liabilities based on their relative fair market values on the date of the acquisition. Goodwill is the excess of the total acquisition cost over the fair value of the assets acquired, less the liabilities assumed.

The amount of goodwill purchased is no longer amortized but tested for impairment. A deferred tax asset or liability is reported in a business combination where the book value differs from the tax basis. Consolidated financial statements are generally required following business combinations.

**CPE NOTE:** When you have completed your study and review of chapters 1 and 2 which comprise this Module, you may wish to take the Quizzer for this Module.

CPE instructions can be found on page 279.

The Module 1 Quizzer Questions begin on page 281. The Module 1 Answer Sheet can be found on pages 307 and 309. For your convenience, you can also take this Quizzer online at **www.cchtestingcenter.com.**

## MODULE 2 — CHAPTER 3
# Intangible Assets

## LEARNING OBJECTIVES

Upon successful completion of this course you will be able to do the following:
- Identify the rules relating to accounting for goodwill
- Comprehend the accounting methods pertaining to research and development costs
- Understand the financial accounting treatment of computer software costs
- Summarize the impairment rules regarding intangible assets

## ACCOUNTING FOR INTANGIBLE ASSETS—OVERVIEW

Although the Sarbanes-Oxley did not specifically change any procedures for accounting for intangible assets, it did impose harsher punishments for those who are not rigorous in insuring that assets are recorded accurately, timely and are all inclusive. In the case of accounting for intangible assets, it is almost impossible for CPA's to not be forced to make some sort of judgment call during the valuation process. For this reason, the responsibility is even more so on the CPA to educate themselves in the appropriate methods of accounting for intangibles.

In addition, some 49% of companies said they relied primarily on intangible assets to create shareholder wealth, yet only 5% had a robust system to measure and track the performance of intangible assets according to a study done by Accenture Ltd. in 2003.( "Intangible Assets and Future Value," Accenture Ltd., 2003 survey of 120 senior executives, www.accenture.com.)

Intangible assets generally lack physical substance. Instead, they confer legal rights or contractual obligations. They are long-term assets, and they include such assets as patents, copyrights, leaseholds, franchises, trademarks, and goodwill. Although assets such as bank accounts, accounts receivable, and investments in stocks and bonds lack physical substance, these assets are not classified as intangible assets.

Intangible assets are usually recorded on the books of the buyer at their fair market value. The best estimate of fair value is cost, when a company acquires the intangible assets by a purchase at arm's length. It can be defined as the amount at which an asset (or liability) could be bought (or incurred) or sold (or settled) in a current transaction between willing parties, that is, other than in a forced or liquidation sale.

Therefore, a company usually records purchased intangibles at their cost. Cost includes all costs necessary to acquire the intangible asset and make it ready for use. Cost includes cash paid, the fair market value of other assets given in exchange, and liabilities incurred in the transaction.

If a company purchases intangible assets in a basket purchase, the total cost to acquire such assets should be allocated to the different assets purchased based on their relative fair market values. If intangible assets are acquired as a contribution to capital, they should be recorded at their estimated fair market value.

The intangible asset goodwill deserves special consideration. Goodwill is not reported as an asset, unless it has been purchased from a third party, because estimates of the fair market value of goodwill are deemed to be too unreliable to be recorded in the accounts.

Before the **Accounting Principles Board (APB)** issued APB Opinion No. 17, intangibles with a limited life were amortized, and those whose useful life was indeterminate were not amortized until it could be determined. APB Opinion No. 17 changed those practices by classifying intangibles as either identifiable or those that lack specific identity. SFAS No. 142 supersedes APB Opinion No. 17 and specifies the accounting and reporting requirements for goodwill and other intangibles as follows:

- A company can purchase intangible assets individually, as part of a group of assets, and as part of a business combination. In addition, a company can develop intangible assets internally. A company usually records acquired intangibles at their fair value, which is typically cost in an arm's length purchase.
- If a company receives an intangible asset as a contribution to capital, it would record the intangible asset at its estimated fair market value.
- If a company acquires an intangible asset in exchange for the company's stock, the company would record the intangible asset at the fair value of the stock or the fair value of the intangible, whichever is more clearly determinable.
- A company amortizes these intangible assets over their finite useful lives, and the company must also test such assets for impairment. A company never amortizes intangibles with indefinite lives, but the company must test such assets for impairment under the provisions of SFAS No. 144.
- A company no longer amortizes goodwill acquired in a business combination. Rather, a company allocates goodwill to reporting units and tests it for impairment according the requirements of SFAS No. 142.

The SEC requires a separate statement for each class of assets that is in excess of 5% of total assets, and the company must state the basis for determining the amount. The company should explain significant changes in a footnote to the financial statements.

## DETERMINING FAIR VALUE

Under simple circumstances, a company records an intangible asset at its acquisition cost just as a company records other long-lived assets. At its March 15, 2006, meeting, the FASB clarified aspects of the guidance included in the October 21, 2005, working draft of a final FASB Statement, *Fair Value Measurements (FVM Statement)*, and discussed the effective date and timing of a final Statement.

The Board clarified that:

- A fair value measurement assumes an orderly transaction to sell or otherwise dispose of an asset or transfer a liability in the principal market for the asset or liability or, in the absence of a principal market, the most advantageous market for the asset or liability.
- The inputs referred to within the fair value hierarchy are market inputs that reflect the assumptions that market participants in the principal (most advantageous) market would use in pricing an asset or liability and differ with respect to the extent to which they are observable. The fair value hierarchy gives the highest priority to observable market inputs (Level 1) and the lowest priority to unobservable market inputs (Level 3).
- A fair value measurement must include all of the assumptions that market participants in the principal (most advantageous) market would consider in pricing the asset or liability, including assumptions about risk if the measurement is based on unobservable market inputs.
- In many cases, a transaction price will represent the fair value of an asset or liability at initial recognition, but not presumptively.

The FVM Statement will be effective for financial statements issued for fiscal years beginning after November 15, 2007, and interim periods within those fiscal years. Earlier application is encouraged if the reporting entity has not yet issued financial statements (annual or interim) for the fiscal year in which the FVM Statement is initially applied.

## DETERMINING THE AMORTIZATION PERIOD

Once fair value is determined, the company then amortizes the cost of an intangible asset over its useful life. At disposition, the difference between the book value of the intangible asset and its selling price represents the gain or loss on disposal.

In recording the amortization, the company debits Amortization Expense and may credit either a contra-asset account such as Accumulated Amortization or credit the intangible asset account directly. Further, the amortization period of an intangible asset is the lesser of its legal or economic life, which may not exceed 40 years.

Generally, the amortization period of an intangible asset is the lesser of its legal or economic useful life. The useful life of an intangible asset to an entity is the period over which the asset is expected to contribute directly or indirectly to the future cash flows of that entity. Factors to consider which are included in Paragraph 11 of Statement 142 are:

- The expected use of the asset by the entity
- The expected useful life of another asset or a group of assets to which the useful life of the intangible asset may relate
- Any legal, regulatory, or contractual provisions that may limit the useful life
- Any legal, regulatory, or contractual provisions that enable renewal or extension of the asset's legal or contractual life without substantial cost (provided there is evidence to support renewal or extension and renewal or extension can be accomplished without material modifications of the existing terms and conditions)
- The effects of obsolescence, demand, competition, and other economic factors (such as the stability of the industry, known technological advances, legislative action that results in an uncertain or changing regulatory environment, and expected changes in distribution channels)
- The level of maintenance expenditures required to obtain the expected future cash flows from the asset (for example, a material level of required maintenance in relation to the carrying amount of the asset may suggest a very limited useful life)
- If no legal, regulatory, contractual, competitive, economic, or other factors limit the useful life of an intangible asset to the reporting entity, the useful life of the asset shall be considered to be indefinite. The term indefinite does not mean infinite.

In addition, FASB does give some specific guidelines for certain types of intangible assets as follows:

- A copyright created on or after January 1, 1978, has a legal life equal to the life of the author plus 70 years (United States Copyright Office Web site: www.loc.gov/copyright). Usually, the economic life of a copyright will be less than its legal life. For patent applications on or after June 8, 1995, utility and plant patents have a legal life of 20 years from the date of the patent application.
- However, design patents have a legal life of 14 years from the date the **United States Patent and Trademark Office** grants the patent. If a patent was in force before June 8, 1995, or it was granted after that date but with an earlier application date, the life is the greater of the 20-year life or 17 years from the date of the grant (United States Patent and Trademark Office Web site: www.uspto.gov).

**EXAMPLE**

Abacus Associates, Inc. incurred $20,000 in the acquisition of a 20-year patent (the maximum legal life granted by the United States Patent and Trademark Office for a patent other than a design patent). At the time, the patent is recorded as an asset:

| | |
|---|---|
| Patent | $20,000 |
| Cash | $20,000 |

Each year, the patent is expensed on a straight-line basis over 17 years (if less than its economic life), and amortization is recorded in one of two ways:

| | |
|---|---|
| Amortization Expense | $ 1,000 |
| Accumulated Amortization | $ 1,000 |

OR

| | |
|---|---|
| Amortization Expense | $ 1,000 |
| Patent | $ 1,000 |

Assuming that the patent becomes worthless during the seventh year (i.e., six years of amortization has been recorded), perhaps due to technological advances obsolescing the patent, the journal entry to record the loss attributable to worthlessness is:

| | |
|---|---|
| Loss on Patent | $14,000 |
| Patent | $14,000 |

On December 21, 2005, FASB released its proposal for an amendment to SFAS No. 142 as it relates to the determination of the useful life and amortization of renewable intangible assets. The term "renewable intangible assets" includes all intangible assets for which a marketplace participant assumes renewal or extension, regardless of whether the contract has explicit provisions that enable renewal or extension. Renewable intangible assets include, but are not limited to, gaming licenses, taxicab medallions, cable franchises, airline route authorities, contracts to manage investments of mutual funds, and FCC licenses. Specifically, the Board decided:

- The provisions of the proposed amendment would be effective for interim and annual periods beginning after June 15, 2006.
- At acquisition, the value of the renewable intangible asset should be attributed to the initial contractual period of use and all future renewal periods based upon the relative value of the discounted cash flows of each period and amortized to expense over those respective periods.
- Incremental and direct costs of renewal should be capitalized and amortized over that renewal period.

- Renewable intangible assets should be subject to a fair-value based test (similar to the impairment test for indefinite lived intangible assets under Statement 142). In the event of an impairment charge, the updated valuation should be utilized for purposes of attributing amortization expense to the remaining renewal periods.
- Paragraph 11(d) of Statement 142 should be retained and modified as follows:

    "Any legal, regulatory, or contractual provisions that enable renewal or extension of the asset's legal or contractual life without substantial cost (provided there is evidence to support renewal or extension and renewal or extension can be accomplished without material modifications of the existing terms and conditions) renewal is reasonably assured)."

- In relation to the determination of the useful life and amortization of intangible assets:
    - An amortization methodology that reflects the "pattern of economic benefit" to a reporting entity should not be specifically developed in order to address the identified practice issues. The Board indicated, however, that use of such an amortization methodology for finite lived intangible assets would not be inconsistent with paragraph 12 of Statement 142.
    - A renewable intangible asset comprises a single asset.

## TESTING IMPAIRMENT OF INTANGIBLES

A company must review identifiable intangibles for impairment when events or circumstances indicate that the current book value may not accurately reflect the recoverable amount of the asset.

In this situation, the entity should determine the estimated future cash flows from use of the asset as well as its residual value. A company must record an impairment loss when there is a difference between the carrying value and the total expected future cash flows However, the amount of the impairment loss equals the excess of the carrying value over the fair value of the intangible.

Only identifiable intangible assets are accounted for using the provisions of SFAS No. 144, which also covers long-lived tangible assets. In certain circumstances and situations, a company may not recover the carrying amount of intangibles over future accounting periods. Some examples include a major decline in the asset's value, a significantly greater than anticipated increase in costs of the asset, and a current period loss with a history or expectation of future losses.

If a company determines that the carrying value of the intangible is not recoverable, then the company must test the asset for possible impairment. The company should divide the assets into asset groups using the lowest level of assets that generate independent cash flows. It is common for this to occur at the enterprise level for intangible assets.

The gross cash inflows are reduced by cash outflows related to the use and later disposition of the asset group. The company then compares the carrying value of the asset group to the undiscounted estimated net cash flows. If the book value is less than the net cash flow amount, the company should test the asset group for impairment.

The additional impairment testing that is required, compares the fair value of the asset group to the related carrying value. If the fair value is less than the book value, the company reports an impairment loss equal to that difference. A company reports an impairment loss on the income statement as a loss from continuing operations.

---

### EXAMPLE

Squareroot Corporation is reviewing its long-lived assets using the provisions of SFAS No. 144, because of current year losses, a history of operating losses, and anticipated future losses. Squareroot's major asset group is identifiable intangibles (e.g., a franchise agreement). The book value of the asset group amounts to $1,000,000, the estimated net future cash flows are $800,000 and the fair value is $750,000.

Squareroot compares the estimated undiscounted future net cash flows to the carrying amount of the assets; so, the carrying amount exceeds the estimated future cash flows by $200,000 ($1,000,000 - $800,000) and the company must compute an impairment loss. The impairment loss equals the difference between the book value and the fair value of the asset group, which is $250,000 in this case ($1,000,000 - $750,000). It is recorded as follows:

| | |
|---|---|
| Estimated Loss from Impairment | $250,000 |
| Franchise | $250,000 |

---

The following are the disclosure requirements of SFAS No. 144 where a company reports an impairment loss in the financial statements:

- Description of the asset
- Situation causing impairment
- Amount of the loss reported in income statement
- Amount of the loss reported as part of income from continuing operations
- If not reported as a separate line item or parenthetically, the caption where the impairment loss is reported
- Method of determining fair value used to compute the loss
- Business segment impacted by the loss

This chapter addresses the provisions of SFAS No. 142 in a later section regarding accounting for goodwill.

## STUDY QUESTIONS

1. When a company purchases an identifiable intangible asset at arm's length, the amount usually treated as fair market value and capitalized as an asset on the books of the buyer is:

   a. Cost
   b. Book value on the books of the seller
   c. Cash paid but not liabilities incurred
   d. Appraised value

2. If a company records an impairment loss for an intangible asset on its books because the asset declined in value during the period, the impairment loss is reported on:

   a. The statement of retained earnings as a prior period adjustment
   b. The income statement as a change in accounting principle
   c. The income statement as a loss from continuing operations
   d. The balance sheet as a reduction in total stockholders equity

3. If a company must record an impairment loss for an intangible asset, the loss equals the excess of the:

   a. Fair value of the intangible over its carrying value
   b. Carrying value of the intangible over its fair value
   c. Carrying value of the intangible over its total expected future net cash flows
   d. Total expected net cash flows from the intangible over its carrying value

4. An intangible asset with a finite useful life should be tested for impairment when its:

   a. Book value is less than the net cash flows related to the use and later disposition of the asset group
   b. Net cash flows related to the use and later disposition of the asset group are less than its book value
   c. Gross cash inflows are greater than its book value
   d. Book value is greater than its gross cash inflows

5. What is the maximum legal life of a copyright?

   a. Life of the author
   b. 20 years
   c. 70 years
   d. Life of the author plus 70 years

**6.** Which of the following does a company *not* have to disclose when it reports an impairment loss on an intangible asset?

**a.** Method of determining the book value of the intangible asset
**b.** Method of determining fair market value used to compute the loss
**c.** Description of the intangible asset
**d.** The situation causing the impairment

---

**NOTE**

Answers to Study Questions, with feedback to both the correct and incorrect responses, are provided in a special section beginning on page **237**.

## ACCOUNTING FOR RESEARCH AND DEVELOPMENT COSTS

A business should typically expense its research and development costs as incurred. Prior to SFAS No. 2 (1974), some companies capitalized and amortized their research and development (R&D) expenditures over arbitrary useful lives. Now, increased comparability of financial statements is achieved by the requirement that companies expense R&D costs as incurred.

In addition, the enterprise should disclose the total amount of research and development costs charged to expense in either the text of the income statement or in the footnotes to the financial statements.

## DEFINITION OF R&D

R&D activities require two determinations:
- Whether the activity constitutes R&D as defined by SFAS No. 2; and
- Proper recognition for the type of activity.

### Definitions

**Research** is defined as an investigation of a critical nature or a planned search with the purpose of discovering new information that will lead to a new or improved service, product, technique, or process.

**Development activities** include conversation of research into a design or blueprint used for a new or improved service, product, technique, or process.

Because this definition is quite broad, the Statement provides complete lists of activities constituting research and development and those not considered R&D. An abbreviated list follows:

**Figure 1: Research and Development Activities**

| Activities Considered R&D | Activities Not Considered R&D |
|---|---|
| Discovery of new information through laboratory research<br><br>A product or process design modification.<br><br>Exploring for ways that new research or knowledge can be applied.<br><br>Testing that is used to evaluate or search for alternative processes or products.<br><br>Design of items, such as tool dies, that relate to new technology. | Changes in design of existing products that are considered periodic or seasonal.<br><br>Activities during commercial production such as routine testing, trouble-shooting, and quality control.<br><br>Activities, considered routine, to improve an existing product.<br><br>Activities of a legal nature that are related to items such as application for patents.<br><br>Design of items, such as tools and dies that are routine in nature. |

## TYPES OF COSTS INCURRED

If a company determines that a cost incurred is considered to be a research and development cost, then proper accounting is dependent on the type of cost incurred. Typically, there are four categories of costs as follows:

1. In the **first category**, the cost represents materials, equipment, or facilities used in the R&D process. A company must expense these costs currently if they have no alternative future use. A company capitalizes such costs if they have a future use. If the company capitalizes the costs, only the current period depreciation on equipment and facilities along with the materials used are expensed currently.
2. The **second category** contains costs incurred to purchase an intangible asset from another enterprise or individual. These costs are treated similarly to those in the first category. If the intangible has no future alternative use, then the company expenses the costs currently. If an alternative future use exists, then the company capitalizes the costs and amortizes them. However, if the intangible has an indefinite life, the company does not amortize the costs but rather tests them for impairment.
3. The **third category** includes indirect costs that are clearly related to R&D activities. A company should expense these costs in the current accounting period.
4. The **fourth** and final category represents personnel services or contractual services provided by others. With the exception of contractual research conducted for another organization, a company charges the costs of these services to expense as incurred.

### EXAMPLE

D&R, a calendar-year corporation, was involved in a research project during the year. D&R used $1,000,000 of materials during the year. The company acquired a patent costing $100,000 which was acquired on January 1 of the year. The patent has alternative uses in the future, over a period of 10 years. The company also acquired equipment with no future uses on January 1 for $30,000 (useful life of five years and no residual value). The company acquired additional equipment on July 1 at a cost of $1,500,000 (it has alternative future uses, 10-year useful life, and no residual value). Salaries of researchers amounted to $500,000. Consulting fees paid to persons outside D&R were $50,000. Overhead allocated to R&D was $15,000.

**Solution:**

| Situation | R&D Costs | Explanation |
|---|---|---|
| Materials | $1,000,000 | Category 1: Materials used charged to income |
| Patent amortized | $10,000 | Category 2: Amortize over 10 years ($100,000/10) |
| Equipment | $30,000 | Category 1: Equipment with no future use is expensed |
| Equipment | $75,000 | Category 1: Equipment with future use is depreciated ($1,500,000/10 x 6/12) |
| Salaries | $500,000 | Category 4: Expense personnel costs |
| Consulting fees | $50,000 | Category 4: Expense fees of outside services |
| Overhead | $15,000 | Category 3: Expense indirect costs allocated to R&D |

## VENTURE ARRANGEMENTS FOR R&D

Many companies engage in venture arrangements for research and development activities. These ventures spread the risk of R&D between two parties or among three or more parties and allow each party to contribute different skills and assets. SFAS No. 68 (1982) provides guidelines to promote consistency of accounting procedures to account for R&D under these circumstances.

The accounting method used in venture arrangements is dependent on whether the enterprise is obligated to repay contributing parties.

If the company is obligated to repay funds regardless of the outcome of the project, then the arrangement is viewed as a borrowing transaction. In this situation, the entity conducting the R&D may be committed to repay funds.

An enterprise is committed to repay monies if any of the following apply:

- The company guarantees or has a contract that commits it to repay.
- The contributors can require the entity to acquire their interest in the venture.

- The contributing parties will receive the entity's debt or equity securities at the conclusion of the venture.

In any of these circumstances, the enterprise must record a liability for funds received and expense R&D costs as incurred, according to the provisions of SFAS No. 2 outlined earlier. If repayment is contingent on successful results from the research activity, the company issuing the advance accounts for the advance of funds as R&D costs at the time of the advance.

---

**EXAMPLE**

Ideas "R" Us, a December 31 year-end business, was involved in two R&D arrangements during the year.

In the first arrangement, Ideas "R" Us performs all R&D activities for the project. The other entities transfer $2 million to Ideas "R" Us on January 1. Repayment of funds advanced to Ideas "R" Us is contingent on whether the research results in success. Research and development costs incurred during the year on this project amount to $1.6 million.

In the second R&D arrangement, Ideas "R" Us transfers $750,000 on April 1 to another corporation responsible for conducting all R&D activities related to a successful patent. Repayment of funds advanced to the R&D corporation is contingent on whether the research results in success.

**Solution:**

Ideas "R" Us makes the following entries during the year.

*January 1:* Record as a liability until the proceeds are used in the research activities.

**Cash $2,000,000**
**Advance under R&D Arrangement $2,000,000**

**Throughout Year:** Record a reduction in the liability as expenses for R&D are incurred. No further entries are required since no liability exists due to the success contingency.

This entry is a summary entry, representing expenses during the year that would normally constitute multiple entries. The costs are not expensed but charged against the advance only.

**Advance under R&D Arrangement $1,600,000**
**Cash $1,600,000**

*April 1:* Since the outside entity is responsible for conducting all R&D and repayment depends on success, Ideas "R" Us must treat the advance as R&D costs at the time of the advance.

**R&D Expense $750,000**
**Cash $750,000**

## STUDY QUESTIONS

**7.** In general, how must a company treat research and development costs?

   **a.** Capitalize them and amortize them over the useful lives of successful projects

   **b.** Expense them as incurred

   **c.** Capitalize them and amortize them over five years

   **d.** Capitalize them and analyze them periodically for impairment

**8.** Which of the following is considered a research and development activity?

   **a.** A product or process design modification

   **b.** Routine activities to improve an existing product

   **c.** Legal activities related to a patent application

   **d.** Activities during production such as testing and quality control

**9.** Which of the following activities is *not* considered a research and development activity?

   **a.** Discovery of new information through laboratory research

   **b.** Exploring for ways that the company can apply new research or knowledge.

   **c.** Testing used to evaluate or search for alternative processes or products

   **d.** Routine design of tools and dies

**10.** How does a company treat the cost of equipment that it purchased during the year for use in a research and development activity?

   **a.** The company capitalizes the cost of the equipment and charges the depreciation on the equipment to Research and Development Expense whether or not the equipment has any future use.

   **b.** The company capitalizes the cost of the equipment and charges the depreciation on the equipment to Research and Development Expense only if the equipment has a future use.

   **c.** The company charges all of the cost of the equipment to Research and Development Expense whether or not the equipment has any future use.

   **d.** The company treats the cost of the equipment as Research and Development Expenses only if the equipment is worthless at the end of three years.

**11.** A company receives a $500,000 payment from another company for use in a research venture arrangement. The company has no obligation to repay any of the $500,000 unless the research is successful. Throughout the year, the company performing the research incurred research expenditures of $300,000. How does the company treat the $300,000 in research expenditures?

**a.** It charges them to Research and Development Expense.

**b.** It charges them to Capitalized Costs Under Research Venture.

**c.** It charges them to Advance Under Research and Development Arrangement.

**d.** It charges them to Cash.

## ACCOUNTING FOR THE COSTS OF COMPUTER SOFTWARE

As a result of **Securities Exchange Commission (SEC) and American Institute of Certified Public Accountants (AICPA)** interest, the growing volume of computer software companies, and the lack of comparability among financial statements of software firms, the **Financial Accounting Standards Board (FASB)** issued SFAS No. 86 (1985).

This Statement specifies the proper accounting and reporting requirements for computer software developed internally and purchased from outside entities for sale, lease, or marketing.

Included in SFAS No. 86 are software programs, a group of computer programs, or computer product enhancement.

Specifically excluded are software programs developed or purchased for internal use and software developed for other entities based on a contractual arrangement.

### Software Products Developed Internally

The appropriate accounting method requires classification of the computer software costs into four different categories:

- **First,** a company must expense software research and development costs as incurred.
- **Second,** after technological feasibility is achieved, a company capitalizes and amortizes software production costs. An entity achieves technological feasibility when the company completes all activities (e.g., coding, testing, and designing) necessary for the entity to determine that it can produce the software product to meet all specifications.
- **Third,** when the software is ready for release to customers, the company capitalizes software inventory costs on a unit-by-unit basis and charges them to Cost of Goods Sold as it sells the software.

- **Fourth**, any other software costs incurred when the company markets the product to customers are expensed when incurred or when the company earns revenue, whichever occurs first.

Examples of software costs are presented in the following chart:

| R&D Costs |
|---|
| Cost of planning |
| Cost of product design |
| Cost of detail program design |
| Cost of achieving technological feasibility |
| Cost of testing software prior to achieving technological feasibility |
| Cost of coding software prior to achieving technological feasibility |
| **Production Costs** |
| Cost of coding after achieving technological feasibility |
| Cost of testing after achieving technological feasibility |
| **Inventory Costs** |
| Cost of duplicating software |
| Cost of software documentation |
| Cost of developing software training materials |
| Cost of physically packaging software for distribution |
| Other Software Costs |
| Cost of software maintenance |
| Cost of software support |

## TECHNOLOGICAL FEASIBILITY

A company must determine technological feasibility to classify R&D costs properly. A detail program design is one that is ready for coding and represents a detail design that takes all requirements to the most detailed form.

From a practical standpoint, if the software package has a detail program design, a company achieves technological feasibility when it satisfies three conditions:

- The entity has finished both the product and the detail program designs.
- The entity has verified that the detail program design is complete and compatible with the product design.
- Either the entity has determined that there are no uncertainties concerning development issues of a high-risk nature, or the entity has resolved such uncertainties.

If the product does not have a detail program design, technological feasibility is established when the entity meets two conditions:

- The entity has finished a product design and a working model of the software.
- The entity has verified that the product design and the working model are complete and compatible.

If, instead, the entity will use the software as an integral part of a software process or product, the costs are considered R&D until two conditions are fulfilled:

- Achievement of technological feasibility for the product
- Completion of all R&D activities associated with the remaining components of the software

In this case, the software costs are not classified as production costs until the entity has achieved technological feasibility and completed all R&D activities.

## ACCOUNTING TREATMENT OF PRODUCTION COSTS

A company capitalizes production costs and amortizes them on a product-by-product basis using an appropriate method.

The correct annual amortization of production costs is equal to the greater of the amounts computed using the following two methods:

- The straight-line method over the useful life of the software product
- The gross revenue ratio method using the following formula:

PCAE = ASR/(ASR + ESR)] x TPC, where
PCAE = Annual production cost amortization expense.
ASR = Actual software revenue recorded for the current year.
ESR = Estimated remaining software revenue to be recorded in future years.
TPC = The smaller of total production costs or net realizable value of the software (future gross revenues from the sale of the product less any costs to complete and dispose of the product, including customer support and software maintenance).

The company must compare the balance in the unamortized production cost account to the net realizable value of the software product on each balance sheet date. If the net realizable value is less than the unamortized production cost balance, the company recognizes a loss for the difference and writes down the unamortized production cost to equal net realizable value. Then, net realizable value is considered the new cost basis for the production costs, and the company computes future amortization using the net realizable value.

**EXAMPLE**

Extuit, Inc., a calendar-year company, is involved in the development of computer software that it will sell to outside customers. Its expected useful life is four years. During the year, X1, Extuit was involved in a software project and incurred the following costs related to the project:

**Costs Incurred Before Technological Feasibility**

| | |
|---|---|
| Cost of coding | $40,000 |
| Cost of testing | $20,000 |
| Cost of planning | $30,000 |
| Cost of achieving technological feasibility | $10,000 |
| Cost of developing product design align | $80,000 |
| Cost of developing a detailed program design | $65,000 |

**Costs Incurred After Technological Feasibility**

| | |
|---|---|
| Cost of coding | $50,000 |
| Cost of software maintenance | $20,000 |
| Miscellaneous software costs after sale | $5,000 |
| Cost of testing | $30,000 |
| Cost of documentation | $20,000 |
| Cost of developing training materials | $60,000 |
| Cost of duplicating software | $20,000 |
| Cost of packaging software | $25,000 |
| Cost of customer support | $25,000 |

**Estimated revenues for Extuit's product are:**

| | |
|---|---|
| Year X2 | $300,000 |
| Year X3 | $400,000 |
| Year X4 | $300,000 |
| Year X5 | $600,000 |

## SOLUTION

**Step 1:** Classify the various software costs into R&D, production, inventory, and other software costs. Before this is possible, the company must determine the date of technological feasibility. Then, all costs incurred before this date are classified as R&D and expensed as incurred.

Thus, R&D costs are $245,000 (all costs incurred before technological feasibility). The costs incurred after the company achieves technological feasibility to produce the product master software are classified as production costs and capitalized on a product-by-product basis; so, the production costs amount to $80,000 (the total of coding and testing costs after technological feasibility).

Other costs incurred to get the product ready for sale, such as those for preparing training materials and documenting and duplicating the software master are inventory costs and are capitalized on a unit-specific basis. The inventory costs in this example total $125,000 (documentation of $20,000, training materials of $60,000, duplicating costs of $20,000, and packaging amounting to $25,000).

Costs incurred after the company sells the product are classified as other software costs and expensed as incurred or when the company recognizes the related revenue, whichever occurs first. These costs amount to $50,000 in this example (customer support, software maintenance, and miscellaneous costs).

**Step 2:** Amortize the software costs classified as production costs using an acceptable method. Amortization begins on 1/1/X2, when the product is ready for customer use. The annual amortization is the greater of the straight-line amount or the amount determined using the gross revenue ratio method. The straight-line method results in amortization of production costs of $20,000 in X2 ($80,000/4). The gross revenue ratio method yields $15,000, computed as follows:

[ASR/(ASR + ESR)] x TPC = [300/(300+1,300)] x $80,000, where
ASR, actual X2 software revenue is $300,000.

ESR, estimated remaining software revenue to be recorded in future years amounts to $1,300,000.

TPC, the smaller of total production costs, $80,000, or net realizable value of the software, $1, 550,000 (future gross revenues $1,600,000 less costs to complete and dispose of the product, including customer support and software maintenance, $50,000).

**Thus, X2 amortization of production costs is the greater of $20,000 or $15,000 and is recorded as follows:**

| | |
|---|---|
| Amortization of Computer Software Production Costs | $20,000 |
| Computer Software Production Costs | $20,000 |

## PURCHASED SOFTWARE

In addition to developing software internally, a company may purchase software that it will market to outside customers. Most of the accounting rules applicable to internally developed software also apply to purchased software; however, a company may market purchased software as purchased, modified and marketed, used as a part of a product, or purchased for alternative future use.

The accounting treatment is dependent on the existence of a future use, whether the company has achieved technological feasibility, and the integration of the purchased product into a product or process.

Like accounting for R&D expenditures, the concept of alternative future use applies to purchased computer software. In this case, alternative future use indicates that the company uses the product purchased for a project in addition to the software product under consideration.

Also, when purchased software has an alternative use and the company has not achieved technological feasibility on the date of purchase, the company must capitalize the cost of the software and account for it based on use.

This means that the company charges part of the cost of the software to R&D and accounts for the balance based on how the company will use the product in the future.

**Figure 2: Technological Feasibility**

| Time Estimates | Technological Feasibility | |
|---|---|---|
| Future | Technologically Feasible Not Technologically Feasible | Production cost capitalized and amortized using an acceptable method. Capitalized cost at the date of purchase and accounted for based on its use. |
| No Future | Technologically Feasible Not Technologically Feasible | Production cost capitalized and amortized using an acceptable method. R&D cost expensed when incurred. |

Disclosure requirements specify that the company must disclose the balance in the unamortized computer software costs account on the balance sheet. On the income statement, the company must disclose the expensed amounts related to total R&D, amortization of capitalized computer software, and losses from the write down of computer software costs to net realizable value.

Computer software expenses and related R&D costs are classified as normal operating expenses on the income statement. Production costs are classified as long-term assets and amortized, while Inventory is a current asset charged off as sold.

---

**EXAMPLE**

Wearsoft is a calendar-year corporation in the business of purchasing, modifying, and marketing computer software. During X1, Wearsoft purchased three software products:

■ **Software 1:** Technological feasibility is established at the date of purchase and the product has an alternative future use, at a cost of $200,000;

■ **Software 2:** The product requires modification prior to sale, so technological feasibility is not achieved at the date of purchase and there is no alternative future use, at a cost of $160,000;

■ **Software 3:** The software is to be used as an integral part of a software process, with no alternate future use, but achieves technological feasibility on the date of purchase at which time R&D is complete, for a cost of $250,000.

All products were available for customer use on December 31, X1.

**SOLUTION**

**Step 1:** Classify the cost of the software on the date of purchase. For Softwares 1 and 3, the purchase cost is a production cost; and, Software 2 costs are classified as R&D. Software 1 is a production cost because technological feasibility is achieved at the date of purchase. Since both technological feasibility and all R&D activities related to the software process are complete at the date of purchase, Software 3 is classified as a production cost. The cost of Software 2 is charged to R&D due to the alternative future use and because technological feasibility has not been achieved. The entry to record the acquisition of the software products is as follows:

| | |
|---|---|
| R&D Expense | $160,000 |
| Computer Software Production Costs | $450,000 |
| Cash | $610,000 |

## STUDY QUESTIONS

**12.** How must a company treat research and development costs related to a software product developed by the company?

    **a.** Capitalize and amortize the costs over the estimated useful life of the software

    **b.** Expense such costs as incurred

    **c.** Capitalizes such costs as a part of inventory and reports such costs as a part of cost of goods sold when the company sells the software

    **d.** Expense such costs only when the company sells the software

**13.** Which of the following costs is a research and development cost with respect to the development of computer software?

    **a.** Cost of achieving technological feasibility

    **b.** Cost of testing after achieving technological feasibility

    **c.** Cost of software documentation

    **d.** Cost of software maintenance

**14.** Which of the following is an inventory cost?

    **a.** Cost of detail program design

    **b.** Cost of coding after achieving technological feasibility

    **c.** Cost of developing software training materials

    **d.** Cost of software support

**15.** Which of the following is a production cost?

   **a.** Cost of testing before achieving technological feasibility
   **b.** Cost of duplicating software
   **c.** Cost of software support
   **d.** Cost of testing after achieving technological feasibility

**16.** On each balance sheet date, a company must compare the balance in the unamortized production cost account to the:

   **a.** Net realizable value of the software product
   **b.** Accumulated amortization
   **c.** Fair market value of the software product
   **d.** Estimated discounted future cash flows from the software product

**17.** Computer software expenses are classified on the income statement as:

   **a.** Extraordinary items
   **b.** Unusual expenses
   **c.** Normal operating expenses
   **d.** Infrequent expenses

## ACCOUNTING FOR GOODWILL AND OTHER INTANGIBLE ASSETS

SFAS No. 142 specifies the accounting and reporting requirements for goodwill and other intangible assets. Issued in June 2001, SFAS No. 142 supersedes APB Opinion No. 17, AICPA Interpretations related to Opinion No. 17 and ARB No. 43, and amends several other accounting principles. A company records acquired intangible assets at fair market value (or relative fair value, if acquired in a lump-sum purchase), which is usually cost when the company purchases the intangible assets in an arm's length purchase. The company amortizes the costs of these intangible assets over their useful lives if the assets are deemed to have a finite life.

A company determines the useful life of an intangible asset by using the time period that the company estimates the intangible asset will contribute directly or indirectly to future cash flows. A company does not amortize intangibles with indefinite lives but tests them for impairment.

A company does not amortize goodwill acquired in a business combination, but instead allocates the goodwill to reporting units and tests it for impairment. The costs related to internally generated intangibles (except goodwill and those costs determined to constitute research and development costs) are capitalized and amortized under certain conditions.

A company should aggregate intangible assets (except goodwill) and report them as a separate line item in the balance sheet. An enterprise may elect to report individual intangibles separately or by class on the balance sheet. A company should report goodwill, however, as a separate line item on the balance sheet.

A company should report impairment losses and amortization expense related to intangibles on the income statement under income from continuing operations as a line item. If a goodwill impairment loss results from a discontinued operation, the company should report the impairment with discontinued operations.

## ACQUISITION OF INTANGIBLES

A company should report an intangible asset acquired individually, such as the purchase of a patent, Internet domain name, or customer lists, as an asset at its fair market value, which is usually cost in an arm's length purchase.

Generally, the amount of the cash exchanged is considered the fair value. If a company uses noncash assets, liabilities, or equity securities to acquire the intangible asset, the company should use the fair market value of the consideration given or received, whichever is more readily determinable, to record the intangible asset.

When a company purchases an intangible in combination with other assets, the company allocates the acquisition price to the intangible based on its fair market value relative to the fair market values of all assets acquired.

A company should amortize an intangible asset with a finite life over its estimated useful life. However, a company should not amortize an intangible with an indefinite life, but the company should test it for impairment when appropriate.

A company determines the useful life of an asset by estimating the period of time that the asset contributes to future cash flows. Factors to consider when determining useful life include asset use, useful life of related assets, legal limits, legal rights that extend useful life, the impact of obsolescence, and the relationship between maintenance costs and future cash flows.

After a company determines the useful life of an intangible asset, the company amortizes the intangible over that useful life using the amortization method that most accurately reflects the pattern of use.

A company should review the useful life each accounting period. A company should restate any changes attributable to an amended useful life prospectively and amortize the remaining book value over the revised useful life.

---

**EXAMPLE**

On January 1, acquired a patent at cost of $100,000. The patent is estimated to have a useful life of 10 years.

**SOLUTION**

The annual amortization expense for the patent amounts to $10,000. If the asset is used up faster in early years and less in later years, some form of accelerated amortization should be used. If the asset is used up equally each period, then straight-line amortization is appropriate.

### EXAMPLE

A patent has a cost of $100,000, no residual value, and accumulated amortization amounting to $20,000. The estimated useful life was originally 10 years. The revised estimate indicates that only four years remain.

### SOLUTION

The new amortization expense amounts to $20,000 per year ($100,000 less $20,000/4 years). The residual value of an intangible asset is often zero. In actuality, it is the asset's fair market value at the end of its useful life reduced by any expected disposition costs. It is assumed to be zero unless it is expected to have a useful life to another enterprise later, or its future value is readily determinable from existing market transactions. In addition, entities should test the intangible asset for impairment.

## IMPAIRMENT

Impairment results when the company may not recover the carrying value of assets over future accounting periods. In the case of intangibles, this most often occurs when there is a major decline in the asset's fair value.

- The following process is utilized to determine an impairment loss. After dividing the entity's assets into groups using the lowest level of assets that generate independent cash flows, the enterprise should estimate the net cash flows for each asset group. The company should compute the cash flows on a gross basis (not discounted to present value) and include any cash flows related to the use and disposition of the asset group.
- If the cash flow is less than the carrying value of the asset group, the company should test it for possible impairment. This requires a comparison of fair market values of the assets in the potentially impaired group.
- If fair value is less than the carrying amount of the asset group, the company reports an impairment loss equal to the difference between the carrying amount and the fair value.
- The asset is reduced by the loss, and the company amortizes the new basis over the remaining useful life.
- A subsequent recovery in the fair value of the intangible does not result in a reversal of the loss writedown.

> **EXAMPLE**
>
> Pattent Corporation is reviewing its intangibles using the provisions of SFAS No. 144 because the company has a history of operating losses. The company has assets in other categories, but only its intangible asset generates cash flows in the category under consideration.
>
> The carrying amount of the intangible asset is $10 million, with estimated net future cash flows of $8 million, and a fair market value of $7.5 million.
>
> **SOLUTION**
>
> Because of the history of operating losses, Pattent Corporation must assess its intangible for impairment. Because the estimated future net cash flow of $8 million is less than the carrying amount of the asset ($10 million), the company must record an impairment loss.
>
> The amount of the loss is $2.5 million, which is the difference between the carrying value ($10 million), and the fair value of the asset ($7.5 million). The following journal entry records the impairment of the intangible:
>
> | Estimated loss from impairment of intangible | 2,500,000 | |
> |---|---|---|
> | Intangible | | 2,500,000 |

## INTERNALLY GENERATED INTANGIBLES

A company may develop, restore, or maintain an intangible asset. Many of the costs are research and development costs, subject to the provisions addressed in the first section of this chapter.

A company capitalizes the costs related to internally generated intangibles when three conditions are satisfied:

- The costs must be related to an intangible asset that can be specifically identified, such as legal fees connected with obtaining a patent.
- Second, the asset must have a determinable life.
- Third, the intangible must not be inherent in a going concern and related to the enterprise as a whole.

For instance, consider the costs incurred to defend a patent held by the company.

The costs would be identifiable with the patent, have a determinable life, and not be related to the enterprise as a whole.

## GOODWILL

Goodwill exists when the purchasing company pays more for a business than the fair market value of the net assets if purchased separately.

**EXAMPLE**

If the value of a company's net asset is $1 million but the purchase price is $1.4 million, goodwill exists in the amount of $400,000. The company records the payment in excess of fair market value of the assets in the Goodwill account.

This section of this course addresses the subsequent accounting for goodwill and impairment decisions. A company does not amortize goodwill resulting from a business combination. Instead, the company tests it for impairment using the special impairment rules for goodwill contained in SFAS No. 142. The test involves a two-step reporting level basis.

**First**, the company compares the carrying amount of the reporting unit to its fair market value, including goodwill. If the carrying value is less than its fair value, no impairment exists, and the second step is not required. If the fair value is less than the carrying value, impairment is assumed. In this case, the company performs **the second step** to determine the amount of the impairment loss. The fair value of the reporting unit is the amount that a willing buyer would pay the seller. Although a quoted market price is the best estimate of fair market value, the company may use other acceptable methods.

Three methods are possible:

- Prices paid for similar assets and liabilities
- Present value of future cash flows
- Valuation using multiples of earnings or revenue from other operations or activities of an entity, for which the multiples are known and are comparable in nature, scope, or size as the reporting unit for which fair value is being estimated

Rather than computing fair value each accounting period or at a minimum annually, fair value can often be carried forward. If the entity or unit experiences no significant changes, had fair value far in excess of book value in the prior determination, and it is unlikely that the fair value is less than book value, then the company can carry fair value forward.

In the **second step**, the company compares the carrying value of the goodwill to the implied fair value of the goodwill. This implied value is distinguished from the fair value because an estimate is used. One cannot directly determine the fair value of goodwill.

A company computes the implied fair value using the same procedures an entity would use when initially computing goodwill in a business combination.

The price paid for the unit (assumed to be fair market value) is allocated to all assets, including any intangibles. Any excess of price paid over the fair value allocated to the assets is the implied fair value of the goodwill.

So, if the implied fair value of the goodwill is less than the related carrying amount of the goodwill, an impairment loss equals the difference. The loss is limited to the book value of the goodwill. A new basis for the goodwill is created. Reversal of prior impairment losses in subsequent periods is not permitted.

Testing for goodwill impairment under SFAS No. 142 uses a process of assigning assets, liabilities, and goodwill to reporting units. Assets and liabilities assigned may be part of a business combination, purchased separately, or as a part of a group purchase. They are typically assigned to the reporting unit on the date of acquisition.

A company should assign goodwill to reporting units that will benefit from it on the acquisition date, using a method that is reasonable, supportable, and applied on a consistent basis.

An entity should test for impairment of goodwill on least an annual basis, and earlier if evidence suggests that testing is warranted. The company must perform the testing at the same time each year, although each entity within a company may have different test dates during the year.

---

### EXAMPLE

LeadJerr Company computed $1,000,000 of goodwill in a business combination on January 1, X1. The goodwill was allocated to Reporting Units L and J. At the end of X3, the values for each reporting unit are:

| Unit | Fair Value | Book Value | Book Value GW | Fair Value GW |
|------|------------|------------|---------------|---------------|
| L | $20,000,000 | $16,000,000 | $600,000 | $700,000 |
| J | $18,000,000 | $19,500,000 | $400,000 | $375,000 |

**Step 1:** Compare the fair value of the reporting unit with its carrying value. For Unit L, the fair value of $20 million exceeds the $16 million book value; therefore, there is no goodwill impairment. For Unit J, the fair value of $18 million is less than the book value of $19.5 million; so, the company must test goodwill for impairment.

**Step 2:** Compare the fair value to the carrying value of the goodwill. This step is only relevant to Unit J. Unit J's goodwill has a book value of $400,000 and a fair value of $375,000. Since the fair value is less than the carrying value by $25,000, the company reports a goodwill impairment loss on the income statement in the amount of $25,000. The new goodwill carrying value amounts to $975,000 (600,000 + 375,000).

A company should not amortize goodwill computed using the equity method, but the company should test it for impairment under the provisions of APB No. 18. A company should test goodwill from a business combination with a minority interest using the minority interest at the date of acquisition. A company tests subsidiary goodwill for impairment at the subsidiary level, using its reporting units. Only if the goodwill is impaired at the consolidated level does the company report an impairment loss in the consolidated financial statements.

**EXAMPLE**

A company disposes of a part of its business. The fair value of the disposed portion of the business prior to disposition was $100,000. The fair value of the remaining portion of the business after the disposition is $400,000. Goodwill is $1,000. What is the amount of the goodwill allocated to the disposition?

The goodwill allocated to the disposition is $200, {$1,000 x [$100,000/($100,000 + $400,000)]}.

## STUDY QUESTIONS

**18.** Which accounting standard now governs the treatment of goodwill and other intangible assets?

   **a.** APB Opinion No. 17
   **b.** SFAS No. 2
   **c.** SFAS No. 68
   **d.** SFAS No. 142

**19.** Goodwill acquired in a business acquisition must be:

   **a.** Expensed in the year acquired
   **b.** Capitalized and amortized over its useful life
   **c.** Capitalized and amortized over 40 years
   **d.** Capitalized and analyzed for impairment

**20.** Internally generated goodwill is:

   **a.** Not recorded in the accounts
   **b.** Capitalized and amortized over its useful life
   **c.** Capitalized and amortized over 40 years
   **d.** Capitalized and analyzed for impairment

**21.** A company should test for impairment of goodwill at least:

   **a.** Monthly
   **b.** Quarterly
   **c.** Semiannually
   **d.** Annually

**22.** An impairment loss for goodwill equals the excess of its:

   **a.** Carrying value over its implied fair market value
   **b.** Implied fair value over its carrying value
   **c.** Net realizable value over its carrying value
   **d.** Carrying value over its fair value

**23.** The costs incurred to defend a patent held by the company should be:

  **a.** Expensed as incurred
  **b.** Capitalized as a cost of the patent
  **c.** Capitalized and amortized over 40 years
  **d.** Capitalized as a separate asset

**24.** If a loss is recorded for the impairment of goodwill and its value increases in a subsequent period, the company should:

  **a.** Do nothing because reversal of prior impairment losses is not allowed
  **b.** Record a gain from continuing operations
  **c.** Record an extraordinary gain
  **d.** Show the increase as a cumulative change in accounting principle

**25.** Which intangible asset must a company report as a separate line item on the balance sheet?

  **a.** Patent
  **b.** Copyright
  **c.** Goodwill
  **d.** License

MODULE 2 — CHAPTER 4

# Balance Sheet Classifications

## LEARNING OBJECTIVES

After completing this chapter, the participant will be able to:

- Define basic concepts and terms associated with balance sheet classification
- Identify the two common procedures of accounting for uncollectible receivables
- Identify important issues regarding the cash surrender value of life insurance
- Apply liability classification issues
- Identify the key principles of GAAP for compensated absences
- Understand and apply the principles of offsetting assets and liabilities

## OVERVIEW

The distinction between current and noncurrent assets and liabilities in a classified balance sheet is an important feature of financial reporting. There is considerable interest in the liquidity of the reporting enterprise, and the separate classification of current assets and liabilities is an important part of liquidity analysis.

GAAP concerning current assets and current liabilities are found in the following pronouncements:

ARB-43    *Chapter 1A, Receivables from Officers, Employees, or Affiliated Companies Chapter 3A, Current Assets and Current Liabilities*

APB-10    *Omnibus Opinion—1966*

FAS-6    *Classification of Short-Term Obligations Expected to Be Refinanced*

FAS-43    *Accounting for Compensated Absences*

FAS-78    *Classification of Obligations That Are Callable by the Creditor*

FAS-150    *Accounting for Certain Financial Instruments with Characteristics of Both Liabilities and Equity*

FIN-8    *Classification of a Short-Term Obligation Repaid Prior to Being Replaced by a Long-Term Security*

FIN-39    *Offsetting of Amounts Related to Certain Contracts*

FIN-41    *Offsetting of Amounts Related to Certain Repurchase and Reverse Repurchase Agreements*

## BACKGROUND

In the ordinary course of business there is a continuing circulation of capital within the current asset accounts. For example, a manufacturer expends cash for materials, labor, and factory overhead that are converted into finished inventory. After being sold, inventory usually is converted into trade receivables and, on collection of receivables, is converted back to cash. The average time elapsing between expending the cash and receiving the cash back from the trade receivable is called an *operating cycle*. One year is used as a basis for segregating current assets when more than one operating cycle occurs within a year. When the operating cycle is longer than one year, as with the lumber, tobacco, and distillery businesses, the operating cycle is used for segregating current assets. In the event that a business clearly has no operating cycle, the one-year rule is used (ARB-43, Ch. 3A, par. 5).

Frequently, businesses have a *natural business year*, at the end of which the company's activity, inventory, and trade receivables are at their lowest point. This is often the point in time selected as the end of the entity's accounting period for financial reporting purposes.

## STUDY QUESTIONS

1. Which one of the following statements is *false?*

   a. The average time elapsing between expending cash and receiving the cash back from the trade receivable is called an operating cycle.

   b. When the operating cycle is longer than a year, the operating cycle is used for segregating current assets.

   c. One year is used as a basis for segregating current assets when more than one operating cycle occurs within a year.

   d. The lumber, tobacco and distillery industries have an operating cycle of one year.

2. At the end of a business' _____, the company's activity, inventory, and trade receivables are at their low point.

   a. fiscal year

   b. natural business year

   c. official business year

   d. none of the above

**NOTE**

Answers to Study Questions, with feedback to both the correct and incorrect responses, are provided in a special section beginning on page **237**.

## BASIC DEFINITIONS

### Current Assets

Resources that are expected to be realized in cash, sold, or consumed during the next year (or longer operating cycle) are classified as current assets. Current assets are sometimes called circulating or working assets; cash that is restricted as to withdrawal or use for other than current operations is not classified as a current asset (ARB-43, Ch. 3A, par. 6).

There are several basic types of current assets (ARB-43, Ch. 3A, par. 4):

- Cash
  - Includes money in any form. For example, cash on deposit, cash awaiting deposit, and cash funds available for use.
- Cash Equivalents
  - Short-term, highly liquid investments that are (a) readily convertible to known amounts of cash and (b) so near their maturities that they present insignificant risk of changes in value because of changes in interest rates.
- Secondary Cash Resources
  - The most common type of secondary cash resources is marketable securities.
- Receivables
  - Include accounts receivable, notes receivable, and receivables from officers and employees.
- Inventories
  - Includes merchandise, raw materials, work in process, finished goods, operating supplies, and ordinary maintenance material and parts.
- Prepaid Expenses
  - Includes prepaid insurance, interest, rents, taxes, advertising, and operating supplies. Prepaid expenses, unlike other current assets, are not expected to be converted into cash; but, if they had not been paid in advance, they would require the use of current assets during the operating cycle.

### Current Liabilities

Current liabilities are obligations for which repayment is expected to require the use of current assets or the creation of other current liabilities.

> **PRACTICE POINTER**
>
> The definition of current liabilities is based on the asset category from which the liability is expected to be retired rather than on a specific period of time. As a practical matter, most current liabilities are those that are expected to be retired during the period of time encompassed by the definition of current assets. Be careful, however, to identify instances where liabilities that are due in the near future should be classified as noncurrent because they will not require the use of current assets. Examples are short-term obligations expected to be refinanced, and noncurrent liabilities that are near their maturity but that will be paid from noncurrent assets (e.g., bond sinking funds).

There are several basic types of current liabilities (ARB-43, Ch. 3A, par. 7):

- Payables from Operations
  - Includes items that have entered the operating cycle, which include trade payables and accrued liabilities such as wages and taxes.
- Debt Maturities
  - Includes amounts expected to be liquidated during the current operating cycle, such as short-term notes and the currently maturing portion of long-term debt
- Revenue Received in Advance
  - Includes collections received in advance of services, for example, prepaid subscriptions and other deferred revenues. This type of current liability is typically liquidated by means other than the payment of cash.
- Other Accruals
  - Includes estimates of accrued amounts that are expected to be required to cover expenditures within the year for known obligations (a) when the amount can be determined only approximately (provision for accrued bonuses payable) or (b) when the specific person(s) to whom payment will be made is (are) unascertainable (provision for warranty of a product) (ARB-43, Ch. 3A, par. 8).

### Working Capital and Related Ratios

Working capital is the excess of current assets over current liabilities, and it is often used as a measure of the liquidity of an enterprise (ARB-43, Ch. 3A, par. 3).

### Changes in Each Element of Working Capital

The changes in each element of working capital are the increases or decreases in each current asset and current liability over the amounts in the preceding year.

**Illustration of Determining Working Capital**

| | 20X5 | 20X6 | Working Capital Increase or Decrease |
|---|---|---|---|
| Current Assets: | | | |
| Cash | $10,000 | $15,000 | $5,000 |
| Accounts receivable, net | 25,000 | 35,000 | 10,000 |
| Inventory | 50,000 | 60,000 | 10,000 |
| Prepaid expenses | 1,000 | 500 | (500) |
| Total current assets | $86,000 | $110,500 | $24,500 |
| Current Liabilities: | | | |
| Accounts payable | $10,000 | $15,000 | $(5,000) |
| Notes payable-current | 20,000 | 15,000 | 5,000 |
| Accrued expenses | 1,000 | 1,500 | (500) |
| Total current liabilities | $31,000 | $31,500 | $(500) |
| Net working capital | $55,000 | $79,000 | |
| Increase in working capital | | | $24,000 |

The *current ratio*, or *working capital ratio*, is a measure of current position and is useful in analyzing short-term credit. The current ratio is computed by dividing the total current assets by the total current liabilities.

**Illustration of Current Ratio**

| | 20X5 | 20X6 |
|---|---|---|
| Current Assets | $86,000 | $110,500 |
| Current liabilities | (31,000) | (31,500) |
| Working capital | $55,000 | $79,000 |
| Current ratio | 2.8 : 1 | 3.5 : 1 |

The *acid-test ratio* (also called the *quick ratio*) is determined by dividing those assets typically closest to cash by total current liabilities. The assets used to calculate this ratio consist of only the most liquid assets, typically cash, receivables, and marketable securities.

**PRACTICE POINTER**

Only receivables and securities convertible into cash are included; restricted cash and securities are excluded.

**Illustration of Acid-Test Ratio**

|  | 20X5 | 20X6 |
|---|---|---|
| Cash | $10,000 | $15,000 |
| Receivables, net | 25,000 | 35,000 |
| Total *quick* assets | $35,000 | $50,000 |
| Total current liabilities | $31,000 | $31,500 |
| Acid-test ratio | 1.1 : 1 | 1.6 : 1 |

## STUDY QUESTIONS

3. Current assets include all of the following *except:*

    a. Revenue received in advance of services
    b. Secondary cash resources
    c. Inventories
    d. Prepaid expenses

4. Current liabilities include all of the following *except:*

    a. Payables from operations
    b. Revenue received in advance of services
    c. Debt maturities
    d. Prepaid expenses

5. Which of the following is computed by dividing the total current assets by the total current liabilities?

    a. Working capital
    b. Acid-test ratio
    c. Quick ratio
    d. Current ratio

## RECEIVABLES

Accounts receivable are reported in the financial statements at net realizable value. Net realizable value is equal to the gross amount of receivables less an estimated allowance for uncollectible accounts.

Two common procedures of accounting for uncollectible accounts are (a) the direct write-off method and (b) the allowance method.

## Direct Write-Off Method

This method recognizes a bad debt expense only when a specific account is determined to be uncollectible. The conceptual weaknesses of the direct write-off method are:

- Bad debt expense is not *matched* with the related sales.
- Accounts receivable are overstated, because no attempt is made to account for the unknown bad debts included therein.

Ordinarily, the direct write-off method is not considered GAAP, because it results in a mismatching of revenues and expenses (i.e., expenses are recognized in a later period than the revenue to which they relate) and overstates the amount of assets. The method may be acceptable in situations where uncollectible accounts are immaterial in amount.

## Allowance Method

The allowance method recognizes an estimate of uncollectible accounts each period, even though the specific individual accounts that will not be collected cannot be identified at that time. Estimates of uncollectible accounts usually are made as a percentage of credit sales or ending receivables. This method is consistent with FAS-5 (Accounting for Contingencies), as explained below.

Under FAS-5, a contingency exists if, at the date of the financial statements, an enterprise does not expect to collect the full amount of its accounts receivable. Under this circumstance, an accrual for a loss contingency must be charged to income, if both of the following conditions exist:

- It is probable that as of the date of the financial statements an asset has been impaired or a liability incurred, based on information available before the issuance of the financial statements.
- The amount of the loss can be *estimated reasonably.*

If both of the above conditions are met, an accrual for the estimated amount of uncollectible receivables is made even if the specific uncollectible receivables cannot be identified. An enterprise may base its estimate of uncollectible receivables on its prior experience, the experience of other enterprises in the same industry, the debtor's ability to pay, or an appraisal of current economic conditions. Significant uncertainty may exist in the ultimate collection of receivables if an enterprise is unable to estimate reasonably the amount that is uncollectible. If a significant uncertainty exists in the ultimate collection of the receivables, the installment sales method, cost-recovery method, or some other method of revenue recognition should be used. In the event that both of the above conditions for accrual are not met and a loss contingency is at least reasonably possible, certain financial statement disclosures are required by FAS-5.

### Illustration of Accounting for Uncollectible Accounts by the Allowance Method

AMB Co. estimates uncollectible accounts at 1% of credit sales. For the current year, credit sales totaled $1,000,000. The year-end balances in accounts receivable and the unadjusted allowance for uncollectible accounts are $250,000 and $15,000, respectively.

The entry to record uncollectible accounts ($1,000,000 x 1% = $10,000) is as follows:

| Bad debt expense | $10,000 |
|---|---|
| Allowance for uncollectible accounts | $10,000 |

The balance sheet will include accounts receivable of $250,000, allowance for uncollectible accounts of $25,000 ($15,000 + $10,000), and net accounts receivable of $225,000 ($250,000 – $25,000).

When a specific uncollectible account is written off (e.g., $2,100), the following entry is required:

| Allowance for uncollectible accounts | $2,100 |
|---|---|
| Accounts receivable (specific account) | $2,100 |

This entry has no effect on the amount of net accounts receivable, because both the receivables balance and the allowance balance are reduced by the same amount.

If the estimate of uncollectible accounts receivable had been based on the ending balance of accounts receivable, the same procedure would have been followed, except that the existing balance in the allowance would require consideration. For example, if uncollectible accounts were estimated at 9% of the ending balance in accounts receivable, the bad debt expense for the year would be $7,500, computed as follows:

| Required allowance ($250,000 x 9%) | $22,500 |
|---|---|
| Balance before adjustment | (15,000) |
| Required adjustment | $7,500 |

The balance sheet would include accounts receivable of $250,000, an allowance of $22,500, and a net receivables amount of $227,500 ($250,000 – $22,500).

A variation on the previous method is to "age" accounts receivable, a procedure that provides for recognizing an increasing percentage as uncollectible, as accounts become increasingly delinquent. For example, applying this procedure to the $250,000 receivables balance above might result in the following:

| | Within 30 Days | 30 Days Overdue | 60 Days Overdue | Past 60 Days Overdue |
|---|---|---|---|---|
| Accounts receivable balance | $120,000 | $50,000 | $50,000 | $30,000 |
| Uncollectible % | 2% | 7% | 12% | 25% |
| Uncollectible balance | $2,400 | $3,500 | $6,000 | $7,500 |

The total uncollectible balance is $19,400, resulting in the recognition of bad debt expense of $4,400, assuming a previous allowance balance of $15,000 ($19,400 − $15,000 = $4,400).

## STUDY QUESTION

**6.** A conceptual weaknesses of the direct write-off method is:

**a.** Bad debt expense is not matched with the related sales.

**b.** An estimate of uncollectible accounts is recorded each period.

**c.** Accounts receivable are understated.

**d.** Uncollectible accounts usually are estimated using a percentage of credit sales.

### Discounted Notes Receivable

Discounted notes receivable arise when the holder endorses the note (with or without recourse) to a third party and receives a sum of cash. The difference between the amount of cash received by the holder and the maturity value of the note is called the discount. If the note is discounted with recourse, the assignor remains contingently liable for the ultimate payment of the note when it becomes due. If the note is discounted without recourse, the assignor assumes no further liability.

The account "discounted notes receivable" is a contra account, which is deducted from the related receivables for financial statement purposes. The following is the procedure for computing the proceeds of a discounted note:

1. Compute the total maturity value of the note, including interest due at maturity.
2. Compute the discount amount (the maturity value of the note multiplied by the discount rate for the time involved).
3. The difference between the two amounts (1, less 2) equals the proceeds of the note.

### Illustration of Discounted Notes Receivable

A $1,000 90-day 10% note is discounted at a bank at 8% when 60 days are remaining to maturity.

| Maturity - $1,000 + ($1,000 x .10 x 90/360) | $1,025.00 |
| Discount - $1,025 x .08 x 60/360 | (13.67) |
| Proceeds of note | $1,011.33 |

### Factoring

Factoring is a process by which a company converts its receivables into immediate cash by assigning them to a factor either with or without recourse. With recourse means that the assignee can return the receivable to the company and get back the funds paid if the receivable is uncollectible. Without recourse means that the assignee assumes the risk of losses on collections. Under factoring arrangements, the customer may or may not be notified.

### Pledging

Pledging is the process whereby the company uses existing accounts receivable as collateral for a loan. The company retains title to the receivables but pledges that it will use the proceeds to pay the loan.

### STUDY QUESTION

> **7.** A process by which a company converts its receivables into immediate cash by assigning them to another party either with or without recourse is known as:
>
> **a.** Pledging
> **b.** Factoring
> **c.** Discounting
> **d.** Contra account

### CASH SURRENDER VALUE OF LIFE INSURANCE

The proceeds of a life insurance policy usually provide some degree of financial security to one or more beneficiaries named in the policy. Upon death of the insured, the insurance company pays the beneficiary the face amount of the policy, less any outstanding indebtedness.

## Insurable Interest

An owner of an insurance contract must have an insurable interest in the insured individual in order for the contract to be valid. An insurable interest in life insurance need only exist at the time the policy is issued, while an insurable interest in property insurance must exist at the time of a loss. An insurable interest is a test of financial relationship. A husband may insure the life of his wife, an employer the life of an employee, a creditor the life of a debtor, and a partner the life of a copartner.

An investment in a life insurance policy is accounted for at the amount that can be realized by the owner of the policy as of the date of its statement of financial position. Generally, the amount that can be realized from a life insurance policy is the amount of its cash surrender value. The increase in the cash surrender value of an insurance policy for a particular period is recorded by the owner of the policy and the cash surrender value is included as an asset in its statement of financial position. The insurance expense for the same period is the difference between the total amount of premium paid and the amount of increase in the cash surrender value of the policy.

## Illustration of Insurable Interest

An enterprise is the owner and sole beneficiary of a $200,000 life insurance policy on its president. The annual premium is $16,000. The policy is starting its fourth year, and the schedule of cash values indicates that at the end of the fourth year the cash value increases $25 per thousand. The enterprise pays the $16,000 premium, and the journal entry to record the transaction is as follows:

| | |
|---|---|
| Life insurance expense - officers | $11,000 |
| Cash surrender value - life insurance policy (200 x $25) | 5,000 |
| Cash | $16,000 |

The cash surrender value of a life insurance policy is classified either as a current or noncurrent asset in the policy owner's statement of financial position, depending upon the intentions of the policy owner. If the policy owner intends to surrender the policy to the insurer for its cash value within its normal operating cycle, the cash surrender value is classified as a current asset in the statement of financial position. If there is no intention of collecting the policy's cash value within the normal operating cycle of the policy owner, the cash surrender value is classified as a noncurrent asset in the statement of financial position.

## STUDY QUESTION

---

**8.** Which one of the following statements is true?

    **a.** The increase in cash surrender value of a life insurance policy for a particular period is not considered an asset in the owner's statement of financial position.

    **b.** An insurable interest in property insurance must exist at the time of the loss.

    **c.** If a policy owner intends to surrender the policy to the insurer for its cash value within its normal operating cycle, the cash surrender value is classified as a noncurrent asset in the statement of financial position.

    **d.** An insurable interest in life insurance must exist at the time of the loss.

---

## LIABILITY CLASSIFICATION ISSUES

### Current Obligations Expected to Be Refinanced

FAS-6 (Classification of Short-Term Obligations Expected to Be Refinanced) and FIN-8 (Classification of a Short-Term Obligation Repaid Prior to Being Replaced by a Long-Term Security) establish GAAP for classifying a short-term obligation that is expected to be refinanced into a long-term liability or stockholders' equity. FAS-6 applies only to those companies that issue classified balance sheets (FAS-6, par. 7).

A short-term obligation can be excluded from current liabilities only if the company intends to refinance it on a long-term basis and the intent is supported by the ability to refinance that is demonstrated in one of the following ways (FAS-6, pars. 9–11):

- A long-term obligation or equity security whose proceeds are used to retire the short-term obligation is issued after the date of the balance sheet but before the issuance of the financial statements.
- Before the issuance of the financial statements, the company has entered into an agreement that enables it to refinance a short-term obligation on a long-term basis. The terms of the agreement must be clear and unambiguous and must contain the following provisions:
  - The agreement may not be canceled by the lender or investor, and it must extend beyond the normal operating cycle of the company.

> **PRACTICE POINTER**
>
> If the company has no operating cycle or the operating cycle occurs more than once a year, then the one-year rule is used.

- At the balance sheet date and at its issuance, the company was not in violation, nor was there any information that indicated a violation, of the agreement.
- The lender or investor is expected to be financially capable of honoring the agreement.

The amount of short-term obligation that can be reclassified as non-current cannot exceed the actual proceeds received from the issuance of the new long-term obligation or the amount of available refinancing covered by the established agreement. The amount must be adjusted for any limitations in the agreement that indicate the full amount obtainable will not be available to retire the short-term obligation. In addition, if the agreement indicates that the amount available for refinancing will fluctuate, then the most conservative estimate must be used. If no reasonable estimate can be made, then the agreement does not fulfill the necessary requirements and the full amount of current liabilities must be presented (FAS-6, par. 12).

An enterprise may intend to seek alternative financing sources besides those in the established agreement when the short-term obligation becomes due. If alternative sources do not materialize, however, the company must intend to borrow from the source in the agreement (FAS-6, par. 13).

> **PRACTICE POINTER**
>
> If the terms of the agreement allow the prospective lender or investor to set interest rates, collateral requirements, or similar conditions that are unreasonable to the company, the intent to refinance may not exist.

FIN-8 addresses the issue of a short-term obligation that is repaid and is subsequently replaced with a long-term debt obligation or equity securities. Because cash is temporarily required to retire the short-term obligation, the obligation should be classified as a current liability in the balance sheet (FIN-8, par. 3).

Any *rollover agreements* or *revolving credit agreements* must meet the above provisions to enable a company to classify the related short-term obligations as noncurrent (FAS-6, par. 14). The financial statements must contain a note disclosing the amount excluded from current liabilities and a full description of the financial agreement and new obligations incurred or expected to be incurred or the equity securities issued or expected to be issued (FAS-6, par. 15).

### Callable Obligations

FAS-78 (Classification of Obligations That Are Callable by the Creditor) establishes GAAP for the current/noncurrent classification in the debtor's balance sheet of obligations that are payable on demand or callable by the creditor.

FAS-78 is applied to a classified balance sheet to determine whether the obligation should be classified as current or noncurrent for balance sheet purposes. FAS-78 is applied to both classified and unclassified balance sheets to determine the maturity dates of obligations disclosed by notes. For example, an unclassified balance sheet may contain a note disclosure of the maturity dates of obligations, despite the fact that the obligations are not classified in the unclassified balance sheet, or may not be identified separately from other obligations in the unclassified balance sheet (FAS-78, par. 4).

At the debtor's balance sheet date, an obligation may, by its terms, be payable on demand. This includes long-term obligations that are callable because a violation of an objective acceleration clause in a long-term debt agreement may exist at the date of the debtor's balance sheet. Such callable obligations must be classified as a current liability at the debtor's balance sheet date unless (FAS-78, par. 5):

- The creditor has waived the right to demand payment for a period that extends beyond one year (or the debtor's normal operating cycle if longer), or
- The debtor has cured the violation after the balance sheet date, but prior to the issuance date of the financial statements, and the obligation is not callable for a period that extends beyond one year (or the debtor's normal operating cycle if longer).

A long-term debt agreement may provide for a grace period that commences after the occurrence of a violation of an objective acceleration clause. FAS-78 requires that such an obligation be classified as a current liability at the debtor's balance sheet date, unless the two criteria above are met and, in addition, the unexpired grace period extends beyond one year (or the debtor's normal operating cycle if longer) (FAS-78, par. 5).

> **OBSERVATION**
>
> FAS-78, which amends ARB-43, Chapter 3A, requires that an obligation be classified as current or noncurrent, based solely on whether the legal terms of the loan agreement require payment within one year (or the operating cycle if longer).

A creditor may have waived the right to demand payment on a specific obligation for a period that extends beyond one year (or the operating cycle if longer). In this event, the debtor shall classify the obligation as a noncurrent liability.

### Acceleration Clauses

An *objective acceleration* clause in a long-term debt agreement is one that contains objective criteria that the creditor must use as the basis for calling part of the loan or the entire loan, such as a specified minimum amount of working capital or net worth requirement.

In the event of a violation of an objective acceleration clause, most long-term obligations become immediately callable by the creditor, or become callable after a grace period that is specified in the loan agreement. When this occurs, the creditor can demand payment of part or all of the loan balance, in accordance with the terms of the debt agreement.

A subjective acceleration clause is one that permits the lender to unilaterally accelerate part or all of a long-term obligation. For example, the debt agreement might state that "if, in the opinion of the lender, the borrower experiences recurring losses or liquidity problems, the lender may at its sole discretion accelerate part or all of the loan balance.…".

Acceleration clauses are accounted for in the same manner as other loss contingencies. If it is *probable* that the subjective acceleration clause will be exercised by the creditor, the amount of the long-term obligation that is likely to be accelerated shall be classified as a current liability by the debtor. On the other hand, if it is only *reasonably* possible that the subjective acceleration clause will be exercised by the creditor, note disclosure may be all that is required. Finally, if the possibility of subjective acceleration is *remote*, no disclosure may be required.

### Employers' Accounting for Defined Benefit Pension and Other Postretirement Plans an Amendment of FASB Statements No. 87, 88, 106, and 132(R)

An exposure draft of a new SFAS was issued by FASB on March 31, 2006 regarding "Employers' Accounting for Defined Benefit Pension and Other Postretirement Plans an amendment of FASB Statements No. 87, 88, 106, and 132(R). This proposed Statement is intended to improve existing reporting for defined benefit postretirement plans by requiring an employer that is a business entity to:

■ Recognize in its statement of financial position the overfunded or underfunded status of a defined benefit postretirement plan measured as the difference between the fair value of plan assets and the benefit obligation. For a pension plan, the benefit obligation would be the projected benefit obligation; for any other postretirement benefit plan, such as a retiree health care plan, the benefit obligation would be the accumulated postretirement benefit obligation.

■ Recognize as a component of other comprehensive income, net of tax, the actuarial gains and losses and the prior service costs and credits that arise during the period but pursuant to FASB Statements No. 87, Employers' Accounting for Pensions, and No. 106, Employers' Accounting for Postretirement Benefits Other Than Pensions, are not recognized as components of net periodic benefit cost. Amounts recognized in accumulated other comprehensive income would be adjusted as they are subsequently recognized as components of net periodic benefit cost pursuant to the recognition and amortization provisions of Statements 87 and 106.

- Recognize as an adjustment to the opening balance of retained earnings, net of tax, any transition asset or transition obligation remaining from the initial application of Statement 87 or 106. Those amounts would not be subsequently amortized as a component of net periodic benefit cost.
- Measure defined benefit plan assets and defined benefit plan obligations as of the date of the employer's statement of financial position.
- Disclose additional information in the notes to financial statements about certain effects on net periodic benefit cost in the upcoming fiscal year that arise from delayed recognition of the actuarial gains and losses and the prior service costs and credits.

This proposed Statement also would apply to a not-for-profit organization or an entity that does not report other comprehensive income but would tailor its requirements to reflect their alternative reporting formats. This proposed Statement would amend Statement 87, FASB Statement No. 88, Employers' Accounting for Settlements and Curtailments of Defined Benefit Pension Plans and for Termination Benefits, Statement 106, and FASB Statement No. 132 (revised 2003), Employers' Disclosures about Pensions and Other Postretirement Benefits, and other related accounting literature.

### Disclosure Requirements

An employer that is a business entity that sponsors one or more defined benefit pension or other postretirement benefit plans shall disclose:

- For each period for which a statement of income is presented, the net actuarial gain or loss and the prior service cost or credit recognized in other comprehensive income, separated into amounts initially recognized in other comprehensive income, and amounts subsequently recognized as adjustments to other comprehensive income as those amounts are recognized as components of net periodic benefit cost pursuant to the recognition and amortization provisions of Statements 87 and 106.
- For each period for which a statement of financial position is presented, the amount of net actuarial gain or loss and the prior service cost or credit included in accumulated other comprehensive income.
- Separately, the estimated portion of the net actuarial gain or loss and the prior service cost or credit in accumulated other comprehensive income that will be recognized as a component of net periodic benefit cost over the fiscal year that follows the most recent statement of financial position presented.

### Effective Dates

For all entities, both public and nonpublic, the requirement to recognize the funded status of a defined benefit postretirement plan and the related disclosure requirements would be effective for fiscal years ending after December

15, 2006. Retrospective application would be required unless retrospective application is impracticable as defined by this proposed Statement.

For a public entity that measures plan assets and benefit obligations as of a date other than the date of its statement of financial position, the requirement to change that date to the year-end reporting date would be applied for fiscal years beginning after December 15, 2006. For a nonpublic entity, including a not-for-profit organization, that measures plan assets and benefit obligations as of a date other than the date of its statement of financial position, the requirement to change that date to the year-end reporting date would be applied for fiscal years beginning after December 15, 2007.

If the employer enters into a transaction that results in a settlement or experiences an event that causes a curtailment of the plan in the last quarter of the fiscal year that precedes the change in measurement date, the related gain or loss would be recognized in earnings in the last quarter of that fiscal year. The proposed amendments related to the measurement date would not be permitted to be applied retrospectively.

## COMPENSATED ABSENCES

FAS-43 (Accounting for Compensated Absences) establishes GAAP for employees' compensated absences and is concerned only with the proper accrual of the liability for compensated absences rather than the allocation of such costs to interim accounting periods.

FAS-43 does not apply to the following (FAS-43, par. 2):

- Severance or termination pay
- Stock or stock options issued to employees
- Deferred compensation
- Postretirement benefits
- Group insurance, disability pay, and other long-term fringe benefits
- Certain sick pay benefits that accumulate

Compensated absences arise from employees' absences from employment because of illness, holiday, vacation, or other reasons. When an employer expects to pay an employee for such compensated absences, a liability for the estimated probable future payments must be accrued if all the following conditions are met (FAS-43, par. 6):

1. The employee's right to receive compensation for the future absences is attributable to services already performed by the employee.
2. The employee's right to receive the compensation for the future absences is vested, or accumulates.
3. It is probable that the compensation will be paid.
4. The amount of compensation is reasonably estimable.

The fact that an employer meets the first three conditions and not the fourth condition must be disclosed in the financial statements.

Vested rights are those that have been earned by the employee for services already performed. They are not contingent on any future services by the employee and are an obligation of the employer even if the employee leaves the employer. Rights that accumulate are nonvesting rights to compensated absences that are earned and can be carried forward to succeeding years. Rights that accumulate increase an employee's benefits in one or more years subsequent to the year in which they are earned. An employer does not have to accrue a liability for nonvesting rights to compensated absences that expire at the end of the year in which they are earned, because they do not accumulate (FAS-43, par. 13).

Nonvesting sick pay benefits that accumulate and can be carried forward to succeeding years are given special treatment by FAS-43. If payment of nonvesting accumulating sick pay benefits depends on the future illness of the employee, an employer does not have to accrue a liability for such payments. The reasons cited in FAS-43 for this exception are (a) the cost/benefit rule, (b) the materiality rule, and (c) the reliability of estimating the days an employee will be sick in succeeding years. This exception does not apply in circumstances in which the employer pays the sick pay benefits even though the employee is not actually sick. An employer's general policy for the payment of nonvesting accumulating sick pay benefits should govern the accounting for such payments (FAS-43, par. 7).

---

**PRACTICE POINTER**

One issue that must be resolved in recognizing the expense and liability for compensated absences is the rate of compensation to use—the current rate or the rate expected to apply when the compensated absence is taken by the employee. In situations in which the rate of compensation increases rapidly and/or a long period of time lapses between the time the compensated absence is earned and taken by the employee, the rate of compensation used may be significant. FAS-43 does not provide guidance on this issue. Other authoritative standards may provide some help in making this decision. For example, net periodic pension cost is determined in FAS-87 (Employers' Accounting for Pensions) based on the projected benefit obligation, which includes expected future increases in compensation. If the difference in the amount of liability for compensated absences, when measured by the current and expected future rates of compensation, is material, the latter more faithfully measures the obligation and expense of the employer.

---

Once a total amount of liability for compensated absences is determined, the amount expected to require the use of current assets should be classified as a current liability. The remaining balance should be presented as a noncurrent liability.

## Sabbatical Leave

An entity may provide its employees with a compensated benefit known as a sabbatical leave whereby the employee is entitled to time off after working for that entity for a specified period of time.

For example, when an employee provides 5 years of service to an entity, the employee is eligible to take 4 weeks off as a sabbatical. During the sabbatical, the individual continues to be a compensated employee of the entity; however, the employee is not required to perform any duties for the entity.

Based on the example above, if an employee terminates employment with the entity before working the full five years, they are not entitled to compensation for the unused sabbatical (that is, the right does not vest over the eight year period as the term is defined in FAS 43). Similarly, if after working five years the employee terminates employment prior to taking the earned leave, they are entitled to no benefit. The sabbatical may also have a limited life once eligibility has been attained.

EITF 06-2, *Accounting for Sabbatical Leave and Other Similar Benefits Pursuant to FASB Statement No. 43*, "Accounting for Compensated Absences" was issued March 16, 2006, in response to questions which have been raised with respect to the interpretation of paragraph 6(b) of FAS 43 on whether, in the absence of a vesting condition, a sabbatical leave actually accumulates. Footnote 2 of paragraph 6 of FAS 43 provides a definition of accumulate and states:

> **NOTE**
>
> For purposes of this Statement, accumulate means that earned but unused rights to compensated absences may be carried forward to one or more periods subsequent to that in which they are earned, even though there may be a limit to the amount that can be carried forward.

Since a sabbatical leave does not typically have a vesting condition, some have questioned whether, based on the definition provided in FAS 43, it should be accrued over the term of the service period. Therefore, diversity exists with respect to the interpretation of accumulate.

The Task Force reached a consensus that "an employee's right to a compensated absence under a sabbatical or other similar benefit arrangement (a) that requires the completion of a minimum service period and (b) in which the benefit does not increase with additional years of service accumulates pursuant to paragraph 6(b) of Statement 43 for arrangements in which the individual continues to be a compensated employee and is not required to perform duties for the entity during the absence. Therefore, assuming all of the other conditions of paragraph 6 of Statement 43 are met, the compensation cost associated with a sabbatical or other similar benefit arrangement should be accrued over the requisite service period."

The Task Force reached a consensus that this Issue should be applied in financial reports for fiscal years beginning after the date the consensus is ratified by the Board. At its June 28, 2006 meeting, the FASB ratified the consensuses reached by the Task Force regarding this issue.

Entities should recognize the effects of applying the consensus on this Issue, warns FASB, "as a change in accounting principle through retrospective application to all prior periods unless it is impracticable to do so. This should include the recognition of:

- The cumulative effect of the change to the new accounting principle on periods prior to those presented reflected in the carrying amounts of assets and liabilities as of the beginning of the first period presented
- An offsetting adjustment, if any, made to the opening balance of retained earnings (or other appropriate components of equity or net assets in the statement of financial position) for that period
- Adjustments to financial statements for each individual prior period presented to reflect the period-specific effects of applying the new accounting principle

If the cumulative effect of applying the change in accounting principle to all prior periods can be determined but it is impracticable to determine the period-specific effects of that change on all prior periods presented, the cumulative effect of the change should be applied to the carrying amounts of assets and liabilities as of the beginning of the earliest period to which the new accounting principle can be applied. An offsetting adjustment, if any, should be made to the opening balance of retained earnings (or other appropriate components of equity or net assets in the statement of financial position) for that period.

If it is impracticable to determine the cumulative effect of applying a change in accounting principle to any prior period, the new accounting principle should be applied as if the change was made prospectively as of the earliest date practicable.

Upon application of this Issue, the following should be disclosed:

- A description of the prior-period information that has been retrospectively adjusted, if any
- The effect of the change on income from continuing operations, net income (or other appropriate captions of changes in the applicable net assets or performance indicator), any other affected financial statement line item, and any affected per-share amounts for the current period and for any prior periods retrospectively adjusted
- The cumulative effect of the change on retained earnings or other components of equity or net assets in the statement of financial position as of the beginning of the earliest period presented.

## UNCERTAIN TAX POSITIONS

The FASB issued an Exposure Draft on July 14, 2005, *Accounting for Uncertain Tax Positions* that would interpret FASB Statement No. 109, *Accounting for Income Taxes.* This proposal seeks to reduce the diversity in practice associated with certain aspects of the recognition and measurement requirements related to accounting for income taxes. Specifically, the proposal would require that a tax position meet a "probable recognition threshold" for the benefit of an uncertain tax position to be recognized in the financial statements. The FASB is proposing that a company would use the definition of probable as described in FASB Statement No. 5, *Accounting for Contingencies.* Companies would recognize in their financial statements the best estimate of the effect of a tax position only if that position is probable of being sustained on audit by the appropriate taxing authorities, based solely on the technical merits of the position. The proposal would apply broadly to all tax positions accounted for under Statement 109, including those that pertain to assets and liabilities acquired in a business combination.

The FASB is proposing that the guidance in this interpretation be effective for the first fiscal year ending after December 15, 2005. Only tax positions that meet the probable recognition test when adopting the proposal would be recognized. The population of tax positions to be reviewed upon adoption includes all for which the statute of limitations is still open at the date of adoption. Any required transition adjustments would be recorded in the period of change using a cumulative catch-up adjustment. Accordingly, as proposed, a calendar year-end company would be required to adopt this interpretation in its 2005 financial statements with any required transition adjustment being recorded on the last day of the period the proposal is adopted (e.g., December 31, 2005 if adopted in the fourth quarter). Restatement of previously issued interim or annual financial statements would not be permitted.

## STUDY QUESTION

---

**9.** Which one of the following statements regarding FAS-43 is *false?*

    **a.** It is concerned only with the proper accrual of the liability for compensated absences rather than the allocation of such costs to interim accounting periods.

    **b.** It establishes GAAP for employees' compensated absences.

    **c.** It applies to severance pay and postretirement benefits.

    **d.** It applies to compensated absences due to illness, holiday or vacation.

---

## OFFSETTING ASSETS AND LIABILITIES—GENERAL

*Offsetting* is the display of a recognized asset and a recognized liability as one net amount in a financial statement. If the amount of the recognized asset is the same as the amount of the recognized liability, then the net or combined amount of both is zero, and, as a result, no amount would appear in the financial statement. If the two amounts are not the same the net amount of the two items that have been offset is presented in the financial statement and classified in the manner of the larger item.

APB-10 (Omnibus Opinion—1966) discusses the general principle of offsetting in the balance sheet in the context of income tax amounts. APB-10 includes the following statements:

- Offsetting assets and liabilities in the balance sheet is improper except where a right of setoff exists.
- This includes offsetting cash or other assets against a tax liability or other amounts owed to governments that are not, by their terms, designated specifically for the payment of taxes.
- The only exception to this general principle occurs when it is clear that a purchase of securities that are acceptable for the payment of taxes is in substance an advance payment of taxes that are payable in the relatively near future.

The general principle of financial reporting, which holds that offsetting assets and liabilities is improper except where a right of setoff exists, usually is considered in the context of unconditional receivables from and payables to another party. FIN-39 (Offsetting of Amounts Related to Certain Contracts) extends this general principle to *conditional* amounts recognized for contracts under which the amounts to be received or paid or the items to be exchanged depend on future interest rates, future exchange rates, future commodity prices, or other factors.

FIN-39 specifies four criteria that must be met for the right of setoff to exist (FIN-39, par. 5):

- Each party owes the other party specific amounts.
- The reporting party has the right to set off the amount payable, by contract or other agreement, with the amount receivable from the other party.
- The reporting party intends to set off.
- The right of setoff is enforceable at law.

**OBSERVATION**

The importance of managerial intent is apparent in the third criterion, which states that the reporting party **intends** to set off its payable and receivable. When all of these conditions are met, the reporting entity has a valid right of setoff and may present the net amount of the payable or receivable in the balance sheet.

Generally, debts may be set off if they exist between mutual debtors, each acting in its capacity as both debtor and creditor. State laws and the U.S. Bankruptcy Code may impose restrictions on or prohibitions against the right of set off in bankruptcy under certain circumstances.

### Illustration of Offsetting Assets and Liabilities

The offsetting of assets and liabilities is an important issue to consider when determining financial statement presentation of current assets and current liabilities. Anytime items are set off, information that would otherwise be available is lost. In addition, important financial statement relationships may be altered when assets and liabilities are set off. Consider the following example:

| Current Assets | |
| --- | --- |
| Receivable from M Co. | $100 |
| Other assets | 400 |
| | $500 |
| Current Liabilities | |
| Payable to M Co. | $75 |
| Other liabilities | 175 |
| | $250 |
| Current ratio (500/250) | 2:1 |

Now, consider the same situation, except the $75 payable to M Co. is offset against the $100 receivable from M Co.:

| Current Assets | |
| --- | --- |
| Net receivable from M Co.     ($100 - $75) | $25 |
| Other assets | 400 |
| | $425 |
| Current Liabilities | |
| Other liabilities | $175 |
| Current ratio (425/175) | 2.4 : 1 |

When offsetting is applied, the individual amounts of the receivable and payable are not presented, and only the net amount of $25 is present in the balance sheet. Further, the current ratio is significantly altered by the offsetting activity. This is a simple example, but it illustrates the impact of offsetting, and thus its importance as a financial statement reporting issue.

Many sources of authoritative accounting standards specify accounting treatments that result in offsetting or in a balance sheet presentation that has an effect similar to offsetting. FIN-39 is not intended to modify the accounting treatment in any of those particular circumstances.

The specific sources of GAAP that are covered by this exemption are (FIN-39, par. 7):

- FASB Statements and Interpretations
- APB Opinions
- Accounting Research Bulletins
- FASB Technical Bulletins
- AICPA Accounting Interpretations
- AICPA Audit and Accounting Guides
- AICPA Industry Audit Guides
- AICPA Statements of Position

### Offsetting in Repurchase and Reverse Repurchase Agreements

FIN-41 (Offsetting Amounts Related to Certain Repurchase and Reverse Repurchase Agreements) provides specific guidance as to when payables under repurchase agreements can be offset with receivables under reverse repurchase agreements. These criteria are (FIN-41, par. 3):

1. The agreements are executed with the same counterparty.
2. The agreements have the same settlement date, set forth at inception.
3. The agreements are executed in accordance with a master netting arrangement.
4. The securities under the agreements exist in "book entry" form and can be transferred only by means of entries in the records of the transfer system operator or securities custodian.
5. The agreements will be settled on a securities transfer system that operates in the manner described below, and the enterprise must have associated banking arrangements in place. Cash settlements for securities transferred are made under established banking arrangements that provide that the enterprise will need available cash on deposit only for any net amounts that are due at the end of the business day.

   It must be probable that the associated banking arrangements will provide sufficient daylight overdraft or other intraday credit at the settlement date for each of the parties.
6. The enterprise intends to use the same account at the clearing bank (or other financial institution) to settle its receivable (i.e., cash inflow from the reverse purchasing agreement) and its payable (i.e., cash outflow to settle the offsetting repurchase agreement).

If these six conditions are met, the enterprise has the option to offset. That choice must be applied consistently.

The third criterion refers to a "master netting arrangement." A master netting arrangement exists if the reporting entity has multiple contracts, whether for the same type of conditional or exchange contract or for different types of contracts, with a single counterparty that are subject to a contractual agreement that provides for the net settlement of all contracts through a single payment in a single currency in the event of default on or termination of any one contract (FIN-39).

The fourth criterion refers to "book entry" form. FIN-41 sees this as a key element because it provides control over the securities. The controlling record for a "book entry" security is maintained by the transfer system operator. A securities custodian that has a security account with the transfer system operation may maintain "subsidiary" records of "book entry" securities and may transfer the securities within its subsidiary records; however, a security cannot be traded from the account of that custodian to a new custodian without a "book entry" transfer of the security over the securities transfer system. This form of accounting record facilitates repurchase and reverse repurchase agreement transactions on securities transfer systems.

For a transfer system for repurchase and reverse repurchase agreements to meet the fifth criterion, cash transfers must be initiated by the owner of record of the securities notifying its securities custodian to transfer those securities to the counterparty to the arrangement. Under associated banking arrangements, each party to a same-day settlement of both a repurchase agreement and a reverse repurchase agreement would be obligated to pay a gross amount of cash for the securities transferred from its counterparty, but the party would be able to reduce that gross obligation by notifying its securities custodian to transfer other securities to that counterparty the same day (FIN-41, par. 4).

In the fifth criterion, the term probable has the same definition as in FAS-5, meaning that a transaction or event is more likely to occur than not. The phrase "daylight overdraft or other intraday credit" refers to the feature of the banking arrangement that permits transactions to be completed during the day when insufficient cash is on deposit, provided there is sufficient cash to cover the net cash requirement at the end of the day.

## STUDY QUESTION

**10.** The display of a recognized asset and a recognized liability as one net amount in a financial statement is known as:

    **a.** Pledging

    **b.** Offsetting

    **c.** Discounting

    **d.** Contra account

## Liabilities and Equity

In May 2003, the Financial Accounting Standards Board (FASB) issued FASB Statement No. 150 (FAS-150), Accounting for Certain Financial Instruments with Characteristics of Both Liabilities and Equity, which seeks to more clearly define the distinction between liabilities and equity. The approach taken is to specifically define liabilities and require that all other financial instruments be classified as equity in the balance sheet. The FASB states that FAS-150 (Accounting for Certain Financial Instruments with Characteristics of Both Liabilities and Equity) is generally consistent with its conceptual framework, specifically FASB Concepts Statement No. 6, Elements of Financial Statements, which provides definitions of the various elements of the statement of financial position (balance sheet), income statement, and statement of cash flows.

FAS-150 establishes standards for issuers of financial instruments with characteristics of both liabilities and equity related to the classification and measurement of those instruments. It requires the issuer to classify a financial instrument as a liability, or asset in some cases, which was previously classified as equity. The classification standards are generally consistent with the definition of liabilities in FASB Concepts Statement No. 6 and with the FASB's proposal to revise that definition to encompass certain obligations that a reporting entity can or must settle by issuing its own equity shares.

## Distinction Between Liabilities and Equity

FAS-150 requires an issuer to classify the following instruments as liabilities, or assets in certain circumstances:

- A financial instrument issued in the form of shares that is mandatorily redeemable in that it embodies an unconditional obligation that requires the issuer to redeem the shares by transferring the entity's assets at a specified or determinable date(s) or upon an event that is certain to occur
- A financial instrument other than an outstanding share that, at its inception, embodies an obligation to repurchase the issuer's equity shares, or is indexed to such an obligation, and that requires or may require the issuer to settle the obligation by transferring assets
- A financial instrument other than an outstanding share that embodies an unconditional obligation that the issuer must or may settle by issuing a variable number of equity shares if, at inception, the monetary value of the obligation is based solely or predominantly on any of the following:
  - A fixed monetary amount known at inception (e.g., a payable to be settled with a variable number of the issuer's equity shares)
  - Variations in something other than the fair value of the issuer's equity shares (e.g., a financial instrument indexed to the S&P 500 and settleable with a variable number of the issuer's equity shares)
  - Variables inversely related to changes in the fair value of the issuer's equity shares (e.g., a written put option that could be net share settled)

FAS-150 applies to issuers' classification and measurement of freestanding financial instruments, including those that comprise more than one option or forward contract. It does not apply to features that are embedded in a financial instrument that is not a derivative in its entirety. In applying the classification provisions of FAS-150, nonsubstantive or minimal features are to be disregarded.

### Required Disclosures

Issuers of financial instruments are required to disclose the nature and terms of the financial instruments and the rights and obligations embodied in those instruments. That disclosure shall include information about any settlement alternatives in the contract and identify the entity that controls the settlement alternatives.

For all outstanding financial instruments within the scope of FAS-150, and the settlement alternative(s), the following information is required to be disclosed by issuers:

- The amount that would be paid, or the number of shares that would be issued and their fair value, determined under the conditions specified in the contract if the settlement were to occur at the reporting date
- How changes in the fair value of the issuer's equity shares would affect those settlement amounts
- The maximum amount that the issuer could be required to pay to redeem the instrument by physical settlement, if applicable
- The maximum number of shares that could be required to be issued, if applicable
- That a contract does not limit the amount that the issuer could be required to pay or the number of shares that the issuer could be required to issue, if applicable
- For a forward contract or an option indexed to the issuer's equity shares, the forward price or option strike price, the number of the issuer's shares to which the contract is indexed, and the settlement date(s) of the contract

### Illustration of Applying FAS-150

**Mandatorily redeemable financial instruments.** Financial instruments issued in the form of shares that embody unconditional obligations of the issuer to redeem the instruments by transferring its assets at a specified or determinable date(s) or upon an event that is certain to occur are required to be classified as liabilities. This includes certain forms of trust-preferred securities and stock that must be redeemed upon the death or termination of the individual who holds them. Although some mandatorily redeemable instruments are issued in the form of shares, those instruments are classified as liabilities under FAS-150 because of the embodied obligation on the part of the issuer to transfer its assets in the future:

> **EXAMPLE**
>
> **Statement of Financial Position**
>
> | | |
> |---|---:|
> | Total assets | $5,000,000 |
> | Liabilities other than shares | $4,200,000 |
> | Shares subject to mandatory redemption | 800,000 |
> | Total Liabilities | $5,000,000 |
>
> **Notes to Financial Statements**
>
> Shares subject to mandatory redemption:
>
> | | |
> |---|---:|
> | Common stock | $600,000 |
> | Retained earnings attributed to those shares | 200,000 |
> | | 800,000 |

**Certain obligations to issue a variable number of shares.** FAS-150 requires liability classification if, at inception, the monetary value of an obligation to issue a variable number of shares is based solely or predominantly on any of the following:

- A fixed monetary amount known at inception
- Variations in something other than the fair value of the issuer's equity shares
- Variations inversely related to changes in the fair value of the issuer's equity shares

> **EXAMPLE**
>
> An entity may receive $500,000 in exchange for a promise to issue a sufficient number of shares of its own stock to be worth $525,000 at a specified future date. The number of shares to be issued to settle the obligation is variable, depending on the number required to meet the $525,000 obligation, and will be determined based on the fair value of the shares at the settlement date. The instrument is classified as a liability under FAS-150.

**Freestanding financial instruments.** FAS-150 requires certain provisions of FAS-150 to be applied to a freestanding instrument in its entirety:

> **EXAMPLE**
>
> An issuer has two freestanding instruments with the same counterparty: (1) a contract that combines a written put option at one strike price and a purchased call option at another strike price on its equity shares; and (2) outstanding shares of stock. The primary requirements of FAS-150 are applied to the entire freestanding instrument that includes both a put option and a call option. It is classified as a liability and is measured at fair value. The outstanding shares of stock are not within the scope of FAS-150.

## Disclosure Standards

Current assets and current liabilities must be identified clearly in the financial statements, and the basis for determining the stated amounts must be disclosed fully (ARB-43, Ch. 3A, par. 3). The following are the more common disclosures that are required for current assets and current liabilities in the financial statements or in notes thereto:

- Classification of inventories and the method used (FIFO, LIFO, average cost, etc.)
- Restrictions on current assets
- Current portions of long-term obligations
- Description of accounting policies relating to current assets and current liabilities

Accounts receivable and notes receivable from officers, employees, or affiliated companies, if material, must be reported separately in the financial statements (ARB-43, Chapter 1A, par. 5).

---

**CPE NOTE:** When you have completed your study and review of chapters 3 and 4 which comprise this Module, you may wish to take the Quizzer for this Module.

CPE instructions can be found on page 279.

The Module 2 Quizzer Questions begin on page 289. The Module 2 Answer Sheet can be found on pages 311 and 313. For your convenience, you can also take this Quizzer online at **www.cchtestingcenter.com.**

MODULE 3 — CHAPTER 5

# Accounting and Financial Reporting: Current Developments

## LEARNING OBJECTIVES

Upon completion of this chapter the practitioner should be able to:

■ Understand the selected Emerging Issues Task Force (EITF) consensus opinions discussed in the chapter, namely:

EITF Issue No. 04-5
EITF Issue No. 04-8
EITF Issue No. 04-10
EITF Issue No. 04-12
EITF Issue No. 05-2
EITF Issue No. 05-5
EITF Issue No. 05-6
EITF Issue No. 05-7
EITF Issue No. 05-8

■ Apply other EITF consensus opinions and pending issues
■ Identify the current developments in accounting and financial reporting

## FASB EMERGING ISSUES TASK FORCE (EITF)— SELECTED ISSUES

### Background

In 1984, the FASB EITF was formed to assist the FASB in the early identification of emerging issues affecting financial reporting and of problems in implementing authoritative pronouncements. The EITF essentially acts to resolve many interpretive issues under existing authoritative GAAP literature that are beyond the scope of the FASB board.

The FASB EITF consists of 13 voting members including senior technical partners of major national CPA firms, as well as representatives of major associations of preparers of financial statements such as the Financial Executives Institute, the Business Roundtable, and the Institute of Management Accountants. The FASB's Director of Research and Technical Activities serves as Task Force Chairman. The SEC's Chief Accountant and a member of the AICPA's Accounting Standards Executive Committee participate in Task Force meetings as observers. A quorum consists of 10 appointed members or their substitutes. The EITF usually meets every eight weeks with all meetings announced by the FASB in ACTION ALERT, along with a listing of topics on the agenda. EITF consensus opinions are published in the *EITF Abstracts*.

Generally, the SEC follows the EITF consensus opinions. In fact, the SEC Chief Accountant has formally stated that he would challenge any accounting principle that differs from the EITF consensus opinions.

EITF consensus opinions have the full effect of GAAP and are positioned in Category C of the GAAP hierarchy as defined in SAS No. 69, *The Meaning of "Present Fairly in Conformity With Generally Accepted Accounting Principles" in the Independent Auditor's Report.*

The EITF meets approximately every eight weeks with its consensus opinions published in the *EITF Abstracts.*

Although historically EITF consensus opinions have been rather specialized and narrow, in the past few years, opinions have been much broader in scope, and universally applicable to businesses across many industries.

### Selected EITF Consensus Opinions

Several important EITF consensus opinions have been issued in the past three years, most of which are not discussed in this chapter. This chapter addresses selected EITF consensus opinions that the author believes have broader appeal to the reader. A table of the most recent EITF consensus opinions is included the Summary of FASB EITFs section.

### EITF ISSUE NO. 04-5: *Determining Whether a General Partner, or the General Partners as a Group, Controls a Limited Partnership or Similar Entity When the Limited Partners Have Certain Rights*

#### Background

There has been a continuing debate in practice as to how to evaluate whether a partnership should be consolidated by one of its partners. Recent guidance provided by FIN 46R regarding kick-out rights in terms of evaluating variable interest entities has initiated the debate again as to what considerations are relevant in determining whether a general partner should consolidate a limited partnership.

Current practice as to the consolidation of a limited partnership by a general partner is typically covered by SOP 78-9, *Accounting for Investments in Real Estate Ventures,* which provides guidance on accounting for investments in real estate ventures, including investments in corporate joint ventures, general partnerships, limited partnerships, and undivided interests.

Outside of SOP 78-9, there is little guidance in terms of assessing whether a limited partner's rights are *important rights* that, under SOP 78-9, might preclude a general partner from consolidating a limited partnership. As a result, there are differing views about what rights constitute important rights.

#### Issue

When should a sole general partner consolidate a limited partnership?

## Consensus Opinion

(Tentative subject to final vote)

## Scope

The scope of the issue is limited to limited partnerships or similar entities (such as limited liability companies that have governing provisions that are the functional equivalent of a limited partnership) that are not variable interest entities under FIN 46R.

The issue does not apply to a general partner that, under GAAP, carries its investment in the limited partnership at fair value with changes in the fair value reported in a statement of operations or financial performance.

> **NOTE**
>
> If an enterprise is required to apply the consolidation guidance included in ARB No. 51 and FASB No. 94 to its investment in a limited partnership, it is within the scope of this issue. This issue does not change current guidance in Issue No. 00-1, Investor Balance Sheet and Income Statement Display under the Equity Method for Investments in Certain Partnerships and Other Joint Ventures, on when it is appropriate for a general partner to use the pro rata method of consolidation for its investment in a limited partnership.

**Multiple general partners.** When a limited partnership has multiple general partners, the determination of which, if any, general partner within the group should consolidate the limited partnership is based on an analysis of the relevant facts and circumstances.

- Entities under common control are considered to be a single general partner in applying the guidance of this issue.

## General Rules of the Issue

A general partner that controls a limited partnership should consolidate the partnership into its financial statements. There is a presumption that general partners *control* a limited partnership regardless of the extent of the general partners' ownership interest in the limited partnership. The presumption that general partners control a partnership is overcome (the general partners *do not control* the limited partnership) if the limited partners have either:

- **Substantive kick-out rights:** The substantive ability to dissolve (liquidate) the limited partnership or otherwise remove the general partners without cause, or,
- **Substantive participating rights:** The ability to effectively participate in certain actions of the limited partnership.

### Substantive Kick-out Rights

Determining whether kick-out rights are substantive should be based on consideration of all relevant facts and circumstances.

**Substantive kick-out rights must have *both of the following character-istics:*** The kick-out rights can be exercised by a single limited partner or a vote of a *simple majority* (or a lower percentage) of the limited partner voting interests held by parties other than the general partners, entities under common control with the general partner(s), and other parties acting on behalf of the general partner(s).

The limited partners holding the kick-out rights have the ability to exercise those rights if they chose to do so; that is, there are *no significant barriers* to the exercise of the rights. Such barriers include, but are not limited to:

■ Kick-out rights subject to conditions that make it unlikely they will be exercisable, for example, conditions that narrowly limit the timing of the exercise

■ Financial penalties or operational barriers associated with dissolving (liquidating) the limited partnership or replacing the general partners that would act as a significant disincentive for dissolution (liquidation) or removal

■ The absence of an adequate number of qualified replacement general partners or the lack of adequate compensation to attract a qualified replacement

■ The absence of an explicit, reasonable mechanism in the limited partnership agreement or in the applicable laws or regulations, by which the limited partners holding the rights can call for and conduct a vote to exercise those rights

■ The inability of the limited partners holding the rights to obtain the information necessary to exercise them.

> **NOTE**
>
> Kick-out rights that can be exercised by a single limited partner would be substantive (assuming no barriers to exercise the kick-out rights exist) even if the partnership agreement requires that more than a simple majority of the limited partners voting interests are required to exercise the kick-out right. In assessing whether a single limited partner has the ability to remove the general partners, consideration should be given as to whether other parties, including related parties under FASB No. 57, may be acting with the limited partner in exercising their kick-out rights.
>
> The EITF observed that a kick-out right that contractually requires a vote in excess of a simple majority (e.g., a supermajority) of the limited partners voting interests to remove the general partners may still be substantive if the general partners could be removed in every possible voting scenario in which a simple majority of the limited partners voting interests vote for removal. That is, there is no combination of limited partners voting interests that represents at least a simple majority of the limited partners voting interests that cannot remove the general partners.

**A limited partner's withdrawal right is not a kick-out right:** A limited partner's unilateral right to withdraw from the partnership in whole or in part (withdrawal right) that does not require dissolution or liquidation of the entire limited partnership would not overcome the presumption that the general partners control the limited partnership. The requirement to dissolve or liquidate the entire limited partnership upon the withdrawal of the limited partner(s) is not required to be contractual for a withdrawal right to be considered as a potential kick-out right.

> **NOTE**
>
> If a limited partnership is economically compelled to dissolve or liquidate upon the withdrawal of a limited partner, the withdrawal right is considered to be a potential kick-out right.

If it is determined that the limited partners do have substantive kick-out rights, presumption of control by the general partners would be overcome and each of the general partners would account for its investment in the limited partnership using the equity method of accounting.

### Substantive participating rights

Limited partners' rights (whether granted by contract or by law) that would allow limited partners to effectively participate in the following actions of the limited partnership should be considered *substantive participating rights* and would overcome the presumption that the general partners control the limited partnership.

- Selecting, terminating, and setting the compensation of management responsible for implementing the limited partnership's policies and procedures.
- Establishing operating and capital decisions of the limited partnership, including budgets, in the ordinary course of business.
- Any other actions where the limited partners are allowed to effectively participate in the decisions that occur as part of the ordinary course of the limited partnership's business and that are significant factors in directing and carrying out the activities of the limited partnership.

> **NOTE**
>
> In evaluating the limited partners' rights to determine whether they are substantive, "participation" means the ability of the limited partners to approve or block actions proposed by the general partners. The general partners must have the limited partners' agreement to take actions outlined above in order for the rights to be substantive participating rights. Participation does not require the ability to initiate actions.

> Limited partners' rights that appear to be participating rights but that by themselves are not substantive would not overcome the presumption of control by the general partners in the limited partnership. The likelihood that the veto right will be exercised by the limited partners should not be considered when assessing whether a limited partner right is a substantive participating right.

Factors used in evaluating whether limited partners' rights that appear to be participating are *substantive rights* (e.g., these rights provide for effective participation in significant decisions):

- The levels at which decisions are made as stated in the limited partnership agreement.

> **NOTE**
>
> Any matters that can be put to a vote must be considered to determine if the limited partners have substantive participating rights by virtue of their ability to vote on matters submitted to a vote of the limited partnership. Determination of whether matters that can be put to a vote of the limited partners, or the vote of the limited partnership as a whole, are substantive should be based on a consideration of all relevant facts and circumstances

- Relationships between the general and limited partners (other than investment in the common limited partnership) that are of a related-party nature (as defined in FASB No. 57) should be considered in determining if the participating rights of the limited partners are substantive.

> **EXAMPLE**
>
> If the limited partner is a member of the immediate family of the general partners, then the rights of the limited partner likely would not overcome the presumption of control by the general partners.

- The degree to which certain limited partners' rights that deal with operating or capital decisions are significant.
  - Limited partners' rights related to items that are not considered significant for directing and carrying out the activities of the limited partnership's business are not substantive participating rights and would not overcome the presumption of control by the general partners. Examples of such limited partners' rights relate to decisions about location of the limited partnership's headquarters, name of the partnership, selection of auditors and accounting principles, etc.

- The fact that certain limited partners' rights provide for the limited partners to participate in significant decisions that would be expected to be made in certain business activities in the ordinary course of business, should not overcome the presumption that the general partners have control, if it is remote (The term "remote" is based on the FASB No. 5 definition, meaning the chance of the event occurring is slight.) that the event or transaction that requires the limited partners' approval will occur.
- Whether the general partners have a contractual right to buy out the interest of the limited partners (a call option).
  - If a buyout is prudent, feasible, and substantively within the control of the general partners, the general partner's contractual right to buy out the limited partners demonstrates that the participating right of the limited partners is not a substantive right.
  - It would not be prudent, feasible, and substantively within the control of the general partners to buy out the limited partners if the limited partners control technology that is critical to the limited partnership, or they are the principal source of funding for the limited partnership.
  - The existence of such call options negates the participating rights of the limited partners to approve or veto an action of the general partners.

**Exclusion of Protective Rights.** Rights that would allow the limited partners to block the following partnership actions would be considered protective (rather than participating) rights and would not overcome the presumption of control by the general partners:

- Amendments to the limited partnership agreement
- Pricing on transactions between the general partners and the limited partnership and related self-dealing transactions
- Liquidation of the limited partnership initiated by the general partners or a decision to cause the limited partnership to enter bankruptcy or other receivership.
- Acquisitions and dispositions of assets that are not expected to be undertaken in the ordinary course of business. (Such rights expected to be made in the ordinary course of business are participating rights).
- Issuance or repurchase of limited partnership interests.

### Assessing Individual Limited Partners Rights

Following in the table are examples that demonstrate how to assess whether the rights of the limited partners should be considered *protective or participating* and, if participating, whether the rights are *substantive*.

| Rights of limited partners | Type of Right | | Conclusion |
|---|---|---|---|
| | Protective Right | Substantive Participating Right | |
| Approval of acquisitions and dispositions of assets in the ordinary course of business | No | Yes | The presumption that the general partners control the limited partnership is overcome. GP does not consolidate partnership. |
| Approval of acquisitions and dispositions of assets not in the ordinary course of business | Yes | No | The presumption that the general partners control the limited partnership is not overcome. GP consolidates partnership. |
| Approval to incur additional indebtedness to finance activities in the ordinary course of business | No | Yes | The presumption that the general partners control the limited partnership is overcome. GP does not consolidate partnership. |
| Approval to incur additional indebtedness to finance activities not in the ordinary course of business | Yes | No | The presumption that the general partners control the limited partnership is not overcome. GP consolidates partnership. |
| Rights to block customary or expected dividends or other distributions | No | Yes | The presumption that the general partners control the limited partnership is overcome. GP does not consolidate partnership. |
| Rights to block extraordinary distributions | Yes | No | The presumption that the general partners control the limited partnership is not overcome. GP consolidates partnership. |
| Rights to approve or veto a new or broader collective-bargaining agreement where the union workforce does not represent a substantial portion of the partnership's work force | No | No | Although the right is participating, the work force is not substantial enough to make the right substantive. The presumption that the general partners control the limited partnership is not overcome. GP consolidates partnership. |
| Rights to approve or veto a new or broader collective-bargaining agreement where the union workforce represents a substantial portion of the partnership's work force | No | Yes | The presumption that the general partners control the limited partnership is overcome. GP does not consolidate partnership. |
| Rights to the initiation or resolution of lawsuits *not* in the ordinary course of business. | Yes | No | The presumption that the general partners control the limited partnership is not overcome. GP consolidates partnership. |

| Rights to initiate or resolve lawsuits *in the ordinary course of business,* such as in the insurance industry | No | Yes | The presumption that the general partners control the limited partnership is overcome. GP does not consolidate partnership |
|---|---|---|---|
| Right to veto the annual operating budget | No | Yes | The presumption that the general partners control the limited partnership is overcome. GP does not consolidate partnership. |
| Selecting, terminating, and setting the compensation of management | No | Yes | The presumption that the general partners control the limited partnership is overcome. GP does not consolidate partnership. |

### Initial Assessment and Reassessment of Limited Partners' Rights

The assessment of limited partners' rights and their impact on the presumption of control of the limited partnership by the general partners should be made when an investor(s) becomes a general partner(s) and should be reassessed if:

- There is a change to the terms or in the exercisability of the right of the limited partners or general partners,
- The general partners increase or decrease their ownership of limited partnership interests, or
- There is an increase or decrease in the number of outstanding limited partnership interests.

### Transition Rules

For general partners of all new limited partnerships formed, and for existing limited partnerships for which the partnership agreements are modified, the guidance of this Issue is effective after June 29, 2005.

For all other limited partnerships, the effective date is no later than the beginning of the first reporting period in the fiscal years beginning after December 15, 2005, and the application of either Transition Method A or B would be acceptable:

- **Transition Method A:** Issue is applied in financial statements issued for the first reporting period in fiscal years beginning after December 15, 2005.

  The effect of initially applying the Issue for existing limited partnership agreements is accounted for similar to a change in accounting principle under APB No. 20, *Accounting Changes*, with a cumulative effect. Other transition rules apply.

- **Transition Method B:** Restate the financial statements for prior periods under APB No. 20 and apply the change to all existing limited partnership agreements based on the facts and circumstances at the time each investment was made and it should consider changes made in later periods. Other transition rules apply.

## EITF ISSUE NO. 04-8: *The Effect of Contingently Convertible Debt on Diluted Earnings per Share*

### Issue

The issue is, in connection with earnings per share, when the dilutive effect of contingently convertible instruments should be included in diluted earnings per share.

### Background

Contingently convertible debt instruments, commonly referred to as "Co-Cos," are financial instruments that add a contingent feature to a convertible debt instrument. Co-Cos are generally convertible into common shares of the issuer after the common stock price has exceeded a predetermined threshold for a specified time period (market price trigger). Currently, most issuers of Co-Cos exclude the potential dilutive effect of the conversion feature from diluted EPS until the market price contingency is met. Co-Cos typically carry a lower interest rate than conventional, nonconvertible debt. In some structures, these instruments permit the issuer to recognize little or no interest costs.

### Consensus Opinion

All instruments that have embedded conversion features (such as contingently convertible debt, convertible preferred stock, and Instrument C in EITF Issue No. 90-19, with a market-based contingency) that are contingent on market conditions indexed to an issuer's share price should be included in diluted earnings per share computations (if dilutive) regardless of whether the market conditions have been met. The consensus includes instruments that have more than one contingency if one of the contingencies is based on market conditions indexed to the issuer's share price and that instrument can be converted to shares based on achieving a market condition- that is, the conversion is not dependent on a substantive non-market-based contingency.

The consensus should be applied to reporting periods ending after the effective date, December 15, 2004, and should be applied retroactively to instruments outstanding at the date of adoption of this consensus. Diluted EPS of all prior periods presented for comparative purposes should be restated to conform to the consensus guidance.

Other transition guidance is provided and not included in this chapter.

### STUDY QUESTIONS

> **1.** In accordance with EITF Issue 04-5, a general partner's control over a limited partnership is deemed to be overridden if the limited partners have certain substantive participating rights. *True or False?*

2.  Under EITF 04-5, in evaluating the limited partners' rights to determine whether they are substantive, "participation" means the ability of the limited partners to approve or block actions proposed by the general partners. ***True or False?***

3.  In accordance with EITF Issue 04-5, factors used in evaluating whether limited partners' rights that appear to be participating are substantive rights (e.g., these rights provide for effective participation in significant decisions) include the levels at which decisions are made as stated in the limited partnership agreement. ***True or False?***

4.  All instruments that have embedded conversion features (such as contingently convertible debt, convertible preferred stock, and Instrument C in EITF Issue No. 90-19, with a market-based contingency) that are contingent on market conditions indexed to an issuer's share price should not be included in diluted earnings per share computations (if dilutive) regardless of whether the market conditions have been met. ***True or False?***

---

**NOTE**

Answers to Study Questions, with feedback to both the correct and incorrect responses, are provided in a special section beginning on page **237**.

## EITF ISSUE NO. 04-10: *Determining Whether to Aggregate Operating Segments That Do Not Meet the Quantitative Thresholds*

### Issue

The issue is how an enterprise should evaluate the aggregation criteria in paragraph 17 of FASB Statement No.131, when determining whether operating segments that do not meet the quantitative thresholds may be aggregated in accordance with paragraph 19 of the same statement.

### Background

FASB No. 131, Disclosures about Segments of an Enterprise and Related Information, requires that a public business enterprise report financial and descriptive information about its reportable operating segments. Operating segments are components of an enterprise about which separate financial information is available that is evaluated regularly by the chief operating decision maker in deciding how to allocate resources and in assessing performance. Typically, financial information is required to be reported on the basis that it is used internally for evaluating segment performance and deciding how to allocate resources to segments.

Paragraph 18 provides certain quantitative thresholds for applying FASB No. 131, while paragraph 19 permits an entity to combine information about a segment with other operating segments that do not meet the quantitative thresholds to produce a reportable segment only if the operating segments share a majority of the aggregation criteria found in paragraph 17.

Paragraph 17 of FASB No. 131 permits two or more operating segments to be aggregated into a single operating segment if aggregation is consistent with the objective and basic principles of FASB No. 131, if the segments have similar economic characteristics, and if the segments are similar in certain areas. Questions have arisen regarding how an enterprise should consider the aggregation criteria listed in paragraph 17 in applying the guidance of paragraph 19 to operating segments that do not meet the quantitative thresholds.

### Consensus Opinion

Operating segments that do not meet the quantitative thresholds can be aggregated only if aggregation is consistent with the objective and basic principles of FASB No. 131, the segments have similar economic characteristics, and the segments share a majority of the aggregation criteria in sections (a) through (e) of paragraph 17 of FASB No. 131.

The Task Force agreed that the consensus in this Issue should be applied for fiscal years ending after September 15, 2005, and that the corresponding information for earlier periods, including interim periods, should be restated unless it is impractical to do so.

### EITF ISSUE NO. 04-12: *Determining Whether Equity-Based Compensation Awards Are Participating Securities*

#### Issue

Whether unvested instruments issued as equity-based compensation (including options and nonvested stock) that provide the right to participate in dividends or dividend equivalents with common stock of the issuer are "participating securities" if the right to the dividends is contingent on factors other than employee service and the passage of time.

#### Background

FASB No. 128, *Earnings per Share*, provides guidance on the calculation and disclosure of EPS. The Statement requires the use of the two-class method of computing EPS for those entities with ***participating securities*** or multiple classes of common stock.

#### Consensus Opinion

The EITF generally agreed that unvested instruments issued as equity-based compensation (including options and nonvested stock) are not participating securities if the right to dividends is contingent on factors other than employee service and the passage of time. However, they were asked to reach a consensus on Issue 1.

## EITF ISSUE NO. 04-13: *Accounting for Purchases and Sales of Inventory with the Same Counterparty*

### Background

An entity may sell inventory to another entity in the same line of business from which it also purchases inventory. The purchase and sale transactions may be part of the same contractual arrangement or separate arrangements. The inventory may be in the form of raw materials, work-in-progress, or finished goods.

### Issue 1

Under what circumstances should two or more transactions with the same counterparty(ies) be viewed as a single nonmonetary transaction within the scope of APB No. 29?

### Issue 2

If nonmonetary transactions within the scope of APB No. 29 are exchanges of inventory within the same line of business under Issue 1 above, are there circumstances under which the transactions should be recognized at fair value?

### Consensus Opinion

**Issue 1:**  Inventory purchase and sales transactions with the same counterparty that are entered into *in contemplation of one another* should be combined and treated as a single exchange under APB No. 29 (carrying value used to record purchased goods).

In situations in which an inventory transaction is legally contingent upon the performance of another inventory transaction with the same counterparty, the two are in contemplation of one another and should be combined in applying APB No. 29.

The issuance of invoices and the exchange of offsetting cash payments is not a factor in determining whether two or more inventory transactions with the same counterparty should be considered as a single nonmonetary inventory transaction within the scope of APB No. 29.

The following factors may indicate that a purchase transaction and a sales transaction with the same counterparty were entered into *in contemplation of one another.*

| Factor indicating two transactions were entered into in contemplation of each other | Comments |
| --- | --- |
| There is a legal right of offset of obligations between counterparties involved in inventory purchase and sales transactions. | The ability to offset receivables and payables related to separately documented inventory transactions indicates there is a link between them. |
| Inventory purchase and sales transactions with the same counterparty are entered into simultaneously. | An inventory purchase transaction simultaneously entered into with another inventory sales transaction with the same counterparty is an indication that the transactions were entered into in contemplation of one another. |
| Inventory purchase and sales transactions were at off-market terms. | If a company enters into an off-market inventory transaction with a counterparty, it is an indication that the transaction is linked to, and entered into, in contemplation of another inventory transaction with that same counterparty. |
| There is relative certainty that reciprocal inventory transactions with the same counterparty will occur. | A company may sell inventory to a counterparty and enter into another arrangement with that same counterparty whereby that counterparty may, but is not contractually required to, deliver an agreed-upon inventory amount. |

**Issue 2:** Nonmonetary exchange whereby finished goods inventory is transferred in exchange for the receipt of raw materials or work-in-progress (WIP) inventory within the same line of business should be recognized at fair value if:

- Fair value is determinable within reasonable limits and,
- The transaction has commercial substance, as defined by FASB No. 153.

**Definition of commercial substance.** A nonmonetary exchange has commercial substance if the entity's future cash flows (FASB Concept Statement No. 7, Using Cash Flow Information and Present Value in Accounting Measurements, may assist in evaluating changes in future cash flows) are expected to significantly change as a result of the exchange.

Cash flows are expected to significantly change if either of the following criteria is met:

- The *configuration (risk, timing and amount) of the future cash flows* of the asset(s) received *differs significantly* from the configuration of the future cash flows of the asset(s) transferred, or
- The *entity-specific value* of the asset(s) received differs from the entity-specific value of the asset(s) transferred, and the difference is significant in relation to the fair values of the assets exchanged.

All other nonmonetary exchanges involving inventory within the same line of business should be recognized at the carrying amount of the inventory transferred.

The following are examples where the inventory would be recognized at the carrying amount of the inventory transferred and not at fair value.

- Transfer of raw materials or WIP for raw materials, or
- Transfer of finished goods for finished goods.

The classification of a type of inventory for purposes of this Issue should be the same classification that an entity uses for external financial reporting purposes.

**Disclosures.** An entity should disclose the amount of revenue and costs (or gains/losses) associated with inventory exchanges recognized at fair value.

**Effective date.** The consensus should be applied to transactions completed in reporting periods *beginning after March 15, 2006*, whether pursuant to arrangements that were in place at the date of initial application of the consensus or arrangements executed subsequent to that date. The carrying amount of the inventory that was acquired under these types of arrangements covered by the Consensus Opinion prior to the initial application of the consensus and that still remains in an entity's balance sheet at the date of initial application of the consensus should not be adjusted for this consensus. Early application is permitted in periods for which financial statements have not been issued.

---

### EXAMPLE 1

**Sale and purchase of inventory between two manufacturers**

**Facts:** Manufacturer A has a longstanding relationship with Manufacturer B, whereby each will buy and sell inventory from each other on an as-needed basis at market prices.

Manufacturer A sells materials to B based on a purchase order from B. Two days later, B sells materials to A based on a separate purchase order from A.

Neither transaction was predicated on the occurrence of the other transaction occurring through either an implied arrangement or a contractual one. Historically, A has sold twice as much in value to B as B has sold to A. Both of these transactions are gross-cash settled at market prices.

**Conclusion:** As a result, the inventory purchase and sales transactions should not be considered a single exchange in applying APB No. 29 (at book value). Instead, the transactions should be treated as two separate transactions recorded at market value.

This assessment is supported by the following factors:

- The reciprocal inventory and purchase and sale transactions were not negotiated between the two parties at the same time.
- There is no correlation between the value of goods delivered to B to the value of the goods received from B.
- A's inventory purchase and sales transactions were not entered into in contemplation of one another.

### EXAMPLE 2

**Sale and purchase of inventory between auto dealers**

**Facts:** Dealer A has excess inventory of cars and does not have enough pickup trucks for near term demand.

Dealer B has excess inventory of pickup trucks and not enough cars.

A and B negotiate an arrangement whereby A sells a specified number of cars to B. Although not committed to do so, B may deliver pickup trucks of equivalent value at wholesale prices to A as consideration for the cars.

A must purchase pickup trucks from B if B chooses to deliver the trucks the following week.

Historically, B has always delivered trucks to A under these arrangements.

At the time A delivers cars to B, A believes B will ship trucks the following week.

Each transaction is separately documented and gross-cash settled at wholesale prices on the date of delivery.

**Conclusion:** From A's perspective, the transactions with B should be treated as a *single nonmonetary exchange under APB No. 29.* The trucks received should be recorded at the *carrying value* of the cars given.

The reason is because A entered into the sales transaction with B *in contemplation of a reciprocal inventory purchase transaction* from B. This conclusion is based on the following factors:

- As a condition of selling inventory to B, A must accept delivery of trucks from B at a later date if B chooses to make such a delivery.
- The mutual agreement between A and B is "off-market" at wholesale prices.
- When A enters into the arrangement with B, A fully expects to purchase the trucks; that is, there is relative certainty that reciprocal inventory transactions with the same counterparty (B) will occur

The fact that each transaction is recorded gross and separately documented has no impact on whether the transaction should be treated as a single exchange under APB No. 29.

## STUDY QUESTIONS

**5.** EITIF Issue No. 04-10 deals with the issue as to how an enterprise should evaluate the aggregation criteria in paragraph 17 of FASB Statement No.131, when determining whether operating segments that do not meet the quantitative thresholds may be aggregated in accordance with paragraph 19 of the same statement. *True or False?*

**6.** Unvested instruments issued as equity-based compensation (including options and nonvested stock) that provide the right to participate in dividends or dividend equivalents with common stock of the issuer are "participating securities" if the right to the dividends is contingent on factors other than employee service and the passage of time. *True or False?*

**7.** In accordance with EITF Issue 04-13, Inventory purchase and sales transactions with the same counterparty that are entered into in contemplation of one another should be  treated as two separate transactions. *True or False?*

**8.** Nonmonetary exchange whereby finished goods inventory is transferred in exchange for the receipt of raw materials or work-in-progress (WIP) inventory within the same line of business should be recognized at fair value if fair value is determinable within reasonable limits and the transaction has commercial substance, as defined by FASB No. 153. *True or False?*

## EITF ISSUE NO. 05-2: *The Meaning of "Conventional Convertible Debt Instrument" in EITF Issue No. 00-19, "Accounting for Derivative Financial Instruments Indexed to, and Potentially Settled in, a Company's Own Stock"*

### Background

FASB No. 133, *Accounting for Derivative Instruments and Hedging Activities*, provides guidance on the bifurcation of embedded derivatives within a host contract, such as bonds, insurance policies, and leases, that do not meet the definition of a derivative in its entirety. Under FASB No. 133, one of three criteria for bifurcation is that a separate instrument with the same terms as the embedded derivative instrument would be a derivative instrument subject to the requirements of FASB No. 133.

Moreover, FASB No. 133 identifies those contracts that should not be considered and accounted for as derivative instruments.  Paragraph 11(a) of FASB No. 133 states that contracts issued or held by the reporting entity that are both a) indexed to its own stock and b) classified in stockholders' equity in its balance sheet should not be considered derivative instruments.

EITF Issue No. 00-19, *Accounting for Derivative Financial Instruments Indexed to, and Potentially Settled in, a Company's Own Stock*, provides guidance in determining whether an embedded derivative would be classified in stockholders' equity in accordance with FASB No. 133 if it were freestanding. However, EITF Issue No. 00-19 has an exception when evaluating whether a *conventional convertible debt instrument* in which the holder may only realize the value of the conversion option by exercising the option and receiving the entire proceeds in a fixed number of shares or the equivalent amount of cash contains an embedded derivative indexed to the company's own stock that would require bifurcation.

Since the issuance of EITF Issue No. 00-19, the variety of contractual terms included in convertible debt instruments has increased significantly. Examples of such changes in terms include contingent conversion features (such as single or multiple triggers), variable conversion ratios, and call options. Although the EITF references the term conventional convertible debt instrument, the EITF does not define this term. Thus, there is the question as to whether an instrument that contains some of the above-noted contractual terms should be considered "conventional instruments" that qualify for the EITF Issue No. 00-19 exception.

A similar issue exists in evaluating whether convertible preferred stock with debt-like features, such as convertible preferred stock with a mandatory redemption date, qualifies for the EITF Issue No. 00-19 exception.

## Issue 1

Should the exception to EITF Issue No. 00-19 for conventional convertible debt instruments be removed or further clarified?

### Consensus Opinion

The EITF concluded that the exception in EITF Issue No. 00-19 for conventional convertible debt instruments should be retained.

## Issue 2

Should a contingency related to the exercise of a conversion option impact the assessment of whether an instrument is conventional for evaluating the exception in EITF Issue No. 00-19?

### Consensus Opinion

Instruments that provide the holder with an option to convert into a fixed number of shares (or equivalent amount of cash at the discretion of the issuer) for which the ability to exercise the option is based on the passage of time or a contingent event should be considered conventional in applying EITF Issue No. 00-19. Instruments that contain standard antidilution provisions would not preclude a conclusion that the instrument is convertible into a fixed number of shares. Standard antidilution provisions are those that result in adjustments to the conversion ratio in the event of an equity restructuring transaction (as defined in FASB No. 123R) that are designed to maintain the value of the conversion option.

### Issue 3

Can convertible preferred stock with a mandatory redemption date qualify for the exception in EITF Issue No. 00-19?

### Consensus Opinion

Convertible preferred stock with a mandatory redemption date may qualify for the exception in EITF Issue No. 00-19 if the economic characteristics indicate that the instrument is more akin to debt than equity. An entity should consider the guidance found in FASB No. 133 in assessing whether the instrument is more akin to debt or equity. Note further that if the preferred stock is more akin to equity than debt, an equity conversion feature would be "clearly and closely related" to that host instrument.

For instruments that are within the scope of this Issue, entities should include the applicable disclosures required in FASB No. 129.

The consensus opinion in this issue should be applied to new instruments entered into and instruments modified in periods beginning after Board ratification of the consensus, on June 29, 2005.

### EITF ISSUE NO. 05-5: *Accounting for Early Retirement or Postemployment Program with Specific Features (Such as Terms Specified in Altersteilzeit Early Retirement Arrangements)*

### Background

This issue addresses specific features in the Altersteilzeit (ATZ) arrangements. The ATZ arrangement is an early retirement program in Germany designed to create an incentive for employees, within a certain age group, to transition from full or part-time employment into retirement before their legal retirement age.

Typical features of the ATZ arrangement include the following:

- An employee must sign an ATZ contract with the employer and can sign the ATZ contract before being eligible to begin working under the arrangement.
- An employer is required to allow participation in the ATZ arrangement without restriction until participation reaches 5 percent of the total work force. After 5 percent participation is achieved, an employer has the right to determine whether employees are accepted into the ATZ arrangement.

- An employee is required to work a minimum period of time with any employer before being eligible for the arrangement, with prior employment with the present employer not being necessary.
- The ATZ arrangement typically offers two alternative arrangements for participating employees:
  - *Type 1:* Participant works 50 percent of the normal full time schedule for each year of the entire ATZ period and receives 50 percent of his or her salary each year,
  - *Type II:* Participant works full time for half of the ATZ period and then does not work for the remaining half and receives 50 percent of his or her salary each year during the entire ATZ period.
- Under both types of arrangements, participants receive an annual bonus which generally equals about 10-15 percent of the most recent regular pay before the start of the ATZ period. Thus the regular combined paid compensation will normally equal about 60-65 percent of the participant's most recent regular pay prior to the start of the ATZ period.
- In order to receive the bonus, employees must provide service to the employer for the required portion of the ATZ period. If the participant dies, voluntarily leaves the company, or is otherwise terminated before fulfilling the service period requirement, the contract will be unwound and the total compensation received will be adjusted to the amount that the participant would have received if he or she had not participated in the ATZ arrangement. For example, if an employee enters into a four-year Type II arrangement and leaves the company after one year, the employee will receive for the one year worked, all of his or her pre-ATZ period annual salary and will not receive any ATZ bonus.
- During the inactive period under the Type II arrangement, participants are legally under a work contract with the employer (considered employees); however, an employee is not permitted to return to active work. Otherwise, the employer would lose any government subsidy.

Under a Type 1 arrangement, an employer can claim the subsidy for a replacement worker hired during the entire ATZ period. For a Type II arrangement, an employer could only claim the subsidy for a replacement worker hired during the inactive ATZ period. The reimbursement each year during the inactive period would be equivalent to two years of bonus payments and additional contributions made into the German government pension scheme.

### Issue 1

How should an entity account for the bonus feature and additional contributions into the German governmental pension scheme under a Type II ATZ arrangement?

## Consensus Opinion

The bonus feature and the additional contributions into the German government pension scheme under a Type II ATZ arrangement should be accounted for as a postemployment benefit under FASB No. 112. An entity should recognize the additional compensation over the period from the point at which the employee signs the ATZ contract until the end of the active service period.

## Issue 2

How should an entity account for the governmental subsidy under Type I and Type II ATZ arrangements?

## Consensus Opinion

The employer should recognize the government subsidy when it meets the necessary criteria and is entitled to the subsidy.

## Transition

The consensus should be applied for fiscal periods beginning after December 15, 2005, and report as a change in accounting estimate affected by a change in accounting principle under FASB No. 154. A company should provide the disclosures required by FASB No. 154.

## EITF ISSUE NO. 05-6: *Determining the Amortization Period for Leasehold Improvements Purchased after Lease Inception or Acquired in a Business Combination*

### Background

FASB No. 13, *Accounting for Leases*, requires that a lessee determine the lease term at the inception of a lease. A lease term is a fixed noncancelable term of the lease plus all periods covered by bargain renewal options or for which failure to renew the lease imposes a penalty on the lessee in such an amount that a renewal appears to be  reasonably assured.

Once the lease term is determined, an entity can classify the lease as either capital or operating, and the period over which to recognize straight-line rents.

**Amortization of capital leases.** Paragraph 11(b) of FASB No. 13 requires that assets recognized under capital leases be amortized in a manner consistent with the lessee's normal depreciation policy except that the amortization period is limited to the lease term (including renewal periods that are reasonably assured). That is, the lessee does not expect to receive any economic benefits from those leased assets in periods that are not reasonably assured of renewal.

**Leasehold improvements related to operating leases.** FASB No. 13 does not address the amortization of leasehold improvements related to operating leases. Consequently, in practice, most entities follow the guidance found in Paragraph 11(b) of FASB No. 13 related to amortization of capital leases as follows:

> Amortized the leaseholds in a manner consistent with the lessee's normal depreciation policy except that the *amortization period is limited to the lease term* (including renewal periods that are reasonably assured).

Paragraph 9 of FASB No. 13 states that the lease term for purposes of lease classification cannot be changed unless either a) the provisions of the lease are modified in a manner that results in the lease being considered a new agreement, or, b) the lease is extended or renewed beyond the existing lease term.

In practice, questions have arisen as to whether the amortization period for leasehold improvements that are placed in service significantly after the beginning of the lease and not contemplated at or near the beginning of a lease can extend beyond the lease term that was determined at the lease inception.

Moreover, a similar question has arisen about leases assumed in a business combination. Paragraphs 12 and 13 of Interpretation 21 to FASB No. 13 require that the acquiring entity retain the lease classification used by the acquired entity, unless certain conditions found in Paragraph 9 are satisfied. Therefore, questions have been raised as to whether the amortization period for leasehold improvements acquired in a business combination can extend beyond the lease term that was determined by the acquiree at lease inception.

### Scope of EITF Issue 05-6

This issue applies to the amortization period for leasehold improvements in operating leases that are either:
- Placed in service significantly after the beginning of the initial lease term and not contemplated at the beginning of the lease term, or
- Acquired in a business combination.

The issue does not apply to:
- Amortization of intangible assets that may be recognized in a business combination for the favorable or unfavorable terms of a lease relative to market prices.
- Preexisting leasehold improvements.

### Issue 1

What is the amortization period for leasehold improvements acquired in a business combination?

## Issue 2

What is the amortization period of leasehold improvements (related to an operating lease) that are placed in service significantly after and not contemplated at the beginning of the lease term?

### Consensus Opinion

**Issue 1:** Leasehold improvements acquired in a business combination should be amortized over the *shorter of* the useful life of the assets or the term that includes reacquired lease periods and renewals that are deemed to be reasonably assured at the date of acquisition.

**Issue 2:** Leasehold improvements that are placed in service significantly after and not contemplated at or near the beginning of the lease term should be amortized over the *shorter of* the useful life of the assets or the term that includes reacquired lease periods and renewals that are deemed to be reasonably assured at the date the leasehold improvements are purchased.

### Effective Date

The consensus should be applied to leasehold improvements that are purchased or acquired in reporting periods beginning after June 29, 2005. Early application is permitted in periods for which financial statements have not been issued.

## EITF ISSUE NO. 05-7: *Accounting for Modifications to Conversion Options Embedded in Debt Instruments and Related Issues*

### Background

Previously, when an issuer modified previously issued convertible debt, there were differing views on whether to include the change in the fair value of an embedded conversion option in the analysis to determine whether a substantial modification had occurred under EITF Issue No. 96-19, Debtor's Accounting for a Modification or Exchange of Debt Instruments.

### Issue 1

Is the change in the fair value of an embedded conversion option that results from a modification of a convertible debt instrument be included in the analysis of whether there has been a substantial change in the terms of the debt instrument to determine if a debt extinguishment has occurred under EITF Issue No. 96-19?

### Consensus Opinion

An entity should include, upon the modification of a convertible debt instrument, the change in fair value of the related embedded conversion option in the analysis to determine whether a debt instrument has been extinguished under EITF Issue No. 96-19. The change in the fair value of an embedded conversion option should be calculated as the difference between the fair value of the embedded conversion option immediately before and after the modification and it should be included in the Issue 96-19 analysis because there is a direct correlation between the value of an embedded conversion option and the yields demanded on a convertible debt instrument. Because the determination of whether an extinguishments or modification has occurred focuses solely on a differential cash flow analysis, the EITF agreed to amend Issue 96-19 to include non-cash changes to the conversion terms under the consensus opinion.

### Issue 2

In modifications that do not result in a debt extinguishments under Issue 96-19, does the modification to a convertible debt instrument that changes the fair value of an embedded conversion option affect subsequent recognition of interest expense for the associated debt instrument?

### Consensus Opinion

The modification of a convertible debt instrument should affect subsequent recognition of interest expense for the associated debt instrument for changes in the fair value of the embedded conversion option. The change in the fair value of an embedded conversion option should be calculated as the difference between the fair value of the embedded conversion option immediately before and after the modification. The value exchanged by the holder for the modification of the conversion option should be recognized as a discount or premium, with a corresponding increase or decrease in additional paid-in capital.

### Issue 3

In modifications that do not result in a debt extinguishment under Issue 96-19, should the issuer recognize a beneficial conversion feature or reassess an existing beneficial conversion feature if upon modification of a convertible debt instrument, the embedded conversion option is in-the-money and the intrinsic value of the embedded conversion option has increased?

### Consensus Opinion

The issuer should not recognize a beneficial conversion feature or reassess an existing beneficial conversion feature upon modification of a convertible debt instrument. The only value associated with the modification of an embedded conversion option (feature) that should be accounted for is the change in the fair value of the embedded conversion option discussed in Issue 2.

## Transition

The consensus of this issue should be applied to future modifications of debt instruments beginning in the first interim or annual reporting period beginning after December 15, 2005. Early application is permitted in periods for which financial statements have not yet been issued. Further, disclosures required by FASB No. 154 should be made excluding those disclosures that require the effects of retroactive application.

## EITF ISSUE NO. 05-8: *Income Tax Consequences of Issuing Convertible Debt with a Beneficial Conversion Feature*

### Background

A company may issue a convertible debt security with a nondetachable conversion feature which is not accounted for separately under APB No. 14, *Accounting for Convertible Debt and Debt Issued with Stock Purchase Warrants.* Yet, when a company issues a convertible debt security with a nondetachable conversion feature that is in-the-money, that conversion feature is required to be accounted for separately as a beneficial conversion feature and recognized and measured separately by allocating to additional paid-in capital a portion of the proceeds equal to the intrinsic value of the conversion feature. In accordance with the U. S. Federal Income Tax Code, the entire amount of proceeds received at issuance of the debt is included in the tax basis of the convertible debt security.

### Issue 1

Does the issuance of convertible debt with a beneficial conversion feature result in a basis difference for purposes of applying FASB No. 109, *Accounting for Income Taxes.*

### Consensus Opinion

The issuance of convertible debt with a beneficial conversion feature results in a basis difference for purposes of applying FASB No. 109.

### Issue 2

If the issuance of convertible debt with a beneficial conversion feature results in a basis difference, is that basis difference a temporary difference under FASB No. 109?

### Consensus Opinion

The basis difference that results from the issuance of convertible debt with a beneficial conversion feature is a temporary difference for purposes of applying FASB No. 109d.

## Issue 3

If the issuance of convertible debt with a beneficial conversion feature results in a temporary difference under FASB No. 109, should the recognition of the deferred tax liability for the temporary difference of the convertible debt be recorded as an adjustment to additional paid-in capital or through the recording of a deferred charge by analogy to the accounting model in Example 4 of Issue No. 98-11, *Accounting for Acquired Temporary Differences in Certain Purchase Transactions That Are Not Accounted for as Business Combinations.*

### Consensus Opinion

The recognition of deferred taxes for the temporary difference of the convertible debt with a beneficial conversion feature should be recorded as an adjustment to additional paid-in capital.

### Transition

This issue should be applied to financial statements beginning in the first interim or annual reporting period beginning after December 15, 2005, and should be applied by retrospective application under FASB No. 154 to all instruments with a beneficial conversion feature accounted for under Issue 00-27, *Application of Issue No. 98-5 to Certain Convertible Instruments.* The Issue would also be applicable to debt instruments that were converted or extinguished in prior periods but are still presented in the financial statements. Early application is permitted for periods for which financial statements have not been issued.

## SUMMARY OF FASB EMERGING ISSUES TASK FORCE OPINIONS (EITFS)

The following is a summary of the most recent FASB EITF Consensus Opinions.

### Issued EITF Consensus Opinions

| Issue Number | Title |
|---|---|
| 05-1 | Accounting for the Conversion of an Instrument That Becomes Convertible upon the Issuer's Exercise of a Call Option. |
| 05-2 | The Meaning of Conventional Convertible Debt Instrument in EITF Issue No. 00-19, Accounting for Derivative Financial Instruments Indexed to, and Potentially Settled in, a Company's Own Stock. |
| 05-3 | Accounting for Rental Costs Incurred during the Construction Period (withdrawn) |
| 05-4 | The Effect of a Liquidated Damages Clause on a Financial Instrument. |
| 05-5 | Accounting for Early Retirement or Postemployment Program with Specific Features (Such as Terms Specified in Altersteilzeit Early Retirement Arrangements) |

| 05-6 | Determining the Amortization Period for Leasehold Improvements Purchased after Lease Inception or Acquired in a Business Combination |
| 05-7 | *Accounting for Modifications to Conversion Options Embedded in Debt Instruments and Related Issues* |
| 05-8 | Income Tax Consequences of Issuing Convertible Debt with a Beneficial Conversion Feature |
| 06-01 | Accounting for Consideration Given by a Service Provider to Manufacturers or Resellers of Equipment Necessary for an End-Customer to Receive Service from the Service Provider |
| 06-02 | Accounting for Sabbatical Leave and Other Similar Benefits Pursuant to FASB Statement No. 43 |
| 06-03 | How Taxes Collected from Customers and Remitted to Governmental Authorities Should Be Presented in the Income Statement (That Is, Gross Versus Net Presentation) |
| 06-04 | Accounting for Deferred Compensation and Postretirement Benefit Aspects of Endorsement Split-Dollar Life Insurance Arrangements |
| 06-05 | Accounting for Purchases of Life Insurance - Determining the Amount That Could Be Realized in Accordance with FASB Technical Bulletin No. 85-4, "Accounting for Purchases of Life Insurance" |
| 06-06 | Application of EITF Issue No. 05-7, "Accounting for Modifications to Conversion Options Embedded in Debt Instruments and Related Issues" |

## STUDY QUESTIONS

**9.** The bonus feature and the additional contributions into the German government pension scheme under a Type II ATZ arrangement should be accounted for as a postemployment benefit under FASB No. 112. An entity should recognize the additional compensation over the period from the point at which the employee signs the ATZ contract until the end of the active service period. *True or False?*

**10.** In accordance with EITF Issue No. 05-6, leasehold improvements acquired in a business combination should be amortized over the shorter of the useful life of the assets or the term that includes reacquired lease periods and renewals that are deemed to be reasonably assured at the date of acquisition. *True or False?*

**11.** In EITF Issue No. 05-7, an entity should not include, upon the modification of a convertible debt instrument, the change in fair value of the related embedded conversion option in the analysis to determine whether a debt instrument has been extinguished under EITF Issue No. 96-19. *True or False?*

**12.** In EITF Issue No. 05-8, the EITF reached a consensus that the issuance of convertible debt with a beneficial conversion feature results in a basis difference for purposes of applying FASB No. 109. *True or False?*

## FASB STAFF POSITIONS (FSPS)

Beginning in 2003, the FASB staff introduced the FASB Staff Position (FSP) as a mechanism through which to issue application guidance similar to that previously issued in Staff Implementation Guides and Staff Announcements.

FSPs may also be used to make narrow and limited revisions to Statements of Interpretations that would have previously been made through Technical Bulletins, such as delaying the effective date of a particular statement.

In general, the comment deadline for a FSP is 30 days with a shorter period of not less than 15 days being used in limited cases.

Following is a list of FSPs issued to date:

**Final Fasb Staff Positions (FSPs) Issued to Date**

| FSP | Description |
| --- | --- |
| **FSP FAS 13-1** | Accounting for Rental Costs during a Construction Period (October 6, 2005) |
| **FSP FAS 13-2** | Accounting for a Change or Projected Change in the Timing of Cash Flows Relating to Income Taxes Generated by a Leveraged Lease Transaction (July 13, 2006) |
| **FSP FAS 19-1** | Accounting for Suspended Well Costs (April 4, 2005) |
| **FSP FAS 97-1** | Situations in Which Paragraphs 17(b) and 20 of FASB Statement No. 97, Accounting and Reporting by Insurance Enterprises for Certain Long-Duration Contracts and for Realized Gains and Losses from the Sale of Investments, Permit or Require Accrual of an Unearned Revenue Liability (June 18, 2004) |
| **FSP FAS 106-1** | Accounting and Disclosure Requirements Related to the Medicare Prescription Drug, Improvement and Modernization Act of 2003 (January 12, 2004) |
| **FSP FAS 106-2** | Accounting and Disclosure Requirements Related to the Medicare Prescription Drug, Improvement and Modernization Act of 2003 (May 19, 2004) |
| **FSP FAS 109-1** | Application of FASB Statement No. 109, Accounting for Income Taxes, to the Tax Deduction on Qualified Production Activities Provided by the American Jobs Creation Act of 2004 (December 21, 2004) |
| **FSP FAS 109-2** | Accounting and Disclosure Guidance for the Foreign Earnings Repatriation Provision within the American Jobs Creation Act of 2004 (December 21, 2004) |
| **FSP FAS 115-1 and FAS 124-1** | The Meaning of Other-Than-Temporary Impairment and Its Application to Certain Investments (November 3, 2005) |
| **FSP FAS 123(R)-1** | Classification and Measurement of Freestanding Financial Instruments Originally Issued in Exchange for Employee Services under FASB Statement No. 123(R) (August 31, 2005) |
| **FSP FAS 123(R)-2** | Practical Accommodation to the Application of Grant Date as Defined in FASB Statement No. 123(R) (October 18, 2005) |
| **FSP FAS 123(R)-3** | Transition Election Related to Accounting for the Tax Effects of Share-Based Payment Awards (November 10, 2005) |

| FSP | Description |
|---|---|
| **FSP FAS 123(R)-4** | Classification of Options and Similar Instruments Issued as Employee Compensation That Allow for Cash Settlement upon the Occurrence of a Contingent Event  (February 3, 2006) |
| **FSP FAS 129-1** | Disclosure Requirements under FASB Statement No. 129, Disclosure of Information about Capital Structure, Relating to Contingently Convertible Securities (April 9, 2004) |
| **FSP FAS 140-1** | Accounting for accrued interest receivable related to securitized and sold receivables under Statement 140 (April 14, 2003) |
| **FSP FAS 140-2** | Clarification of the Application of Paragraphs 40(b) and 40(c) of FASB Statement No. 140 (November 9, 2005) |
| **FSP FAS 141-1 and FAS 142-1** | Interaction of FASB Statements No. 141, Business Combinations, and No. 142, Goodwill and Other Intangible Assets, and EITF Issue No. 04-2, "Whether Mineral Rights Are Tangible or Intangible Assets" (April 30, 2004) |
| **FSP FAS 142-2** | Application of FASB Statement No. 142, Goodwill and Other Intangible Assets, to Oil- and Gas-Producing Entities (September 2, 2004) |
| **FSP FAS 143-1** | Accounting for Electronic Equipment Waste Obligations (June 8, 2005) |
| **FSP FAS 144-1** | Determination of Cost Basis for Foreclosed Assets under FASB Statement No. 15, Accounting by Debtors and Creditors for Troubled Debt Restructurings, and the Measurement of Cumulative Losses Previously Recognized under Paragraph 37 of FASB Statement No. 144, Accounting for the Impairment or Disposal of Long-Lived Assets (November 11, 2003) |
| **FSP FAS 146-1** | Determining Whether a One-Time Termination Benefit Offered in Connection with an Exit or Disposal Activity Is, in Substance, an Enhancement to an Ongoing Benefit Arrangement (September 3, 2003) |
| **FSP FAS 150-1** | Issuer's Accounting for Freestanding Financial Instruments Composed of More Than One Option or Forward Contract Embodying Obligations under FASB Statement No. 150, Accounting for Certain Financial Instruments with Characteristics of both Liabilities and Equity (October 16, 2003) |
| **FSP FAS 150-2** | Accounting for Mandatorily Redeemable Shares Requiring Redemption by Payment of an Amount that Differs from the Book Value of Those Shares, under FASB Statement No. 150, Accounting for Certain Financial Instruments with Characteristics of both Liabilities and Equity (October 16, 2003) |
| **FSP FAS 150-3** | Effective Date, Disclosures, and Transition for Mandatorily Redeemable Financial Instruments of Certain Nonpublic Entities and Certain Mandatorily Redeemable Noncontrolling Interests under FASB Statement No. 150, Accounting for Certain Financial Instruments with Characteristics of both Liabilities and Equity (November 7, 2003) |
| **FSP FAS 150-4** | Issuers' Accounting for Employee Stock Ownership Plans under FASB Statement No. 150, Accounting for Certain Financial Instruments with Characteristics of both Liabilities and Equity (November 7, 2003) |
| **FSP FAS 150-5** | Issuer's Accounting under Statement 150 for Freestanding Warrants and Other Similar Instruments on Shares That Are Redeemable (June 29, 2005) |

| FSP | Description |
|---|---|
| **FSP FIN 45-1** | Accounting for Intellectual Property Infringement Indemnifications under FASB Interpretation No. 45, Guarantor's Accounting and Disclosure Requirements for Guarantees, Including Indirect Guarantees of Indebtedness of Others (June 11, 2003) |
| **FSP FIN 45-2** | Whether FASB Interpretation No. 45, Guarantor's Accounting and Disclosure Requirements for Guarantees, Including Indirect Guarantees of Indebtedness of Others, Provides Support for Subsequently Accounting for a Guarantor's Liability at Fair Value (December 10, 2003) |
| **FSP FIN 45-3** | Application of FASB Interpretation No. 45 to Minimum Revenue Guarantees Granted to a Business or Its Owners (November 10, 2005) |
| **FSP FIN 46(R)-4** | Technical Correction of FASB Interpretation No. 46 (revised December 2003), Consolidation of Variable Interest Entities, Relating to Its Effects on Question No. 12 of EITF Issue No. 96-21, "Implementation Issues in Accounting for Leasing Transactions involving Special-Purpose Entities" (April 30, 2004) |
| **FSP FIN 46(R)-5** | Implicit Variable Interests under FASB Interpretation No. 46 (revised December 2003), Consolidation of Variable Interest Entities (This FSP is applicable to both nonpublic and public reporting enterprises. This issue commonly arises in leasing arrangements among related parties, and in other types of arrangements involving related parties and previously unrelated parties.) (March 3, 2005) |
| **FSP FIN 46(R)-6** | Determining the Variability to Be Considered in Applying FASB Interpretation No. 46(R) (April 13, 2006) |
| **FSP FTB 85-4-1** | Accounting for Life Settlement Contracts by Third-Party Investors (March 27, 2006) |
| **FSP APB 18-1** | Accounting by an Investor for Its Proportionate Share of Accumulated Other Comprehensive Income of an Investee Accounted for under the Equity Method in Accordance with APB Opinion No. 18 upon a Loss of Significant Influence (July 12, 2005) |
| **FSP EITF 85-24-1** | Application of EITF Issue No. 85-24, "Distribution Fees by Distributors of Mutual Funds That Do Not Have a Front-End Sales Charge," When Cash for the Right to Future Distribution Fees for Shares Previously Sold Is Received from Third Parties (March 11, 2005) |
| **FSP EITF 00-19-1** | Application of EITF Issue No. 00-19 to Freestanding Financial Instruments Originally Issued as Employee Compensation (May 31, 2005) (Superseded by FSP FAS 123(R)-1) |
| **FSP EITF 03-1-1** | Effective Date of Paragraphs 10–20 of EITF Issue No. 03-1, "The Meaning of Other-Than-Temporary Impairment and Its Application to Certain Investments" (September 30, 2004) |
| **FSP SOP 78-9-1** | Interaction of AICPA Statement of Position 78-9 and EITF Issue No. 04-5 (July 14, 2005) |
| **FSP SOP 94-6-1** | Terms of Loan Products That May Give Rise to a Concentration of Credit Risk (December 19, 2005) |
| **FSP AAG INV-1 and SOP 94-4-1** | Reporting of Fully Benefit-Responsive Investment Contracts Held by Certain Investment Companies Subject to the AICPA Investment Company Guide and Defined-Contribution Health and Welfare and Pension Plans (December 29, 2005) |

## PRACTICE ISSUES: Cash Flow Shenanigans

### Presentation of Customer Notes Receivable on the Statement of Cash Flows

A recent study indicates that companies are inconsistently accounting for the change in customer notes receivable as it relates to the statement of cash flows.

More specifically, in certain industries it is common for companies to engage in sales involving notes receivable with their customers.

Examples include:

- Notes receivable arising from a floor-planning financing arrangement
- Installment sale receivables
- Franchise receivables
- Lease receivables arising from sales-type lease transactions

Many companies are including the change in notes receivable in the investing activities section of the statement of cash flows, instead of the operating activities section. In doing so, cash from operations may increase significantly.

---

**EXAMPLE**

Assume the following:

| | |
|---|---|
| Net sales | $10,000,000 |
| Operating expenses | 7,000,000 |
| Net income | $3,000,000 |

Of the $10,000,000 of sales, $6,000,000 is collected in cash and the remaining $4,000,000 remains in notes receivable.

**Scenario 1:** The $4,000,000 of change in notes receivable is presented in the operating activities section. The statement of cash flows is presented as follows:

| Cash from operating activities: | |
|---|---|
| Net income | $3,000,000 |
| Adjustments: | |
| Change in notes receivable | (4,000,000) |
| Cash used in operating activities | $(1,000,000) |

**Scenario 2:** The $4,000,000 of change in notes receivable is presented in the investing activities section. The statement of cash flows is presented as follows:

| Cash from operating activities: | |
|---|---|
| Net income | $3,000,000 |
| Adjustments: | 0 |
| Cash used in operating activities | $3,000,000 |
| **Cash used in investing activities:** | |
| Change in notes receivable | (4,000,000) |

By presenting the change in notes receivable in the investing activities section, it appears that the company has generated $3,000,000 of operating cash flow and then invested it in investing activities.

### Does Fasb No. 95 Require the Change in Customer Notes Receivable to be Classified in the Operating Activities Section?

FASB No. 95, *Statement of Cash Flows*, is not clear as to whether customer notes receivable should be presented in the operating activities section, although FASB No. 95 deals with a similar situation related to installment sales by stating:

> "A somewhat difficult classification issue arises for installment sales...for which...cash inflows....may occur several years after the date of transaction....The board agreed that all cash collected from customers should be classified as operating cash flows (paragraph 95 of FASB No. 95)."

Although FASB No. 95 addresses the collection of an installment sale, it does not specifically address the change in notes receivable. Instead, it does state that all cash collected from customers should be classified as operating cash flows, including notes receivable.

### The Georgia Tech Financial Analysis Lab Study

In 2004, The Georgia Institute of Technology published a report entitled *Cash-Flow Reporting Practices for Customer-Related Receivables* (the Study). The Study was supplemented with an update on the Study issued in February 2005.

The Study considered the accounting treatment by selected companies of the change in customer notes receivable in the statement of cash flows.

| Companies Presenting the Change in Notes Receivable in the Investing Activities Section | | | |
|---|---|---|---|
| Company | Year | Change in notes receivable presented in investing activities | Reported cash provided by operating activities |
| Ford Motor | 2003 | $(2,878,000) | $20,195,000 |
| General Motors | 2003 | (4,058,000) | 7,600,000 |
| Harley-Davidson | 2003 | (133,958) | 935,553 |
| 7-Eleven | 2003 | (2,411) | 534,511 |
| Federal Signal | 2003 | (5,118) | 75,377 |
| Nortel | 2003 | 31,000 | (761,000) |
| Paccar | 2003 | (27,800) | 818,700 |
| Textron | 2003 | 14,000 | 848,000 |

Reproduced with permission of Georgia Tech College of Management, from Cash-Flow Reporting Practices for Customer-Related Notes Receivable, April 2004 and February 2005.

**NOTE**

After publishing the above report, the SEC sent a letter to the CFOs of the companies they believed may have presented the changes in customer-related notes receivable as investing cash flow. In the letter, the SEC noted that such a presentation was not in conformity with GAAP and called for the firms to change their reporting practices by reclassifying the changes in the operating activities section.

## Cash flow reporting for insurance proceeds

**Question:** How should insurance proceeds received in connection with a claim for damage or destruction of property, plant and equipment be presented in the statement of cash flows?

**Response:** An inconsistency in cash flow reporting practices is the categorization of insurance proceeds related to property, plant and equipment. In practice, some companies report such proceeds as inflows in the operating activities section of the statement, which is incorrect and overstates cash flows from operating activities.

FASB No. 95, *Statement of Cash Flows*, requires that insurance proceeds received that are a direct result to investing activities, such as damage or destruction to equipment, should be recorded in the investing activities section of the statement of cash flows. The theory is that such proceeds are the same as a sale of assets.

More specifically, FASB No. 95 defines *cash inflows from operating activities* to include:

"All other cash receipts that do not stem from transactions defined as investing or financing activities, such as amounts received to settle lawsuits, proceeds of insurance settlements *except for those that are directly related to investing or financing activities, such as from destruction of a building*, and refunds from suppliers."

The FASB No. 95 definition states that insurance settlement proceeds are included in operating activities except for settlements related to the destruction of or damage to a building or equipment, which are included in investing activities.

Thus, insurance related to inventory, and business interruption insurance proceeds should be presented in the operating activities section of the Statement. Because many claims are a combination of damage to equipment, inventory, as well as a portion of business interruption insurance, these proceeds should be split between operating and investing activities.

| Insurance proceeds related to | Presented as |
| --- | --- |
| PP&E damaged or destroyed | Investing activities |
| Inventory damaged or destroyed | Operating activities |
| Business interruption insurance | Operating activities |

Consider the following example:

**EXAMPLE**

In 20X2, Company X has a fire that damages its manufacturing plant and equipment, and inventory. The Company receives an insurance recovery settlement in the amount of $5 million for the following claim:

| | |
| --- | --- |
| Equipment destroyed | $3,000,000 |
| Inventory damaged or destroyed | 1,200,000 |
| Business interruption, including lost profits during the down time | 800,000 |
| | $5,000,000 |

The carrying value of the assets destroyed were $1,200,000 for inventory and $1,700,000 for equipment, resulting in a $1,300,000 gain on the transaction as follows:

| | |
|---|---:|
| Insurance proceeds—equipment and inventory | $4,200,000 |
| Carrying value: | |
|   Inventory | (1,200,000) |
|   Equipment | (1,700,000) |
| Gain | $1,300,000 |
| Business interruption insurance income | $800,000 |

At December 31, 20X2, the company received $4,000,000 of the insurance proceeds with the remaining $1,000,000 received in 20X3. The $1,000,000 receivable relates to the equipment.

Entries related to the transaction follow:

| | | |
|---|---:|---:|
| Entry in 20X2 | | |
| Cash | 4,000,000 | |
| Insurance receivable | 1,000,000 | |
|   Inventory | | 1,200,000 |
|   Equipment (cost less accumulated) | | 1,700,000 |
|   Gain on insurance proceeds | | 1,300,000 |
|   Business interruption insurance income | | 800,000 |
| | | |
| Entry in 20X3 | | |
| Cash | 1,000,000 | |
|   Insurance receivable | | 1,000,000 |

The presentation should be made as follows:

**Company X**
**Statements of Income**
**For the Years Ended December 31, 20X3 and 20X2**

| | 20X2 | 20X3 |
|---|---:|---:|
| Net sales | $XX | $XX |
| Cost of sales | XX | XX |
| Gross profit on sales | XX | XX |
| Operating expenses | XX | XX |
| Net operating income | XX | XX |
| Other income: | XX | XX |
|   **Gain on insurance recovery- equipment-inventory** | 1,300,000 | XX |
|   **Business interruption insurance** | 800,000 | XX |
| Net income before taxes | XX | XX |
| Income taxes | XX | XX |
| Net income | $XX | $XX |

**Company X**
**Statements of Cash Flows**
**For the Years Ended December 31, 20X3 and 20X2**

| | 20X2 | 20X3 |
|---|---|---|
| **Cash provided by operating activities:** | | |
| Net income | $XX | XX |
| Adjustments: | | |
| Depreciation and amortization | | |
| Deferred income taxes | | |
| **Gain on insurance recovery- equipment-inventory** | **(1,300,000)** | **0** |
| | XX | XX |
| **Proceeds from insurance related to inventory** | **$1,200,000** | **0** |
| Cash provided by operating activities | XX | XX |
| **Cash provided by investing activities:** | | |
| **Proceeds from insurance related to equipment** | **3,000,000** | |
| **Increase (decrease) in insurance settlement receivable** | **(1,000,000)** | **1,000** |
| Cash provided by operating activities | XX | XX |

**NOTE**

In the above example, the change in the insurance settlement receivable is presented in investing activities because it relates to the equipment portion of the settlement. Because the proceeds are recorded in investing activities, the corresponding receivable should also be recorded in investing activities. If a portion of the receivable is related to the inventory or business interruption insurance recovery, the change in that receivable should be presented in the operating activities section.

### How are Companies Classifying Insurance Proceeds in Practice?

The only study found on the matter was published in 2005 entitled *Cash-Flow Reporting Practices for Insurance Proceeds Related to PP&E* (Georgia Tech College of Management June 2005). This Study concluded that there is a lack of consistency in the classification of insurance proceeds received from damage to property, plant, and equipment (PP&E). In particular, the Study's author identified several companies that had insurance proceeds related to PP&E that were clearly classified as part of operating activities in the statement of cash flows, as summarized in the following table:

## Classification of Insurance Proceeds
## from PP&E as Part of Operating Activities

| Company | Operating CF as reported including ins proceeds- PP&E | Insurance proceeds adjustment | Operating CF Excluding insurance proceeds | % change |
|---|---|---|---|---|
| Arch Chemicals (2004) | $88,100,000 | 3,300,000 | $84,800,000 | 4% |
| Cherokee International (2005) | 3,979,000 | 158,000 | 3,821,000 | 4% |
| Eagle Picher (2003) | (958,000) | 7,848,000 | (8,806,000) | 819% |
| Finish Line  (2004) | 57,799,000 | 1,228,000 | 56,571,000 | 2% |
| Gulfport Energy (2003) | 9,382,000 | 2,510,000 | 6,872,000 | 27% |
| Home Products Intl. (2005) | (8,030,000) | 1,059,000 | (9,089,000) | 13% |
| Network Equipment (2003) | (1,786,000) | 3,451,000 | (5,237,000) | 193% |
| Spacehab (2003) | 19,780,000 | 17,667,000 | 2,113,000 | 89% |

Reproduced with permission of Georgia Tech College of Management, from Cash-Flow Reporting Practices for Insurance Proceeds Related to PP&E, June 2005.

### Dealing with the Impairment of Real Estate Held for Use

FASB No. 144, *Accounting for the Impairment or Disposal of Long-Lived Assets* requires a company to recognize an impairment loss on a long-lived asset when the carrying amount of a long-lived asset exceeds its fair value. FASB No. 144 applies to both personal and real property.

Recently, there has been a softening in real estate values due to numerous factors including an overall building glut (supply exceeds demand) and a slight uptick in interest rates. The result is that for the first time since the issuance of FASB No. 144 in 2002, companies may start to have real estate that is impaired and need to be tested for that impairment. Rarely in the past decade has this issue been considered in most financial statement engagements.

Specifically, FASB No. 144 states that an impairment loss exists when the carrying amount of real estate exceeds its fair value.

There are essentially three steps to applying the impairment test:
- Step 1: Perform a Review of Events and Changes in Circumstances
- Step 2: Test for Impairment
- Step 3: Measure the Impairment Loss

### Step 1: Perform a Review of Events and Changes in Circumstances

An impairment test of real estate is performed only if there is an indication that impairment might exist. Thus, an annual test is typically not required in a strong real estate market, since there is unlikely to be events and changes in circumstances that would indicate impairment.

Real estate is tested whenever events or changes in circumstances indicate that its carrying amount may not be recoverable. In Step 1, the entity reviews all of the events and changes in circumstances to determine if a potential impairment exists- that is, the carrying amount of the asset(s) may not be recoverable.

Examples of events and changes in circumstances that might warrant a test include:

- Significant decline in the market price of the real estate or similar real estate
- Continued decline in rental rates and vacancies
- Failure to meet debt service on a regular basis
- Change in the use of the property
- Known environmental contamination
- Legal changes such as rent control or use restrictions

If any of the above factors are known to exist, a test for impairment should be performed.

### Step 2: Test for Impairment

If based on a review of the events and changes in circumstances in Step 1 indicates that there might be impairment (e.g., carrying value may not be recoverable), Step 2 should be performed.

The formula for testing for impairment of the real estate is as follows:

The carrying amount of the real estate is compared with the estimated future undiscounted cash flows to be generated from use of and ultimate disposition of the real estate

| Estimated future cash flows | $\geq$ | Carrying amount of the real estate | $=$ | No impairment exists (no further action required) |
| Estimated future cash flows | $<$ | Carrying amount of the real estate | $=$ | Impairment exists Go to Step 3 and measure the impairment |

### Step 3: Measure the impairment

If, based on Step 2, estimated future cash flows are less than the carrying amount of the real estate, the real estate carrying amount is not recoverable. Therefore, asset impairment must be measured in Step 3.

Formula for measuring impairment:

Carrying amount of the real estate
Less: Fair value of the real estate
Equals: Impairment loss

If the carrying amount is less than the fair value of the real estate, an impairment loss is recorded as follows:

| Impairment loss | xx | |
| Real estate | | xx |

After an impairment loss is recognized, *the reduced carrying amount shall become the new cost* and is depreciated over the real estate's remaining useful life. Restoration of previously recognized impairment losses is *prohibited*.

---

**EXAMPLE**

Harry owns a commercial office building in downtown Boston. He purchased the property in the height of the real estate market. Presently, there is a glut of vacant commercial space and events and circumstances suggest that the building might be impaired.

| Assume: | |
|---|---|
| Carrying amount of all assets and liabilities of the asset group | $2,000,000 |
| Estimated net cash flows per year | $110,000 |
| Remaining useful life of the building | 30 years |
| Fair value of the building | $1,100,000 |

**Step 1: Perform a review of events and changes in circumstances**

Presently, there is a glut of vacant commercial space and events and circumstances suggest that the building might be impaired. Thus, a test for impairment should be performed under Step 2.

**Step 2: Test for impairment**

Estimated annual future cash flows  $110,000 x 30 years = $3,300,000

$$\text{Estimated future cash flows } \$3,300,000 \quad < \quad \text{Carrying amount } \$2,000,000 \quad = \quad \text{NO IMPAIRMENT}$$

**Step 3:  Measure the Impairment Loss**

Not applicable: Step 2 did not result in impairment.

If Step 3 had been done, the impairment loss would have looked like this:

| Carrying amount of all assets and liabilities | $2,000,000 |
|---|---|
| **Fair value (above)** | **1,100,000** |
| Impairment loss | $(900,000) |

**Conclusion:** The real estate has declined to the extent that the fair value of $1,100,000 is less than the carrying amount of $2,000,000. However, that decline in value is not recorded as an impairment loss. The reason is because Step 2 did not result in impairment. The estimated future cash flows of $3,300,000 exceed the carrying amount of $2,000,000. Because the remaining useful life of the real estate is 30 years, cash flows for the impairment test are accumulated over a 30-year period, resulting in ample cash flow to exceed the carrying amount and, thus, avoid having to measure impairment in Step 3. This example is in contrast to a test for impairment of machinery or equipment, where cash flows must be accumulated using a much shorter remaining life of perhaps five years.

Let's review the steps to testing and measuring an impairment of real estate.

### Step 1: Perform a Review of the Events and Change in Circumstances

As previously noted, events and changes in circumstances that suggest that real estate might be impaired include:

- Significant decline in the market price of the real estate or similar real estate
- Continued decline in rental rates and vacancies
- Failure to meet debt service on a regular basis
- Change in the use of the property
- Known environmental contamination
- Legal changes such as rent control or use restrictions

If any of the above factors are known, a test for impairment should be performed.

### Step 2: Test for Impairment

In testing for impairment, there are a few issues that are indigenous to real estate. Annual net cash flows should include:

- Net operating income (rental income less operating expenses) before interest, depreciation and amortization, but *after principal payments.*

**NOTE**

The cash flows should reflect estimated increases or decreases in rental income and operating expenses over the remaining useful life of the property.

- Estimated capital expenditures needed to maintain the property over the remaining useful life, such as:
  - Roof replacement every 8 years
  - Apartment renovation during turnovers
  - Painting and porch replacement

> **NOTE**
>
> Capital expenditures that would increase the future service potential of the asset (e.g., qualify the property for an alternative use) are not included in the future cash flows.

- Salvage (residual) value at the end of the life of the real estate assuming the real estate is sold. The residual value should be *net of selling costs such as commissions,* and should reflect the payoff of any remaining mortgages on the property at the expected time of sale.
  Salvage value formula:

| | |
|---|---|
| Estimated sell price at the end of the asset's useful life | $xx |
| Less: estimated costs to sell the property including, commissions, advertising, etc. | (xx) |
| Less: Mortgage payoff at estimated time of sale | (xx) |
| Salvage value (net) | $xx |

The cash flow formula is summarized like this.

| | Annual net cash flow |
|---|---|
| Net operating income before interest, depreciation and amortization* | $xx |
| − Principal payments on mortgages secured by real estate | (xx) |
| − Estimated reserves for capital expenditures and replacements needed to maintain the property | (xx) |
| + Salvage value at the end of the asset's life, assuming the real estate is sold  (net of costs to sell) | xx |
| **NET CASH FLOW** | $xx |

* Rental income less cash operating expenses, accrual basis.

**The remaining useful life should be the remaining life in the hands of the entity.** The remaining useful depreciable life is a strong indicator of the remaining life for purposes of computing cash flows. If an entity plans to sell the property within a certain period of time (e.g., next five years), the remaining useful life should not exceed the estimated remaining time that the entity plans to hold the property. The ability to obtain renewed or replacement financing should be a factor in determining the remaining useful life of the asset.

### Step 3: Measure the Impairment

If there is an impairment determined in Step 2, the real estate impairment loss must be measured. If the real estate is rental property, the best way to determine fair value is to use a capitalization rate.

---

**EXAMPLE 1**

Net operating income / Capitalization rate = Fair value of real estate

---

If the property is land, fair value should be determined based on the quoted market price or price for similar land.

---

**EXAMPLE 2**

The following example illustrates a more complex application of FASB No. 144 to real estate.

**Facts:** Company X is a real estate company that has 100 commercial and residential rental properties.

Property C is a residential rental property that was purchased 12 years ago at the height of the real estate market. Management believes that the real estate might be impaired. The neighborhood in which the property is located has deteriorated significantly since the date of purchase, resulting in declining rents and higher-than-usual vacancies. Management believes that in the future, the property may be located in a valuable location where a downtown redevelopment may occur. As a result, Management has decided to hold onto the property indefinitely.

When the property was purchased, X obtained a 20-year commercial mortgage. For GAAP purposes, management has selected 39 years as the useful life, which is consistent with management's intent to use the property and, coincidentally the same life as the tax life. Specific details follow:

---

| Carrying amount: | |
|---|---|
| Land | $500,000 |
| Building | 7,200,000 |
| Fixtures and appliances | 100,000 |
| Total | $7,800,000 |
| | |
| Mortgage on property | (1,000,000) |
| Net carrying amount of asset group | $6,800,000 |
| Remaining useful life (based on depreciation schedule) | 27 years* |
| Fair value of asset group | 2,500,000** |

\* Original life 39 years less 12 years depreciation = 27 years remaining.
\*\* NOI $350,000/ 10% capitalization rate = $3,500,000 less mortgage balance $(1,000,000) = $2,500,000.

### ESTIMATED FUTURE CASH FLOWS

| Year | Operating cash flows* | Capital expenditures** | NOI | Principal payments | Salvage value of assets*** | Total undiscounted cash flows |
|---|---|---|---|---|---|---|
| 1 | $400,000 | ($50,000) | $350,000 | $(50,000) | $0 | $300,000 |
| 2 | 250,000 | (50,000) | 200,000 | (50,000) | 0 | 150,000 |
| 3 | 250,000 | (50,000) | 200,000 | (50,000) | 0 | 150,000 |
| 4 | 250,000 | (50,000) | 200,000 | (50,000) | 0 | 150,000 |
| 5 | 250,000 | (50,000) | 200,000 | (50,000) | 0 | 150,000 |
| 6 | 250,000 | (50,000) | 200,000 | (50,000) | 0 | 150,000 |
| 7 | 250,000 | (50,000) | 200,000 | (50,000) | 0 | 150,000 |
| 8 | 250,000 | (50,000) | 200,000 | (50,000) | 0 | 150,000 |
| 9 | 250,000 | (50,000) | 200,000 | (50,000) | 0 | 150,000 |
| 10 | 250,000 | (50,000) | 200,000 | (50,000) | 0 | 150,000 |
| 11-15 | 1,250,000 | (250,000) | 1,000,000 | (250,000) | 0 | 750,000 |
| 16-20 | 1,250,000 | (250,000) | 1,000,000 | (250,000) | 0 | 750,000 |
| 21-25 | 1,000,000 | (250,000) | 750,000 | 0 | 0 | 750,000 |
| 26 | 200,000 | (50,000) | 150,000 | 0 | 0 | 150,000 |
| 27 | 200,000 | (50,000) | 150,000 | 0 | 1,500,000 | 1,650,000 |
| | $6,550,000 | $(1,350,000) | $5,200,000 | $(1,000,000) | $1,500,000 | $5,700,000 |

**Calculations:**
\* Rental income less operating expenses (real estate taxes, insurance, maintenance, utilities, management). Excludes depreciation, amortization and interest.
\*\* Estimated capital expenditures to maintain the existing property such as roof replacement, windows, apartment renovation.
\*\*\* Estimated salvage at the end of the property's life:

Year 27 NOI $150,000/10% capitalization rate = $1,500,000 estimated value in year 27.

### Step 1: Perform a Review of Events and Changes in Circumstances

Management believes that property C might be impaired. The neighborhood in which the property is located has deteriorated significantly since the date of purchase, resulting in declining rents and higher-than-usual vacancies. Thus, a test for impairment should be performed under Step 2

### Step 2: Test for Impairment

Estimated future cash flows $5,700,000 $<$ Carrying amount $6,800,000 $=$ IMPAIRMENT

Because the estimated future cash flows is less than the carrying amount of the property, there is an impairment, and Step 3 must be performed to measure the impairment loss.

### Step 3: Measure the Impairment Loss

| | |
|---|---|
| Carrying amount of the property | $6,800,000 |
| Fair value (above) | - 2,500,000 |
| Impairment loss | $(4,300,000) |

The loss should be allocated to the components of the long-lived assets (building, land and equipment) based on each asset's relative carrying amount as follows:

| Carrying amount | Carrying amount | % of total CV | Allocation of loss | Revised carrying amount |
|---|---|---|---|---|
| Land | $500,000 | 6.4 | $(275,200) | $224,800 |
| Building | 7,200,000 | 92.3 | (3,968,900) | 3,231,100 |
| Fixtures and appliances | 100,000 | 1.3 | (55,900) | 44,100 |
| Total | $7,800,000 | 100% | $(4,300,000) | $3,500,000 |

**Entry for impairment loss:**

| | | |
|---|---|---|
| Impairment loss | 4,300,000 | |
| Land | | 275,200 |
| Building | | 3,968,900 |
| Fixtures and appliances | | 55,900 |

After the assets are written down, the revised carrying amount of the building and fixtures and appliances should be depreciated over the remaining useful life of the assets.

**OBSERVATION**

In computing net cash flows from real estate, the amount of principal payments is deducted in arriving at the net cash flow amount. At first glance, one might think that an accelerated mortgage amortization schedule could result in negative cash flows and, thus, an impairment of real estate. However, this is not the case. Although it is true that an accelerated amortization schedule reduces net cash flows per year, the offset occurs in the year in which the asset is assumed sold. The net salvage value of the real estate is computed after deducting the mortgage balance and costs to sell. Therefore, an accelerated principal schedule results in reductions in cash flows in earlier years, but a smaller or no reduction in the salvage value in later years when the mortgage balance is lower.

## Dealing with the impairment of land

An impairment loss is more likely to be incurred for land as compared with rental property. The reason is primarily due to the fact that land's only cash flow may be from the ultimate disposition of the property, resulting in the carrying amount not being recovered.

**EXAMPLE**

Assume Company X holds land for investment. The only cash flows related to the property are carrying costs (real estate taxes and insurance) and proceeds from the ultimate sale of the property. The Company's plan is to hold the property for another five years and then sell it.

Management is concerned that the asset might be impaired given the deterioration of the surrounding area coupled with the economic downturn. The property was originally purchased for $5,000,000 and presently has a fair value of $3,000,000 as indicated in the table below:

| | |
|---|---|
| Carrying amount | $5,000,000 |
| Fair value | 3,000,000** |

**Based on quoted market value per acre for similar properties in the area.

Management tentatively plans to hold the property for another five years. It believes that, at worst, the fair value of the property will not deteriorate any further and could be sold for $3,000,000 at the end of five years.

Estimated future cash flows over the next five years are as follows:

| | | | | Salvage value of | Total undiscounted |
|---|---|---|---|---|---|
| Year | Operating cash flows* | Capital expenditures | NOI | assets | cash flows |
| 1 | $(50,000) | $0 | $(50,000) | $0 | $(50,000) |
| 2 | (55,000) | 0 | (55,000) | 0 | (55,000) |
| 3 | (60,000) | 0 | (60,000) | 0 | (60,000) |
| 4 | (65,000) | 0 | (65,000) | 0 | (65,000) |
| 5 | (75,000) | 0 | (70,000) | 3,000,000 | 2,930,000 |
| | $(300,000) | 0 | $(300,000) | $      0 | $2,700,000 |

**ESTIMATED FUTURE CASH FLOWS**

* Consists of costs to maintain the property including real estate taxes insurance and maintenance. There is no income.

### Step 1: Perform a Review of Events and Changes in Circumstances

Management is concerned that the asset might be impaired given the deterioration of the surrounding area coupled with the economic downturn.

### Step 2: Test for Impairment

Estimated future cash flows $2,700,000 < Carrying amount $5,000,000 = IMPAIRMENT

### Step 3: Measure the Impairment Loss

| | |
|---|---|
| Carrying amount | $5,000,000 |
| Fair value (above) | -3,000,000 |
| Impairment loss | $(2,000,000) |

Entry for impairment loss

| | | |
|---|---|---|
| Impairment loss | 2,000,000 | |
| Land | | 2,000,000 |

**OBSERVATION**

The above example illustrates how easy it is to record an impairment loss on land versus rental property. Because rental property generates net cash flow over an extended useful life of twenty to thirty years, rarely will a rental property fail the impairment test. That is, future estimated cash flows will most likely exceed the carrying amount, notwithstanding unusual facts and circumstances. The result is that Step 2 does not result in impairment and therefore, Step 3 is not performed to measure impairment.

With respect to non-leased land, the result may be different. It is more likely that land that has declined in value may be written down to recognize an impairment loss. Because non-leased land does not generate annual cash flows exclusive of the net proceeds from the ultimate sale of the land,

It is possible that the future cash flows from ultimate use of the land will be less than the carrying amount, resulting in impairment in Step 2 of the test. Then, Step 3 is performed to measure the impairment in which the carrying amount is written down to the fair value of the land.

## CLARIFYING THE USEFUL LIFE
## OF INTANGIBLE ASSETS—FASB NO. 142

FASB No. 142, *Goodwill and Other Intangibles,* was effective in 2002 and provides three categories of intangible assets which are addressed in this section.

- Goodwill
- Intangible assets (other than goodwill) with *finite lives*
- Intangible assets (other than goodwill) with *indefinite lives*

The following chart summarizes the treatment of these three categories of intangible assets which is discussed in detail further on in this section.

| Goodwill | Intangible Assets Other Than Goodwill | |
|---|---|---|
| | **Finite lives** | **Indefinite lives** |
| Not Amortized | Amortized over useful lives | Not amortized |
| Tested annually for impairment | Tested for impairment only if there is a reason to do so.<br><br>- Refinancing costs<br>- Leasehold improvements<br>- Patents<br>- Copyrights<br>- Franchises with fixed contract terms | Tested annually for impairment<br><br>- Certain trademarks and tradenames<br>- Licenses such as liquor and broadcast<br>- Taxi medallions<br>- Franchises without fixed contract terms<br>- Airport routes |

Goodwill is not amortized but is tested for impairment at least annually. If it is impaired, goodwill is written down and an impairment loss is recorded.

With respect to intangible assets other than goodwill, FASB No. 142 segregates such assets into two categories: intangibles with finite lives and intangibles with indefinite lives.

| Category | Accounting treatment |
|---|---|
| Intangible assets with finite lives | Amortized over their estimated useful lives |
| Intangible assets with indefinite lives | Not amortized until the lives become finite<br>Are tested annually for impairment |

### Intangible Assets with Finite Useful Lives

Since the issuance of FASB No. 142, there has been confusion as to whether certain intangible assets had finite or indefinite lives since the difference is significant.

An intangible asset with a *finite useful life should be amortized over its useful life unless that life is determined to be indefinite* (for purposes of this discussion, a finite life is defined as not having an "indefinite life").

If an intangible asset has a finite useful life, but the precise length of that life is not known, the intangible asset shall be amortized over the best estimate of its useful life.

The method of amortization should reflect the pattern in which the economic benefits of the intangible asset are consumed or used up. If the pattern cannot be reliably determined, the *straight-line method* should be used.

The useful life is the period over which the asset is expected to contribute directly or indirectly to future cash flows of the entity. The useful life is _not_ the period of time that it would take an entity to internally develop an intangible asset that would provide similar benefits.

Pertinent factors to consider in determining the useful life include:

- The expected use of the asset by the entity.
- The expected useful life of another asset or a group of assets to which the useful life of the intangible asset may relate (e.g., mineral rights to depleting assets).
- Any legal, regulatory, or contractual provisions that may limit the useful life.
- Any legal, regulatory, or contractual provisions that enable renewal or extension of the asset's legal or contractual life *without substantial cost* (provided there is evidence to support renewal or extension and renewal or extension can be accomplished *without material modifications of the existing terms and conditions*).
- The effects of obsolescence, demand, competition, and other economic factors (e.g., the stability of the industry, known technological advances, legislative action that results in an uncertain or changing regulatory environment, and expected changes in distribution channels).
- The level of maintenance expenditures required to obtain the expected future cash flows from the asset, such as a material level of required maintenance in relation to the carrying amount of the asset may suggest a very limited useful life.

**EXAMPLE**

R is a retail store that leases retail space in a shopping mall. At the inception of the lease, R spends $200,000 on leasehold improvements. The lease is for 5 years and provides for an additional 5-year option for extension by R. The lease terms provide that once installed the leasehold improvements belong to the landlord and cannot be removed by R at the end of the lease. R expects to exercise the lease option for the additional five-years and all evidence supports R's ability to do so.

**Conclusion:** In determining the useful life of the leasehold improvements, consideration should be given to several factors which include a) the entity's expected use of the asset, b) any extensions of the asset's legal or contractual life *without substantial cost,* and, c) whether the extension can be accomplished *without material modifications* of the existing terms and conditions. In this case, R expects to use the asset for the lease term and for the 5-year extension, meaning that it expects to generate cash flows from use of the asset over a total 10-year period. Second, because the lease provides for a renewal option that can be exercised with minimal cost, the lease option period is considered in determining the useful life. Third, because the extension is part of the lease, it is unilateral and can be accomplished without materials modifications to the existing lease. Thus, the $200,000 leasehold improvements should be amortized over a ten-year period, which includes the five-year option.

**EXAMPLE**

**Change the facts:** Same facts as above except that the company does not like doing business in the mall and does not plan to exercise the additional five-year option.

**Conclusion:** Even though R has the ability to exercise the option, the fact that it does not plan to do so should be considered in determining the useful life. In this case, the leasehold improvements should be amortized over the initial five-year period, not including the additional five-year option period.

**EXAMPLE**

**Change the facts again:** Same facts as the immediate previous examples except that after two years, R changes its mind and decides that it will exercise the option after the five-year period expires.

**Conclusion:** The original useful life of five years has changed so that the revised remaining useful life is eight years (two years remaining on the original lease plus five years on the option). Therefore, the remaining unamortized balance in the leasehold improvements should be amortized over the revised remaining useful life of eight years. The change in the life is treated prospectively without affecting the two previous years.

### Intangible Assets with Indefinite Useful Lives

An intangible asset with an *indefinite life should not be amortized until its life is determined to be no longer indefinite.* If no legal, regulatory, contractual, competitive, economic, or other factors limit the useful life of an intangible asset, the useful life is considered *indefinite.* An intangible asset is deemed to have an indefinite life if there is no legal, regulatory, contractual, competitive, economic, or other factors that limit the useful life of an intangible asset. That is, there is no limit placed on the end of the assets useful life to the reporting entity.

Examples of intangible assets that might have indefinite lives include:

- Certain trademarks and tradenames
- Certain licenses such as liquor and broadcast licenses
- Taxi medallions
- Franchises
- Airport routes

The term "*indefinite*" does not mean "*infinite*" or "indeterminate." A life is indefinite if it extends beyond the foreseeable horizon (e.g., there is *no foreseeable limit* on the period of time over which it is expected to contribute to cash flows of the reporting entity).

An intangible life that has a limited legal life is considered indefinite if:

- Evidence exists to support that the legal life can be renewed indefinitely without substantial cost, and,
- The entity is in compliance with all laws and regulations that permit it to renew in the future.

**EXAMPLE**

Licenses, trademarks and tradenames that have legal lives that can be renewed with minimal cost and no evidence of any objection to that renewal.

If the life subsequently becomes finite, the intangible asset shall then be amortized prospectively over its estimated remaining useful life. Each reporting period, an entity must evaluate whether events and circumstances continue to support an indefinite useful life.

An intangible asset (other than goodwill) that is not amortized should be tested for impairment *annually,* or more frequently on an interim basis if an event or circumstance occurs between annual tests indicating that the asset might be impaired.

> Formula for Annual Impairment Test
>
> Fair value of intangible asset
>
> Less: Carrying value of intangible asset
>
> Equals: Impairment loss

If an impairment loss is recognized, the written down carrying amount of the intangible shall be the asset's new basis for subsequent impairment tests. The reversal of previously recognized impairment losses is prohibited.

### OBSERVATION

With respect to an intangible asset with an indefinite life, the annual test for impairment illustrated above does not follow the impairment test performed under FASB No. 121, as superseded by FASB No. 144. Conversely, intangible assets with finite lives are tested for impairment under FASB No. 121. What is the difference?  FASB No. 121 (144) applies a two-step test for impairment.

## Renewable Licenses

One of the more confusing aspects of FASB No. 142 is the treatment for licenses and other intangibles that can be renewed on a regular basis at minimal cost, such as broadcast or liquor licenses.  Many of these licenses are short-term (from one to three years) and require renewal simply by paying a nominal renewal fee.  Provided the entity is not in violation of certain laws at the time of renewal (e.g., did not sell liquor to minors), the probability of renewal is high. Thus, in viewing the license, it is likely that the license will continue to be renewed in the foreseeable future.

## How Should Such a License be Categorized Under FASB No. 142?

Is it a finite- or infinite-lived asset? Is the life limited to the current renewal period of one to three years, or should the life reflect the future periods for which the license is likely to be renewed? FASB No. 142 states that an intangible life that has a limited legal life is considered indefinite if:

- Evidence exists to support that the legal life can be renewed indefinitely without substantial cost, and,
- The entity is in compliance with all laws and regulations that permit it to renew in the future.

> **EXAMPLE**
>
> Licenses, trademarks and tradenames that have legal lives that can be renewed with minimal cost and no evidence of any objection to that renewal.

If the company can renew a license indefinitely without incurring significant cost, and the company is in compliance with all laws and regulations that allow it to renew the license, then the license has an indefinite life and should not be amortized.

If the life subsequently becomes finite, the intangible asset shall then be amortized prospectively over its estimated remaining useful life.

> **EXAMPLE**
>
> Company X purchases a broadcast license for $1,000,000 which is renewable after three years. At the time of renewal, X is in compliance with all laws and regulations that provide for renewal and such renewal can be made by paying a nominal licensing fee. Unless the Company violates FCC laws and regulations, the company believes the license is renewable indefinitely.
>
> **Conclusion:** The asset has an indefinite life and is not amortized. Instead, it should be tested annually for impairment.

> **EXAMPLE**
>
> **Change the facts:** With two years remaining on its three-year license, the Company has been charged with violating FCC rules and there is concern that its license may not be renewable.
>
> **Conclusion:** Because there is a question as to whether the license can be renewed indefinitely, the life is now finite. The license should be amortized over the remaining number of years in the license period, which is two years.

## RECENT FASB DEVELOPMENTS—INTANGIBLE ASSETS

The FASB has added to its agenda a project that deals with FASB No. 142 and intangible assets. Specifically, the project will address certain aspects of how to determine the useful life of an intangible asset including, but not limited to, how to define the term "substantial cost" with respect to renewable assets. In its July 2006 meeting, the FASB discussed the comment letters received on the project, referred to as proposed FSP FAS 142-d: Amortization and

Impairment of Acquired Renewable Intangible Assets, and decided not to address the issues in the current proposed FSP.

## STUDY QUESTIONS

**13.** Many companies are including the change in notes receivable in the investing activities section of the statement of cash flows, instead of the operating activities section. In doing so, cash from operations may increase significantly. *True or False?*

**14.** FASB No. 95 requires the change in customer notes receivable to be classified in the operating activities section of the cash flow statement. *True or False?*

**15.** The SEC requires the change in customer notes receivable to be classified in the operating activities section of the cash flow statement. *True or False?*

**16.** FASB No. 95, Statement of Cash Flows, requires that insurance proceeds received that are a direct result to investing activities, such as damage or destruction to equipment, should be recorded in the investing activities section of the statement of cash flows. The theory is that such proceeds are the same as a sale of assets. *True or False?*

**17.** FASB No. 95 states that insurance proceeds received in connection with a claim for damage should always be presented in the operating activities. *True or False?*

**18.** FASB No. 144, Accounting for the Impairment or Disposal of Long-Lived Assets requires a company to recognize an impairment loss on a long-lived asset when the carrying amount of a long-lived asset exceeds its fair value. *True or False?*

**19.** Goodwill is amortized. *True or False?*

**20.** An intangible asset with an indefinite life should not be amortized until its life is determined to be no longer indefinite. *True or False?*

MODULE 3 — CHAPTER 6

# FASB 123R: Share-Based Compensation

## LEARNING OBJECTIVES

Upon completion of this chapter, the professional will be able to do the following:

- Be familiar with the background that led to the issuance of FASB No. 123R;
- Identify the types of plans subject to FASB No. 123R;
- Understand how to use the fair value method and option models required by FASB No. 123R; and
- Comprehend the transition rules for implementing FASB No. 123R.

## INTRODUCTION

Accounting for stock options has entered its last phase of a 20-year debate with the FASB's December 2004 issuance of FASB No. 123R, **Share-Based Payment**, an Amendment of FASB Statements No. 123 and 95.

The FASB succumbed to the pressures of Wall Street, Congress, and the financial press by requiring companies to *"expense"* stock options, which is synonymous with using an external fair value method (based on an option model) to value stock options.

Although advocates of expensing options believe they are improving corporate accountability and transparency, what they have not considered is that the FASB's action is likely to make use of traditional stock option plans obsolete.

In anticipation of the FASB's new statement, many companies already have restructured their compensation packages to eliminate stock options altogether as a compensation incentive.

Instead, they have replaced stock options with other forms of compensation—such as restricted stock—that create less of an impact on net income.

## BACKGROUND OF THE STATEMENT

The accounting for stock options has been one of the most controversial GAAP issues in the past decade. In the early 1990s, the issue was debated at length and resulted in the issuance of FASB No. 123, **Accounting for Stock-Based Compensation.**

From 1972 to 1995, the accounting for stock options was addressed by APB No. 25, **Accounting for Stock Issued to Employees.** APB No. 25

required entities to record compensation cost for stock-based employee compensation plans. Under APB No. 25, an employer used an intrinsic method to determine the value of compensation at one *"snapshot"* date, referred to as the measurement date, as follows:

At the measurement date:

| | |
|---|---|
| Fair value (quoted price) of the stock granted | $xx |
| Less: Option price | - (xx) |
| Equals: Discount offer to employees | $xx |

Discount × Number of shares = Compensation cost

The compensation cost was amortized to compensation expense over the number of years the employees were required to work to earn the options (generally the vesting period).

### The Games That Were Played Under APB No. 25

Because APB No. 25 used a *"snapshot"* approach to valuing compensation, companies could easily avoid recording any expense simply by issuing the option with no discount at the measurement date. Assume that the company issued the option at the same price as the fair value on the measurement date ($70).

The calculation of compensation would look like this:

| | |
|---|---|
| FMV at measurement date | $ 70 |
| Option price | - 70 |
| Discount | $ 0   × 10,000 shares = $0 compensation |

A company avoided recording compensation by offering an option price that was at least as high as the fair value at the measurement date. Using APB No. 25's intrinsic method, if no compensation was recorded at the measurement date, the company was not required to remeasure compensation as the fair value of the stock increased in the future.

### The Push to Replace APB No. 25 with FASB No. 123

In the late 1970s and early 1980s, stock options became a much more important component of compensation as the high-tech industry experienced significant growth. A key element for retaining a quality workforce in the high-tech industry was to offer stock options.

As use of stock options expanded, there were concerns that APB No. 25 was outdated and did not reflect the true fair value of the options. That is, the intrinsic method of computing compensation was flawed, in that it could result in no compensation being computed even though there was a true external market value to that option.

In June 1993, the FASB issued an exposure draft requiring entities to implement a fair-value based accounting method for stock compensation plans. The proposed statement would have required all companies to value their stock options using an external optional model (such as the **Black-Scholes Model**) and to record the compensation as expense. The result would have been significant increases in compensation expense for many companies.

This proposed statement was met with extreme opposition and public outcry as members of industry and even Congress challenged the Statement, concerned about its effect on business: a potentially massive depletion of earnings. As a result of the public resentment and political pressures, in October 1993, the FASB issued FASB No. 123, **Accounting for Stock-Based Compensation.**

### The Final Form of FASB No. 123

In its final form, FASB No. 123 represented a compromise between the FASB and industry, in which companies could choose to record compensation expense using an external fair value model or the intrinsic method.

If the intrinsic method was used, the company was required to provide the pro forma fair value information in the footnotes.

Specifically, FASB No. 123, which remained GAAP for stock options until the implementation date of FASB 123R, required the following accounting and disclosure procedures.

### Accounting

An entity had a choice of two methods to account for stock options:

- Implement a fair-value based method for accounting for compensation for employee stock options: Options were valued at the grant date based on their fair value based on an externally generated, option-pricing model such as the Black-Scholes or binomial model; or
- Maintain the existing intrinsic value method used in APB No. 25. If the intrinsic method continued to be used, the entity had to disclose additional pro forma disclosures "as if" the entity had implemented the fair value based method: The pro forma information had to include:
  - Pro forma net income; and
  - Earnings per share (if presented).

Compensation cost for the award of stock options to employees was recognized on a straight-line basis over the period(s) in which the related employee services are rendered by a charge to compensation cost and a corresponding credit to equity (APIC); Disclosures were also required regardless of which method was used.

**Figure 1**

*This diagram depicts the methods that could be used under FASB No. 123.*

### FASB No. 123 Methods—Pre FASB No. 123R
### (Choice of Two Methods)

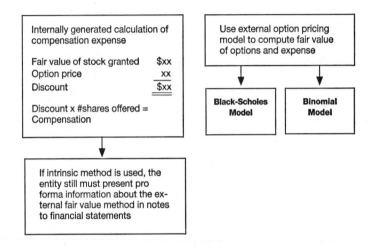

### Pressure on the FASB to Amend FASB No. 123

After approximately one decade of FASB No. 123 being in effect, the FASB reconsidered the accounting for stock options partially based on pressure to replace FASB No. 123 with a new statement that would require the use of the fair value method, that is, remove the choice to use an intrinsic value to measure compensation cost.

In March 2003 the FASB decided to add the stock option project to its agenda with the goal of issuing new accounting rules and disclosures for stock options. The FASB's motivation to consider changing the accounting for stock options was based on several factors, including:

Europe's IASB issued a new standard requiring use of a fair value method (option model). With the FASB and the International Accounting Standards Board (IASB) headed toward convergence of international standards, the FASB had little choice but to follow the IASB's lead in issuing a new standard for stock options.

The results of a FASB survey showed that 76 percent of investors responding were in favor of using an external fair value method to measure stock options, even though 88 percent of responding companies were opposed to such a change. And, with the demise of Enron and the devastation created for its employees, Congress and others wanted to protect employees by changing the accounting and transparency for stock options.

On March 31, 2004, the FASB issued an exposure draft entitled, Shared-Based Payment, an Amendment of FASB Statements No. 123 and 95 and resulted in the issuance of FASB No. 123R, **Share-Based Payment**, in December 2004.

## STUDY QUESTIONS

1. FASB No. 123, the pre-FASB No. 123R GAAP for stock options, allowed companies to choose to record compensation expense using an external fair value model or the intrinsic method. *True or False?*

2. The FASB's motivation to consider changing the accounting for stock options was based on several factors including Europe's IASB issuing a new standard requiring use of a fair value method (option model). With the FASB and IASB headed toward convergence of international standards, the FASB had little choice but to follow the IASB's lead in issuing a new standard for stock options. *True or False?*

**NOTE**

Answers to Study Questions, with feedback to both the correct and incorrect responses, are provided in a special section beginning on page **237**.

## EFFECTIVE DATE OF FASB NO. 123R

The Statement became effective as follows:

- **Publicly held entities that do not file as small business issuers.** As of the beginning of the first interim or annual reporting period beginning after June 15, 2005;
- **Publicly held entities that file as small business issuers.** As of the beginning of the first interim or annual reporting period beginning after December 15, 2005; and
- **Nonpublic entities.** As of the beginning of the first interim or annual reporting period beginning after December 15, 2005.

## EFFECTS OF THE REVISION

FASB No. 123R replaces FASB No. 123, Accounting for Stock-Based Compensation, and supersedes APB No. 25, Accounting for Stock Issued to Employees.

The Statement applies to share-based payment transactions in which an entity acquires goods or services by issuing (or offering to issue) its shares, share options, or other equity instruments.

In such situations, the entity is required to make the following entry:

| | | |
|---|---|---|
| Compensation or other services expense | | XX |
| Additional paid-in capital | XX | |

Examples include:
- Stock options or other equity instruments issued in exchange for employee services rendered; and
- Equity instruments issued for other services rendered or goods received.

Specifically, the Statement does the following:
- Requires that the cost resulting from all share-based payment transactions be recognized in the financial statements using the grant-date fair value as the measurement of cost;
- Requires all entities to apply a fair-value-based measurement method in accounting for share-based payment transactions with employees (except for equity instruments held by ESOPs) and those in which an entity acquires goods or services from nonemployees in share-based payment transactions;
- Provides that fair value is measured based on an observable value, then using an option model (such as the Black-Scholes Model);
- Provides certain exceptions to the fair value measurement method if it is not possible to reasonably estimate the fair value of an award at the grant date;
- Provides a nonpublic entity with the use of modified fair value method (the calculated value method) when it is not practicable to estimate stock volatility in determining fair value;
- Amends FASB No. 95, **Statement of Cash Flows**, to require that excess tax benefits be reported as a cash inflow from a financing activity rather than as a reduction of taxes paid in the operating activities section;
- Establishes criteria as to when a plan is noncompensatory and thus not subject to FASB No. 123R;
- Expands disclosures required for share-based payments; and
- Allows a nonpublic entity to use an intrinsic method to value measure and record instruments that are categorized as liabilities (not as equities).

FASB No. 123R also eliminates the following from FASB No. 123:
- Use of the intrinsic value method for valuing equity awards that was permitted under FASB No. 123; and
- Use of the minimum value method for nonpublic entities that assumed zero volatility in valuing its stock options under FASB No. 123.

## STUDY QUESTIONS

> **3.** FASB No. 123R requires that the cost resulting from all share-based payment transactions be recognized in the financial statements using the grant-date fair value as the measurement of cost. ***True or False?***
>
> **4.** FASB No. 123R maintains use of the intrinsic method for nonpublic entities for share-based equity awards. ***True or False?***

## REQUIREMENT OF THE STATEMENT

### Scope of FASB No. 123R

The Statement applies to all share-based payment transactions in which an entity acquires goods or services by issuing (or offering to issue) its shares, share options, or other equity instruments or by incurring liabilities to an employee or other supplier:

- In amounts based, at least in part, on the price of the entity's shares or other equity instruments; or
- that require or may require settlement by issuing the entity's equity shares or other equity instruments.

The Statement applies to transactions with employees and nonemployees; it does not apply to share-based payment transactions involving an **employee share ownership plan (ESOP)** that is subject to SOP 93-6, **Employers' Accounting for Employee Stock Ownership Plans.**

## STUDY QUESTION

> **5.** FASB No. 123R applies to only certain types of share-based payment transactions in which an entity acquires goods or services by issuing (or offering to issue) its shares, share options, or other equity instruments. ***True or False?***

## RULES OF FASB NO. 123R

### General Rules

The following rules apply to all entities:

- An entity shall recognize the goods acquired or services received in a share-based payment transaction when it obtains the goods or as the services are received; and the entity shall recognize either a corresponding increase in equity or a liability, depending on whether the instruments granted satisfy the equity or liability classification criteria.

- An asset may be recognized before it actually receives the goods or services, if it first exchanges share-based payment for an enforceable right to receive those goods or services. Regardless, the goods or services are not recognized before they are received.

### Employees v. Nonemployees

These rules apply to transactions with employees as opposed to nonemployees:
- For nonemployees, the transaction should be measured and recorded at the fair value of the equity instruments issued or goods or services received, whichever is more determinable; and
- For employees, transactions (e.g., stock options) should be measured based on the fair value of the equity instruments issue.

## STUDY QUESTIONS

**6.** One of the general rules of FASB No. 123R is that an entity shall recognize the goods acquired or services received in a share-based payment transaction when it obtains the goods or as the services are received. *True or False?*

**7.** FASB No. 123R applies to transactions with both employees and non-employees. *True or False?*

### Rules Pertaining to Costs

These rules apply to various types of costs:
- As the goods or services are disposed of or consumed, the entity shall recognize the corresponding cost; and
- Compensation costs related to a share-based award should be recognized over the period during which the employee is required to provide service in exchange for the award (the requisite service period, which is usually the vesting period).

### EXAMPLE

Inventory is purchased by the issuance of equity instruments. The entity should record the inventory at the fair value of equity instruments issued or the inventory, whichever is more determinable. As the inventory is sold, the cost is recognized in the income statement.

**EXAMPLE**

A company purchases employee services in exchange for the issuance of equity instruments. The entity should record the compensation at the fair value of the equity instruments issued. As the services are rendered during the requisite service period, the compensation should be recorded as a cost on the income statement.

**NOTE**

The cost of services or goods may be initially capitalized as part of the cost to acquire or construct another asset, such as inventory or a capital asset. Later on, the cost is recognized on the income statement when the asset is disposed of, consumed, or depreciated/amortized.

The accounting for all share-based payment transactions reflects the rights conveyed to the holder of the instruments and the obligations imposed on the issuer of the instruments, regardless of how those transactions are structured.

**EXAMPLE**

The rights and obligations embodied in a transfer of equity shares to an employee for a note that provides no recourse to other assets of the employee (that is, other than the shares) are substantially the same as those embodied in a grant of equity share options. Such a transaction shall be accounted for as a substantive grant of equity share options.

## Measurement Rules

The following rules pertain to measuring the value of transactions:

- Generally, the objective of accounting for transactions under share-based payment arrangements with employees is to recognize, in the financial statements, the employee services received in exchange for equity instruments issued or liabilities incurred and the related cost to the entity as those services are consumed.
- An entity shall account for the compensation cost from share-based payment transactions with employees using a fair-value-based method as follows:
  - The cost of services received from employees in exchange for awards of share-based compensation shall be measured based on the grant-date fair value of the equity instruments issued or at the fair value of the liabilities incurred;

— The portion of the fair value of an instrument attributed to employee service is net of any amount that an employee pays, or becomes obligated to pay, for that instrument when it is granted.

> **EXAMPLE**
>
> An employee pays $5 at the grant date for an option with a grant-date fair value of $50. The amount attributed to employee service is $45 ($50 – $5).

The grant date is the date at which an employer and an employee reach a mutual understanding of the key terms and conditions of a share-based payment award. The employer becomes contingently obligated on the grant date to issue equity instruments or transfer assets to an employee who renders the requisite service. On the grant date, an employee begins to benefit from, or to be adversely affected by, subsequent changes in the price of the employer's equity shares as follows:

- Awards that are subject to shareholder approval are not deemed to be granted until shareholder approval is obtained unless approval is essentially a formality, such as in the case where management and the members of the board control enough votes to approve the arrangement.
- An individual must be an employee at the grant date. Thus, if an individual has been granted stock options but has not yet begun employment, the grant date is the date on which the individual begins employment.

> **EXAMPLE**
>
> On January 1, 20X5, a company offers a stock option award arrangement to a prospective employee. The individual starts her employment on March 1, 20X5. The grant date is not January 1, 20X5, but rather March 1, 20X5, the date the individual starts her employment.
>
> For equity instruments awarded to employees, the transaction is measured at the grant-date fair value of the equity instruments issued. The fair value of the goods and services received should be used if it is more reliably measurable than the fair value of the equity instruments issued. The estimate of fair value at the grant date of the equity instruments is based on the share price and other pertinent factors (such as expected volatility), and is not remeasured in subsequent periods under the fair value method. The restrictions and conditions inherent in equity instruments awarded to employees are treated differently depending on whether they continue in effect after the requisite service period.

A restriction that continues in effect after an entity has issued instruments to employees—such as the inability to transfer vested equity share options to third parties or the liability to sell vested shares for a period of time—is considered in estimating the fair value of the instruments at the grant date.

The effect of nontransferability and nonhedgeability are taken into account in estimating the fair value of the equity instrument.

A restriction that stems from the forfeitability of instruments to which employees have not yet earned the right (such as the inability either to exercise a nonvested equity share option or to sell nonvested shares) is not reflected in the estimated fair value of the related instruments at the grant date. Those restrictions are taken into account by recognizing compensation cost only for awards for which employees render the requisite service.

No compensation cost is recognized for instruments that employees forfeit because a service condition or a performance condition is not satisfied.

The effect of a market condition is reflected in the grant-date fair value of an award. Compensation cost is recognized for an award with a market condition provided the requisite service is rendered, regardless of when—if ever—the market condition is satisfied.

Factors included and excluded in the measurement of fair value at the grant date are noted in Table 1.

**Table 1. Factors Included and Excluded
in the Measurement of Fair Value**

| Included at the Grant Date | Excluded at the Grant Date |
| --- | --- |
| Restrictions that continue in effect after the entity has issued instruments to employees such as: Inability to transfer vested equity share options to third parties; and Inability to sell vested shares for a period of time. | Restrictions that stem from the forfeitability of instruments to which employees have not yet earned the right, such as: Inability either to exercise a nonvested equity share option; and Inability to sell nonvested shares. |
|  | Reload features and contingent features that require an employee to transfer equity shares earned, or realized gains from the sale of equity instruments earned, to the issuing entity for consideration that is less than fair value on the date of transfer (including no consideration), such as a clawback feature. |

Restrictions stemming from forfeiting instruments to which employees have not yet earned the right are taken into account by recognizing compensation cost only for awards for which employees render the requisite service.

A **nonvested equity share** or **nonvested equity share unit** awarded to an employee shall be measured at its fair value as if it were vested and issued on the grant date.

A **restricted share** awarded to an employee (e.g., a share that will be restricted after the employee has a vested right to it) shall be measured at its fair value, which is the same amount for which a similarly restricted share would be issued to third parties.

Awards classified as liabilities are measured at the fair value of the **liability** issued, as of the grant date. Unlike equity instruments, liabilities are subsequently **remeasured** to their fair values at the end of each reporting period until the liability is settled.

## STUDY QUESTIONS

> **8.** Under FASB No. 123R, the objective of accounting for transactions under share-based payment arrangements with employees is to recognize in the financial statements the employee services received in exchange for equity instruments issued or liabilities incurred and the related cost to the entity as those services are consumed. *True or False?*
>
> **9.** The grant date is the date on which an employee may exercise his or her stock options. *True or False?*
>
> **10.** For equity instruments awarded to employees, the transaction is measured at the grant-date fair value of the equity instruments issued. *True or False?*

### Rules for Determining Fair Value

The objective is to estimate the fair value at the grant date of equity instruments that the entity is obligated to issue when employees have rendered the requisite service and satisfied any other conditions needed to earn the right to benefit from the instruments as follows:

The fair value of an equity share option or similar instrument—for example, certain **share appreciation rights (SARs)**—shall be measured based on the observable market price of identical or similar equity or liability instruments in active markets, if available.

A similar instrument is one whose fair value differs from its intrinsic value; for example, an instrument that has time value such as a **share appreciation right** (SAR) that requires net settlement in equity shares has time value, whereas an equity share does not.

> **EXAMPLE**
>
> Awards to employees of a public entity of shares of its common stock, subject only to a service or performance condition for vesting, should be measured based on the market price of otherwise identical (identical except for the vesting condition) common stock at the grant date.
>
> An estimate of the amount at which similar instruments would be exchanged should factor in expectations of the probability that the service would be rendered and the instruments would vest (e.g., the performance or service conditions would be satisfied).

> **NOTE**
>
> The estimated fair value of instruments at the grant date does not take into account the effect on fair value of vesting conditions and other restrictions that apply only during the requisite service period. The effect of such restrictions is reflected by recognizing compensation cost only for instruments for which the requisite service is rendered. Absent an observable market price, the fair value of an equity share option or similar instrument shall be estimated using a valuation technique, such as an option-pricing model.

## STUDY QUESTIONS

**11.** The effect of nontransferability and nonhedgeability are not taken into account in estimating the fair value of the equity instrument. ***True or False?***

**12.** Factors included in the measurement of fair value at the grant date include restrictions that continue in effect after the entity has issued instruments to employees such as the inability to transfer vested equity share options to third parties and the inability to sell vested shares for a period of time. ***True or False?***

**13.** A nonvested equity share or nonvested equity share unit awarded to an employee shall be measured at its book value as if it were vested and issued on the grant date. ***True or False?***

**14.** With respect to liabilities, awards classified as liabilities are measured at the fair value of the liability issued, as of the grant date. ***True or False?***

**15.** The fair value of an equity share option or similar instrument (such as certain SARs) shall be measured based on the observable market price of identical or similar equity or liability instruments in active markets, if available. ***True or False?***

## VALUATION TECHNIQUES

If observable market prices of identical or similar equity or liability instruments are not available, a valuation technique must be used to measure the grant-date fair value of the equity or liability instruments awarded to employees.

A valuation technique should reflect the one that would be used to determine an amount at which instruments with the same characteristics would be exchanged.

The technique must be:

- Applied in a manner consistent with the fair value measurement objective and the other requirements of the Statement;
- Based on established principles of financial economic theory and generally applied in that field; and
- Reflect all substantive characteristics of the instrument.

A valuation technique used to value employee share options or other similar instruments estimates fair value at a single point in time (the grant date).

**NOTE**

Assumptions used in the valuation technique are based on expectations at the grant date based on information available at the time of measurement. The fair value will change over time as factors used subsequently change, such as share price fluctuations, risk-free interest rate changes, or dividend stream modifications. Changes in the fair value of the instruments do not indicate that the previous expectations used to measure fair value were incorrect. Moreover, the fair value of the instruments at the grant date is not a forecast of what the estimated fair value may be in the future.

### Option Pricing Valuation Models

The Statement does not specify a preference for a particular valuation technique or model in estimating the fair value of employee share options and similar instruments, provided the entity develops reasonable and supportable estimates for each assumption used in the model. Assumptions include the employee share option's expected term, taking into account the contractual term and the effects of employees' expected exercise and post-vesting employment termination behavior.

An entity should change the valuation technique if it concludes that a different technique is likely to result in a better estimate of fair value.

Two types of option-pricing models are identified by the Statement:

- A closed-form model: such as **Black-Scholes-Merton Model**; and
- A lattice model, such as a **Binomial Model**.

### Closed-form Model (Black-Scholes-Merton Model)

A closed-form model:

- Assumes the option exercises occur at the end of an option's contractual term, and expected volatility, dividends and risk-free rates are constant over the option's term;
- Must be adjusted to take account of certain characteristics of employee share options and similar instruments that are not consistent with the models' assumptions (such as the ability to exercise before the end of the options' contractual term); and
- Uses a single weighted-average expected option term.

### Lattice Model (Binomial Model)

A lattice model:

- Can be designed to reflect dynamic assumptions of expected volatility and dividends over the option's contractual term, and estimates of expected options exercise patterns during the options' contractual term, including the effect of blackout periods; and
- More fully reflects the substantive characteristics of a particular employee share option or similar instrument.

### Assumptions Used in an Option-Pricing Model

At a minimum, an option model must include the following requirements:

- Exercise price of the option;
- Expected term of the option, taking into account both the contractual term of the option and the effects of employees' expected exercise and post-vesting employment termination behavior;
- Current price of the underlying share;
- Expected volatility of the price of the underlying share for the expected term of the option;
- Expected dividends on the underlying share for the expected term of the option; and
- Risk-free interest rate for the expected term of the option.

> **NOTE**
>
> Assumptions used in the valuation technique are based on expectations at the grant date based on information available at the time of measurement. The fair value will change over time as factors used subsequently change, such as share price fluctuations, risk-free interest rate changes, or dividend stream modifications. Changes in the fair value of the instruments do not indicate that the previous expectations used to measure fair value were incorrect. Moreover, the fair value of the instruments at the grant date is not a forecast of what the estimated fair value may be in the future.

FASB No. 123R makes the following comments about selected assumptions:

- In estimating expected volatility, dividends, and term of the option, if no amount within the range is more or less likely than any other amount, an average of the amounts in the range (referred to as the expected value) should be used; and
- Historical experience should be used to develop expectations about the future, and should be modified to reflect that the future is reasonably expected to differ from the past.

The assumptions are summarized in Table 2.

A change in the valuation technique or the method of determining appropriate assumptions used in a valuation technique is a change in accounting estimate under APB No. 20, **Accounting Changes**, and should be applied prospectively to new awards.

**Table 2. Assumptions Included in an Option Model**

| Option Model Requirements | Comments |
|---|---|
| Expected term of the option takes into account both the contractual term of the option and the effects of employees' expected exercise and post-vesting employment termination behavior. | Fair value of an employee share option or similar instrument is generally nontransferable and should be based on its expected term, rather than its contractual term. This is because employees typically exercise their options before the end of the options' contractual term. In contrast, the fair value of a traded (transferable) share option is based on its contractual term because rarely is it economically advantageous to exercise, rather than sell, a transferable share option before the end of its contractual term. |
| | The expected term of an employee share option is the period of time for which the instrument is expected to be outstanding (the time from the service inception date to the date of expected exercise or other expected settlement). |
| | Factors that may affect expectations about employees' exercise and post-vesting employment termination behavior include:<br>■ Vesting period of the award-the expected term must at least include the vesting period;<br>■ Employees' historical exercise and post-vesting employment termination behavior for similar grants;<br>■ Expected volatility of the price of the underlying share;<br>■ Blackout periods and other coexisting arrangements such as agreements that allow for exercise to automatically occur during blackout periods if certain conditions are met; and<br>■ Employees' ages, lengths of services, and home jurisdictions. |
| Expected volatility of the price of the underlying share for the expected term of the option. | Volatility is the measure of the amount by which a financial variable (such as share price) has fluctuated (historical volatility) or is expected to fluctuate (expected volatility) during a period. Factors to consider in estimating expected volatility include:<br>■ Volatility of the share price, including changes in that volatility and possible mean reversion of that volatility over the most recent period<br>■ Implied volatility of the share price determined from the market prices of traded options or other traded financial instruments<br>■ For public entities, the length of time an entity's shares have been publicly traded<br>■ Appropriate and regular intervals for price observations<br>■ Corporate and capital structure, such the degree to which an entity is leveraged is directly correlated with the degree of volatility. |

| Option Model Requirements | Comments |
|---|---|
| Expected dividends on the underlying share for the expected term of the option. | An entity may use either its expected yield or its expected payments in its option-pricing model. Further, the historical pattern of dividend increases or decreases (including the effect of dividend protection actions) should be considered in the model. |
| Risk-free interest rate for the expected term of the option. | **U.S. Entity Using an Option on Its Own Shares:**<br><br>■ **Lattice model:** Must use as the risk-free interest rate the implied yields currently available from the U.S. Treasury zero-coupon yield curve over the contractual term of the option if the entity is using the lattice model incorporating the option's contractual term.<br><br>■ **Closed-form model:** Should use the implied yield currently available on U.S. Treasury zero-coupon issues with a remaining term equal to the expected term used as the assumption in the model.<br><br>■ **Non-U.S. Entities:** Use the implied yield currently available on zero-coupon governmental issues denominated in the currency of the market in which the share, or underlying share, which is the basis for the instrument awarded, primarily trades. |

## Reload Options and Contingent Features

The fair value of each award of equity instruments—including an award of options with a reload feature (reload options)—shall be measured separately based on its terms, and the share price and other pertinent factors at the grant date. The effect of a reload feature in the terms of the award shall not be included in estimating the grant-date fair value of the award. Instead, a subsequent grant of reload options shall be accounted for as a separate award when the reload options are granted.

A reload feature provides for automatic grants of additional options whenever an employee exercises previously granted options using the entity's shares, rather than cash, to satisfy the exercise price. At the time of exercise using shares, the employee is automatically granted a new option—a reload option—for the shares used to exercise the previous option.

A contingent feature of an award that might cause an employee to return to the entity either equity instruments earned or realized gains from the sale of equity instruments earned for consideration that is less than the fair value on the date of transfer (including no consideration), such as a clawback feature, shall not be reflected in estimating the grant-date fair value of an equity instrument. Instead, the effect of such contingent feature shall be accounted for if and when the contingent event occurs.

Share-based payments awarded to an employee of the reporting entity by a related party or other holder of an economic interest in the entity, as compensation for services provided to the entity are considered share-based payment transactions accounted for under the Statement unless the transfer is clearly for a purpose other than compensation for services to the reporting entity.

> **NOTE**
>
> The substance of such a related party transaction is that the economic interest holder makes a capital contribution to the reporting entity, and that entity makes a share-based payment to its employee in exchange for services rendered. One example in which such a transfer would not be considered compensation is a transfer to settle an obligation of the economic interest holder to the employee that is unrelated to employment by the entity.

### Special Valuation Exceptions

FASB No. 123R provides two exceptions from the use of the fair value method to value stock options. One involves use by a nonpublic entity of the calculated value method, and one is employed when it is impossible to estimate the fair value at the grant date.

### Use of the Calculated Value Method by a Nonpublic Entity

If a nonpublic entity is unable to reasonably estimate the fair value of its equity share options because it is not practicable for it to estimate the expected volatility of its share price, the entity shall account for its equity share options and similar instruments using the calculated value method.

The calculated value method is only available for use by a nonpublic entity.

Not practicable means that expected volatility cannot be estimated if the entity cannot obtain sufficient historical information about past volatility or other information without undue cost and effort.

The calculated value method determines fair value by using an external historical volatility of an appropriate industry sector index, instead of the expected volatility of the entity's internal share price. The following rules apply to its use: The calculated value method must be used for all equity share options or similar instruments, and in each period, unless the nature of the entity's operations changes so that another index is more appropriate; and

The calculation based on the industry sector index should be made using the daily historical closing values (or, the most frequent observations available of the historical closing values) of the index selected for the period of time prior to the grant date (or service inception date) that is equal in length to the expected term of the option.

If historical closing values are not available for the entire expected term, a nonpublic entity shall use the closing values for the longest period of time available.

**NOTE**

An appropriate industry sector index is one that is representative of the industry sector in which the nonpublic entity operates and that reflects the size of the entity. A weighted index may be appropriate if the entity operates in several industry sectors. In selecting an index, emphasis should be placed on the one that is most closely related to the nature of the entity's operations. However, an entity is precluded from using a broad-based market index like the S&P 500, Russell 3000, or Dow Jones Wilshire 5000 because such indices are too diversified to represent the specific sector in which the nonpublic entity operates.

**OBSERVATION**

FASB No. 123 permitted a nonpublic entity to use a minimum value method by omitting expected volatility from the fair value valuation. With FASB No. 123R, the FASB eliminated use of the minimum value method and, instead, permits a nonpublic entity to use a calculated value method to compute fair value. Under the calculated value method, volatility is reflected into the computation of fair value, but volatility is computed using an appropriate external industry sector index that is representative of the industry sector in which the nonpublic entity operates and that reflects the size of the entity.

### When It Is Not Possible to Estimate Fair Value at the Grant Date

An equity instrument for which it is not possible to reasonably estimate fair value at the grant date shall be accounted for based on its intrinsic value, remeasured at each reporting date through the date of exercise or other settlement, until it can reasonably estimate fair value.

This exception is available to both nonpublic and public entities.

The final measure of compensation cost shall be the intrinsic value of the instrument at the date it is settled. Compensation cost for each period until settlement shall be based on the change in the intrinsic value of the equity instrument in each reporting period.

The entity shall continue to use the intrinsic value method for those instruments even if it subsequently concludes that it is possible to reasonably estimate the fair value.

> **NOTE**
>
> It is usually possible to reasonably estimate the fair value of most equity share options and other equity instruments at the date they are granted. In rare instances, it may not be possible to reasonably estimate the fair value because of the complexity of the instrument's terms. In such a case, use of the intrinsic value method should be used until the time at which fair value can be reasonably estimated. Using the intrinsic value method, the intrinsic value is adjusted at each balance sheet date.

The exposure draft to FASB No. 123R provided a nonpublic entity a choice of using a fair value or intrinsic value to measure compensation cost for a share option plan. In the final statement, the FASB removed the choice to use the intrinsic method, stating that *"two entities should not use different methods to measure and account for their equity share options solely because one is public and the other is not."* Therefore, the FASB concluded that a fair-value-based method should be used for all entities, public and nonpublic, alike, and that the intrinsic value method should not be a choice for nonpublic entities.

However, FASB No. 123R does provide a narrow exception (the second exception, in which the fair value estimate is delayed) that allows any entity (public or nonpublic) to use the intrinsic value method in rare instances in which it cannot measure fair value at the grant date. In such unusual situations, the intrinsic value should be remeasured at each balance sheet date.

### Awards Classified as Liabilities

In determining whether an instrument should be classified as a liability or equity, an entity shall apply GAAP applicable to financial instruments issued in transactions not involving share-based payment.

FASB 150 defines liability as follows:

- Unless otherwise required, an entity shall apply the classification criteria in paragraphs 8-14 of FASB No. 150, **Accounting for Certain Financial Instruments with Characteristics of Both Liabilities and Equity**, as they are effective at the reporting date, in determining whether to classify as a liability a freestanding financial instrument given to an employee in a share-based payment transaction.
- FASB No. 150 does not apply to outstanding shares embodying a conditional obligation to transfer assets, such as shares that give the employee the right to require the employer to repurchase them for cash equal to their fair value (puttable shares).

A puttable (or callable) share awarded to an employee as compensation shall be classified as a liability if either of two conditions is met:

- The repurchase feature permits the employee to avoid bearing the risks and rewards normally associated with equity share ownership for a reasonable period of time from the date the requisite service is rendered and the share is issued, or, It is probable that the employer would prevent the employee from bearing those risks and rewards for a reasonable period of time from the date the share is issued (a period of six months or more is a reasonable period).

- A puttable (or callable) share that does not meet either of the two conditions noted above is classified as equity.

Options or similar instruments on shares shall be classified as liabilities if either of the following conditions is satisfied:

- The underlying shares are classified as liabilities; or
- The entity can be required under any circumstances to settle the option or similar instrument by transferring cash or other assets.

> **NOTE**
>
> One example is an entity that may grant an option to an employee that, upon exercise, would be settled by issuing mandatorily redeemable shares not subject to the deferral in FSP FAS 150-3. Because the mandatorily redeemable share would be classified as a liability under FASB No. 150, the option also would be classified as a liability.

An award may be indexed to a factor in addition to the entity's share price. If the additional factor is not a market, performance, or service condition, the award shall be classified as a liability for purposes of the Statement, and the additional factor shall be reflected in estimating the fair value of the award. The award is classified as a liability even if the entity granting the share-based payment instrument is a producer of the commodity whose price changes are part or all of the conditions that affect an award's vesting conditions or fair value.

Examples include:

- An award of options whose exercise price is indexed to the market price of a commodity, such as gold; and
- A share award that will vest based on the appreciation in the price of a commodity such as gold whereby that award is indexed to both the value of the commodity and the issuing entity's shares.

The accounting for an award of share-based payment shall reflect the substantive terms of the award and any related arrangement.

> **NOTE**
>
> Usually, the written terms provide the best evidence of the substantive terms of an award. However, an entity's past practice may indicate that the substantive terms of an award differ from its written terms. For example, an entity that grants a tandem award under which an employee receives either a stock option or a cash-settled SAR is obligated to pay cash on demand if the choice is the employee's, and the entity thus incurs a liability to the employee.
>
> Conversely, if the choice is the entity's, it can avoid transferring its assets by choosing to settle in stock, and the award qualifies as an equity instrument. However, if an entity that nominally has the choice of settling awards by issuing stock predominately settles in cash, or if the entity usually settles in cash whenever an employee asks for cash settlement, the entity is settling a substantive liability rather than repurchasing an equity instrument.
>
> In determining whether an entity that has the choice of settling an award by issuing equity shares has a substantive liability, the entity also shall consider whether it has the ability to deliver the shares and it is required to pay cash if a contingent event occurs.

A provision that permits employees to effect a broker-assisted cashless exercise of part or all of an award of share options through a broker does not result in liability classification for instruments that otherwise would be classified as equity if two criteria are met:

- The cashless exercise requires a valid exercise of the share options; and
- The employee is the legal owner of the shares subject to the option, even though the employee has not paid the exercise price before the sale of the shares subject to the option.

> **NOTE**
>
> A provision for either direct or indirect (through a net-settlement feature) repurchase of shares issued upon exercise of options (or the vesting of nonvested shares), with any payment due employees withheld to meet the employer's minimum statutory withholding requirements resulting from the exercise, does not, by itself, result in liability classification of instruments that otherwise would be classified as equity. However, if an amount of the minimum statutory requirement is withheld or may be withheld at the employee's discretion, the entire award shall be classified and accounted for as a liability.

> **NOTE**
>
> At the grant date, the measurement objective for liabilities incurred under share-based compensation arrangements is the same as the objective for equity instruments awarded to employees. However, the measurement date for liability instruments is the date of settlement. Accordingly, liabilities incurred under share-based arrangements are remeasured at the end of each reporting period until settlement.

A public entity shall measure a liability award under a share-based payment arrangement based on the award's fair value remeasured at each reporting date until the date of settlement. Compensation cost for each period until settlement shall be based on the change (or portion of change) in the fair value of the liability for each reporting period.

A nonpublic entity shall make a policy decision of whether to measure all of its liabilities incurred under share-based payment arrangements at fair value or to measure all such liabilities at intrinsic value. Regardless of the method used, a nonpublic entity shall remeasure its liabilities under share-based payment arrangements at each reporting date until the date of settlement.

The fair-value-based method is preferable for purposes of justifying a change in accounting principle under APB No. 20, **Accounting Changes**.

## STUDY QUESTION

**16.** FASB No. 123R does not specify a preference for a particular valuation technique or model in estimating the fair value of employee share options and similar instruments. *True or False?*

## RULES FOR EMPLOYEE STOCK PURCHASE PLANS

An **employee stock purchase plan (ESPP)** that satisfies all of the following criteria does not recognize compensation cost and, thus, is a noncompensatory plan not subject to the Statement:

The plan satisfies at least one of the following two conditions:

- The terms of the plan are no more favorable than those available to all holders of the same class of shares; and/or
- Any purchase discount from the market price does not exceed the per-share amount of share issuance costs that would have been incurred to raise a significant amount of capital by a public offering.

> **NOTE**
>
> The Statement indicates that if an entity justifies a purchase discount in excess of 5 percent, it is required to reassess that discount at least annually, and no later than the first share purchase offer during the fiscal year. If upon reassessment the discount is not considered justifiable, subsequent grants using the discount would be compensatory.

Substantially all employees that meet limited employment qualifications may participate on an equitable basis; and the plan incorporates no option features, other than the following:

- Employees are permitted a short period of time, not to exceed 31 days, after the purchase price has been fixed, to enroll in the plan.
- The purchase price is based solely on the market price of the shares at the date of purchase, and employees are permitted to cancel participation before the purchase date and obtain a refund of amounts previously paid, such as those paid by payroll withholdings.

A plan option feature causes the plan to be compensatory and subject to the Statement if there is a provision that establishes a purchase price:

- As an amount based on the lesser of the equity share's market price at the grant date or its market price at the date of purchase; or
- Based on the share's market price at the grant date and that permits a participating employee to cancel participation before the purchase date and obtain a refund of amounts previously paid contains an option feature that causes the plan to be compensatory.

The requisite service period for any compensation cost resulting from an ESPP is the period over which the employee participates in the plan and pays for the shares.

> **EXAMPLE**
>
> Company X offers all full-time employees and all nonemployee shareholders the right to purchase $10,000 of its common stock at a 5-percent discount from its market price at the date of purchase, which occurs in one month. Y estimates the per-share amount of share issuance costs that raise a significant amount of additional capital by a public offering is approximately 8 percent.

In order for a plan to be noncompensatory, it must satisfy at least one of the following two conditions:

- The terms of the plan are no more favorable than those available to all holders of the same class of shares; and/or
- Any purchase discount from the market price does not exceed the per-share amount of share issuance costs that would have been incurred to raise a significant amount of capital by a public offering.

This plan is noncompensatory because its terms are no more favorable than those available to all holders of the same class of shares.

Second, the 5-percent discount does not exceed the 8-percent per-share issuance cost to raise additional capital.

Thus, compensation cost is not measured and recorded under the plan.

## EXAMPLE

Company Y has a dividend reinvestment program based on the following terms:

- The plan permits shareholders the ability to reinvest dividends by purchasing shares of its common stock at a 10-percent discount from its market price on the date that dividends are distributed. The number of shares that can be reinvested by shareholders is based on the number of shares each shareholder presently holds;
- Y offers all full-time employees the right to purchase annually up to $10,000 of its common stock at a 10-percent discount from its market price on the date of purchase. The number of shares that an employee can purchase under the plan is based on the $10,000 limit and not based on the number of shares the employee presently owns, if any;
- Y estimates the per-share amount of share issuance costs that raise a significant amount of additional capital by a public offering is approximately 8 percent; and
- Y's common stock is widely held and many shareholders will not receive dividends totaling at least $10,000 during the annual offering period.

In order for a plan to be noncompensatory, it must satisfy at least one of the following two conditions:

- The terms of the plan are no more favorable than those available to all holders of the same class of shares; and/or
- Any purchase discount from the market price does not exceed the per-share amount of share issuance costs that would have been incurred to raise a significant amount of capital by a public offering.

In this example, neither of the two conditions has been satisfied and, thus, the award plan is compensatory. First, the terms of the plan offered to employees are more favorable than those available to all holders of the same class of shares. Specifically, the number of shares employees may purchase is not based on the number of shares held or dividends received. Instead, it is based on the maximum of $10,000. For all other shareholders, the amount of shares that may be purchased at a discount is limited to the number of shares held and the dividends received from those shares.

Second, the 10-percent discount exceeds the 8-percent per-share issuance cost to raise additional capital.

As a result, the plan offered to employees is not the same as the one offered to all other shareholders in the same class of stock, making the employee plan compensatory. Compensation cost should be measured and recognized under the plan with the entire 10-percent discount being compensation.

## STUDY QUESTION

**17.** An employee stock purchase plan (ESPP) that satisfies certain criteria recognizes compensation cost and, thus, is a compensatory plan subject to FASB No. 123R. *True or False?*

## RECOGNITION OF COMPENSATION COST FOR AN AWARD ACCOUNTED FOR AS AN EQUITY INSTRUMENT

### Recognition of Compensation Cost Over the Requisite Service Period

Compensation cost for an award of share-based employee compensation classified as equity shall be recognized over the requisite service period, with a corresponding credit to equity (such as additional paid-in capital).

The requisite service period is the period during which an employee is required to provide service in exchange for an award, which is typically the vesting period. The period is estimated based on an analysis of the terms of the share-based payment award. The requisite service period may be explicit, implicit, or derived. An explicit service period is one that is stated based on the terms of the share-based payment award.

**EXAMPLE**

A stock option award states that shares vest after three years of service.

An **implicit service** period is one that may be inferred from an analysis of an award's terms, including other explicit service or performance conditions.

**EXAMPLE**

A stock option award vests only upon the completion of a new product design. The design is expected to be completed 18 months from the grant date.

A **derived service** period is one based on a market condition that is inferred from application of certain valuation techniques used to estimate fair value.

**EXAMPLE**

An employee can exercise a stock option award only if the share price doubles at any time during a five-year period. The derived service period can be obtained by using certain valuation techniques that estimate the fair value.

**NOTE**

The requisite service period for an award that contains a market condition can be derived from certain valuation techniques that may be used to estimate grant-date fair value. Moreover, although an award may have one or more service periods, whether explicit, implicit, or derived, it can only have one requisite service period for an accounting period unless it is accounted for as in-substance multiple awards.

An award with a combination of market, performance, or service conditions may contain multiple explicit, implicit, or derived service periods. For such an award, the estimate of the requisite service period is based on an analysis of all vesting and exercisability of conditions, all explicit, implicit, and derived service periods, and the probability that performance or service conditions will be satisfied.

If vesting of an award is based on satisfying both a market condition and a performance or service condition, and it is probable that the performance or service condition will be satisfied, the estimate of the requisite service period is the longest of the explicit, implicit, or derived service periods.

If vesting of an award is based on satisfying either a market condition or a performance or service condition, and it is probable that the performance or service condition will be satisfied, the estimate of the requisite service period is the shortest of the explicit, implicit, or derived service periods.

Following are several examples that illustrate the issues related to the determination of a requisite service period. These examples were adapted from FASB No. 123R.

**EXAMPLE**

On January 1, 20X5, Company X enters into an arrangement with its CEO for 40,000 share options on its stock with an exercise price of $30 per share.

Shares will vest or be forfeited based on the following schedule provided annual performance targets for X's revenue and net income are achieved. The performance targets are defined and quantified at the inception of the award program, January 1, 20X5.

| Date of Vesting | Number of Shares That Vest |
| --- | --- |
| December 31, 20X5 | 10,000 |
| December 31, 20X6 | 10,000 |
| December 31, 20X7 | 10,000 |
| December 31, 20X8 | 10,000 |
| | 40,000 |

The requisite service period is implicit, not explicit. Even though there are explicitly stated vesting dates, the vesting is subject to achieving certain performance targets (e.g., revenue or net income levels).

Although there is one award program, each of the four tranches should be accounted for as a separate award with it own service inception date, grant-date fair value, and a one-year requisite service period.

Each arrangement specifies an independent performance condition (e.g., that year's revenue and net income) for a stated service period and the forfeiture of one year's awards has no effect on future years' awards. Each of the four awards has a grant date of January 1, 20X5.

**EXAMPLE**

On January 1, 20X5, Company X enters into a five-year employment contract with its CEO. The contract provides that the CEO will be given 10,000 fully vested share options at the end of each year (50,000 share options total after five years). The exercise price of each tranche will be equal to the market price at the date of issuance (December 31 of each year within the five-year term).

Each tranche (10,000 shares each) should be accounted for as a separate award with its own service inception date, grant date, and one-year service period.

There are five separate grant dates as the grant date for each tranche is December 31 of each year. The reason is that December 31 of each year is the date when there is a mutual understanding of the key terms and conditions of the agreement (e.g., the exercise price is known and the CEO begins to benefit from, or be adversely affected by, changes in the price of the employer's equity shares).

The service inception date for each award (January 1) precedes the grant date (December 31) because the options are fully vested when they are issued on December 31 and the exercise price is determined at the end of each period.

### EXAMPLE

On January 1, 20X5, Company X grants its CEO 200,000 share options on its stock with an exercise price of $30 per option share.

Vesting (or exercisability) occurs upon both the share price reaching and maintaining at least $70 per share for 30 consecutive trading days, and the completion of eight years of service. X estimates the share price will achieve the $70 per share for 30 consecutive trading dates after six years. The award contains both an explicit service period (eight years related to a service condition) and a derived service period (six years related to a market condition). If vesting of an award is based on satisfying both a market condition and a performance or service condition, and it is probable that the performance or service condition will be satisfied, the estimate of the requisite service period is the longest of the explicit, implicit, or derived service periods. Thus, in this example, the requisite service period over which compensation cost is allocated is eight years (i.e., the longer of eight or six years).

### EXAMPLE

On January 1, 20X5, Company X grants its CEO 200,000 share options on its stock with an exercise price of $30 per option share.

Vesting (or exercisability) occurs upon the earlier of the share price reaching and maintaining at least $70 per share for 30 consecutive trading days, or the completion of eight years of service. X estimates the share price will achieve the $70 per share for 30 consecutive trading dates after six years.

The award contains both an explicit service period (eight years related to a service condition) and a derived service period related to a market condition. The entity should make its best estimate of the derived service period related to the market condition. In this example, the derived service period is 6 years related to the market condition.

If vesting of an award is based on satisfying either a market condition or a performance or service condition, and it is probable that the performance or service condition will be satisfied, the estimate of the requisite service period is the shortest of the explicit, implicit, or derived service periods. In this example, compensation cost is recognized over six years, which is the shorter of the service condition (eight years) and the market condition (six years).

> **EXAMPLE**
>
> Same facts as previous example, except that on February 15, 20X9, X satis-
> fies the market condition ($70 per share for 30 consecutive trading days).
>
> X should immediately recognize any unrecognized compensation cost
> because no further service is required to earn the award.

The service inception date is the beginning of the requisite service period
and is usually the grant date. The service inception date may precede the
grant date if:

- An award is authorized;
- Service begins before a mutual understanding of the key terms and
  conditions of the award are reached; and
- Either the award's terms do not include a substantive future requisite
  service condition that exists at the grant date, or the award contains a
  market or performance condition that if not satisfied during the service
  period preceding the grant date and following the inception of the arrangement, results in forfeiture of the award.

> **NOTE**
>
> Compensation cost is not recognized prior to receiving all necessary ap-
> provals unless such approval is merely a formality or perfunctory. Therefore,
> if service begins but authorization of the award has not been received,
> compensation cost is not recorded until such approval is received.

If the service inception date precedes the grant date, an accrual for compensation cost should be made for the period(s) before the grant date, using
the following rules:

The accrual is based on the fair value of the award at the reporting date
that occurs prior to the grant date.

In the period that includes the grant date, cumulative compensation cost
is adjusted to reflect the cumulative effect of measuring compensation cost
using the fair value at the grant date rather than the fair value previously used
at the service inception date (or any subsequent reporting date).

> **NOTE**
>
> An entity shall make a policy decision about whether to recognize com-
> pensation cost for an award with only service conditions that has a graded
> vesting schedule:

1. on a straight-line basis over the requisite service period for each separately vesting portion of the award as if the award was, in-substance, multiple awards; or

2. on a straight-line basis over the requisite service period for the entire award (e.g., over the requisite service period of the last separately vesting portion of the award).

However, the amount of compensation cost recognized at any date must at least equal the portion of the grant-date value of the award that is vested at that date.

### EXAMPLE

On April 1, 20X5, Company X offers a position to an individual that has been approved by the CEO and board of directors. In addition to salary and other benefits, Company X offers to grant 10,000 shares of Company X stock that vest upon completion of 5 years of service.

The employee accepts the award on April 2, 20X5 and begins providing services to X on June 2, 20X5.

The market price of X's stock is $25 on April 1, 20X5 and $40 on June 2, 20X5.

Thus, the service inception date is June 2, 20X5.

The grant date is also June 2, 2005. Even though the stock options were approved and offered to the individual on April 1, 20X5, the individual was not an employee until he or she started employment on June 2, 20X5.

On the grant date, June 2, 20X5, assume the fair market value is calculated to be $400,000. Once measured, the $400,000 compensation is recognized over the five-year service period.

### EXAMPLE

Same facts as previous example, except required board approval does not occur until August 5, 20X5, two months after employment begins (June 2, 20X5).

The market price of X's stock on August 5 is $38 per share. Both the service inception date and grant date are the same, August 5, 20X5. The service inception date is August 5, and not June 2, because authorization from the board did not occur until August 5. The result is that the fair value is measured at the grant date of August 5, at $380,000 ($38 per share × 10,000 shares = $380,000). Once measured, the $380,000 is recognized over the period August 5, 20X5 to June 2, 20X10.

Further, there is no compensation recorded for the period June 2 through August 4, 20X5, because compensation cost cannot be recognized prior to the service inception date. The service inception date cannot start until all authorizations are received even though an employee may actually start performing the service to earn the awards.

### EXAMPLE

On April 1, 20X5, Company X offers a position to an individual.

On April 1, 20X5, X announces to the employee that it will grant 10,000 shares of Company X stock to the employee on April 1, 20X6 based on the market price of the stock on April 1, 20X6. On April 1, 20X5, the Board of Directors approves the awards plan. There is no substantial service required after April 1, 20X6, to vest in the awards. The employee accepts the award on April 1, 20X5, and immediately begins providing services to X.

The market price of X's stock is as follows:

- $25 on April 1, 20X5;
- $35 on December 31, 20X5; and
- $40 on April 1, 20X6.

X's reporting period ends on December 31 and its effective tax rate is 40 percent. Thus, the service inception date is April 1, 20X5, which is prior to the grant date of April 1, 20X6.

The service inception date is April 1, 20X5 because three requirements are satisfied on that date:

- The award is authorized;
- Service begins before a mutual understanding of the key terms and conditions of the award is reached (e.g., the market price is not known at April 1, 20X5); and
- The award's terms do not include a substantive future requisite service condition that exists at the grant date.

Because there is no future service required after April 1, 20X6, the requisite service period over which compensation cost is recorded is April 1, 20X5 to April 1, 20X6 (the period during which the employee is required to perform service in exchange for the award). The service inception date (April 1, 20X5) precedes the grant date (April 1, 20X6) resulting in an accrual being made for compensation. The accrual is based on the fair value of the award as of the December 31, 20X5, reporting date, which is $35 per share. Entry on December 31, 20X5 (end of the reporting period)

| | |
|---|---|
| Compensation cost | 262,500 (1) |
| Share-based liability | 262,500 |
| Deferred income tax asset | 105,000 (2) |
| Deferred income tax expense | 105,000 |

(1) $35 × 10,000 = $350,000 × 9 months (April 1–December 31, 20X5) = $262,500
(2) $262,500 × 40% = $105,000

On April 1, 20X6 (the grant date), X makes an entry to adjust cumulative compensation cost to reflect the cumulative effect of measuring compensation cost using the fair value at the April 1, 20X6 grant date, rather than the April 1, 20X5, previously used.

| | |
|---|---|
| Compensation cost based on grant date April 1, 20X6: | |
| $40 × 10,000 shares | $400,000 |
| Compensation cost previously recorded based | |
| on December 31, 20X5, market price | |
| | 262,500 |
| Adjustment required: April 1, 20X6 | 137,500 |

Entry on April 1, 20X6 (the grant date):

| | |
|---|---|
| Share-based liability | 262,500 |
| Compensation cost | 137,500 |
| Additional paid in capital | 400,000 |
| Deferred income tax asset | 55,000(1) |
| Deferred income tax expense | 55,000 |

(1) $137,500 × 40% = $55,000

## Amount of Compensation Cost to Be Recognized
## Over the Requisite Service Period

The total amount of compensation cost recognized at the end of the requisite service period for an award of share-based compensation shall be based on the number of instruments for which the requisite service has been rendered (the requisite service period has been completed).

The initial accruals of compensation cost shall be based on the estimated number of instruments for which the requisite service is expected to be rendered. The estimate should be revised if subsequent information indicates the actual number of instruments is likely to differ from previous estimates.

The cumulative effect on current and prior periods of a change in the estimated number of instruments for which the requisite service is expected to be or has been rendered shall be recognized in compensation cost in the period of the change. Accruals of compensation cost for an award with a performance condition shall be made using the probable outcome of that performance condition.

Compensation cost shall be accrued if it is probable that the performance condition will be achieved and shall not be accrued if it is not probable that the performance condition will be achieved. (The definition of probable found in FASB No. 5, **Accounting for Contingencies,** is that the future event or events are likely to occur.)

> **EXAMPLE**
>
> If the number of options or shares an employee earns varies depending on which, if any, of two or more performance conditions are satisfied, compensation cost shall be accrued if it is probable that the performance condition will be satisfied. That assessment should be made by taking into account the interrelationship of those performance conditions.

Previously recognized compensation costs shall not be reversed if an employee share option, or share unit, for which the requisite service has been rendered expires unexercised or unconverted.

### Estimating the Requisite Service Period

An entity shall make an initial best estimate of the requisite service period at the grant date (or at the service inception date if that date precedes the grant date) and shall base accruals of compensation cost on that period. The estimate should be adjusted for changes in circumstances. The initial best estimate and any subsequent adjustment to that estimate of the requisite service period for an award with a combination of market, performance, or service conditions shall be based on an analysis of:

- All vesting and exercisability conditions;
- All explicit, implicit, and derived service periods; and
- The probability that performance or service conditions will be satisfied.

> **NOTE**
>
> For an award meeting the criteria noted above, the initial best estimate of the requisite service period is adjusted depending on both the nature of the conditions and the manner in which they are combined. For example, one consideration is whether an award vests or becomes exercisable when either a market or performance condition is satisfied or whether both conditions must be satisfied.

**Effect of Market, Performance, and Service Conditions
on Recognition and Measurement of Compensation Cost**

An employee's share-based payment award becomes vested at the date that the employee's right to receive or retain equity shares, other equity instruments, or assets under the award is no longer contingent on satisfaction of either a performance condition or a service condition. The Statement requires that an analysis be made of market, performance, or service conditions that are explicit or implicit in the terms of an award, to determine the requisite service period over which compensation cost is recognized and whether recognized compensation cost may be reversed if an award fails to vest or become exercisable. The following definitions apply:

**Market condition.** A condition affecting the exercise price, exercisability, or other pertinent factors used in determining the fair value of an award that relates to the achievement of a specified price of the issuer's shares or a specific amount of intrinsic value indexed solely to the issuer's shares or a specified price of the issuer's shares.

> **EXAMPLE**
>
> Vesting occurs if Company X's stock price reaches $30 per share.

**Performance condition.** A condition affecting the exercise price, exercisability, or other pertinent factors used in determining the fair value of an award that relates to both an employee's rendering service for a specified period of time, and achieving a specified performance target that is defined solely by reference to the employer's own operations or activities.

> **EXAMPLE**
>
> Vesting occurs if the Company's net income is $1 million. Other examples include attaining a specified growth rate in return of assets, obtaining regulatory approval to market a specified product, selling shares in an initial public offering, and a change in control, attaining a growth in EPS, etc.

**Service condition.** A condition affecting the exercise price, exercisability, or other pertinent factors used in determining the fair value of an award that depends solely on an employee rendering service to the employee for the requisite service period. A condition that results in the acceleration of vesting in the event of an employee's death, disability, or termination without cause is a service condition.

> **EXAMPLE**
>
> Vesting occurs if the employee performs five years of employment.

The rules for market, performance, and service conditions that affect vesting or exercisability are as follow:

If an award requires satisfaction of one or more market, performance, or service conditions (or any combination of those factors):

- Compensation cost is recognized only if the performance or service condition is satisfied, even if a market condition is met.
- No compensation cost is recognized if all performance and service conditions are not met.
- If a market condition is satisfied, compensation cost is not recognized unless all performance and service conditions are met.

If vesting is based solely on one or more performance or service conditions, any previously recognized compensation cost is reversed if the performance or service conditions are not satisfied.

> **NOTE**
>
> A market condition is not considered to be a vesting condition, and an award is not forfeited solely because a market condition is not satisfied. Therefore, an entity shall reverse previously recognized compensation cost for an award with a market condition only if the performance and service conditions required are not met, unless the market condition is satisfied prior to the end of the requisite service period, in which case any unrecognized compensation cost should be recognized at the time the market condition is satisfied. Moreover, the effect of a market condition is reflected in estimating fair value of an award at the grant date.

Performance or service conditions that affect vesting are not reflected in estimating the fair value of an award at the grant date because those conditions are restrictions that stem from the forfeitability of instruments to which employees have not yet earned the right.

Market, performance, and service conditions that affect factors other than vesting or exercisability include a grant-date fair value shall be estimated for each possible outcome of such a performance or service condition, and the final measure of compensation cost shall be based on the amount estimated at the grant date for the condition or outcome that is actually satisfied.

> **NOTE**
>
> Market, performance, and service conditions, or a combination of these factors, may affect an award's exercise price, contractual term, quantity, conversion ratio, or other factors that are considered in measuring an award's grant-date fair value.

### When the Condition Is Not Satisfied

Should an entity reverse off previously recognized compensation cost if a market, performance, or service condition is not satisfied (e.g., the award does not vest)?

The Statement provides that compensation cost is reversed if the award fails to vest or become exercisable unless the requisite service is rendered—that is, unless the service and performance conditions are met. Thus, if vesting is not ultimately rendered, any compensation cost previously recorded must be reversed off even if a required market condition has been satisfied. There is an exception whereby compensation cost is not reversed if a market condition is satisfied prior to the end of the requisite service period.

> **EXAMPLE**
>
> Share options vest if the stock price reaches $50 per share (market condition) and five years of service are rendered (service condition). The company records compensation expense over five years. The stock price reaches $50 per share, but the employee leaves after four years, never completing her five years of service.
>
> Once the employee leaves (e.g., the service condition is not met), the compensation previously recorded in the first four years should be reversed even though the market condition (stock price reached $50) was met. The reason is that the service condition (employment of five years) was not satisfied.

> **EXAMPLE**
>
> Assume the same facts as previous example, except the stock price never reaches $50 per share over the five-year period. The employee does satisfy her five-years of service. Compensation expense is recorded over the five-year requisite service period. The compensation recorded over the five years is not reversed off due to the market condition (stock price reaching $50 per share) not being achieved. The reason is that the service condition (five years of service) was achieved.

**EXAMPLE**

Share options vest if the Company's net income grows at least an average of 10 percent per year over five years (performance condition) and five years of service is rendered (service condition). The company records compensation expense over five years. At the end of five years, net income grew an average of only 7 percent and the employee did provide the five years of service.

At the end of the five years, the five years of compensation expense recorded should be reversed. Although the service condition has been satisfied (five years of service rendered), the performance condition has not (net income did not grow an average of 10 percent per year). The Statement requires compensation to be reversed if all performance and service conditions are not met.

## Compensation Cost Not Reversed Off When an Employee Chooses Not to Exercise the Option

FASB No. 123R states that previously recognized compensation cost is not reversed if the option expires unexercised provided the employee performs the requisite service related to the option. The requisite service means the employee satisfies all service and performance conditions required to earn the option. However, any previously recorded deferred income taxes related to the recording of book compensation expense should be reversed because the entity will not receive a future tax deduction from the awards.

**EXAMPLE**

Company X offers an employee options for 1,000 shares of stock that vest after five years of service. The employee has two years after the five-year period to exercise the options. X measures the value of the options and records compensation cost which is recognized over the five-year period.

The employee services the required five-year service period. At the end of the exercise period, the options expire unexercised because the option price exceeds the market price of the stock.

Thus, the compensation recorded over the five-year period should not be reversed once the options expire unexercised because the employee satisfied all service and performance conditions to earn the options. In this case, there was only one service condition (the five years of service) and no performance conditions.

However, deferred income taxes previously recorded should be reversed off since the entity will not receive a tax benefit from the stock options.

### Recognition of Changes in the Fair Value or Intrinsic Value of Awards Classified as Liabilities

Changes in the fair value (or intrinsic value for a nonpublic entity that elects that method) of a liability incurred under a share-based payment arrangement that occur during the requisite service period shall be recognized as compensation cost over that period.

The percentage of the fair value (or intrinsic value) that is accrued as compensation cost at the end of each period shall equal the percentage of the requisite service that has been rendered to that date.

Changes in the fair value (intrinsic value) of a liability that occur after the end of the requisite service period are compensation cost of the period in which the changes occur. Any difference between the amount for which a liability award is settled and its fair value at the settlement date as estimated is an adjustment of compensation cost in the period settled.

### Modifications of Awards of Equity Instruments

A modification of the terms or conditions of an equity award shall be treated as an exchange of the original award for a new award. The transaction is treated as if the entity repurchases the original instrument by issuing a new instrument of equal or greater value, incurring additional compensation cost for any incremental value.

The effects of a modification are measured as follows:

- Incremental compensation cost shall be measured as the excess of the fair value of the modified award over the fair value of the original award immediately before its terms are modified, measured based on the share price and other pertinent factors at that date; and
- Total recognized compensation cost for an equity award shall at least equal the fair value of the award at the grant date unless at the date of the modification the performance or service conditions of the original award are not expected to be satisfied.

The total compensation cost measured at the date of a modification shall be:

- The portion of the grant-date fair value of the original award for which the requisite service is expected to be rendered, or has already been rendered, at that date + The incremental cost resulting from the modification = Total compensation cost;
- Compensation cost shall be subsequently adjusted; and
- A change in compensation cost for an equity award measured at intrinsic value shall be measured by comparing the intrinsic value of the modified award, if any, with the intrinsic value of the original award, if any, immediately before the modification.

> **NOTE**
>
> The effect of the modification on the number of instruments expected to vest shall be reflected in determining incremental compensation cost. The estimate at the modification date of the portion of the award expected to vest shall be subsequently adjusted.

### Other Modifications

Additionally, the following modifications apply:

- **Inducements.** A short-term inducement is accounted for as a modification of the terms of only the awards of employees who accept the inducement. Other inducements are modifications of the terms of all awards subject to them and are accounted for as such;
- **Equity restructurings.** Exchanges of share options or other equity instruments or changes to their terms in conjunction with an equity restructuring or a business combination are modifications under the Statement;

> **NOTE**
>
> Except for a modification to add an antidilution provision that is not made in contemplation of an equity restructuring, accounting for a modification in conjunction with an equity restructuring requires a comparison of the fair value of the modified award with the fair value of the original award immediately before the modification. If the amounts are the same, no incremental compensation cost is recognized.

- **Repurchases or cancellations of awards of equity instruments.** The amount of cash or other assets transferred (or liabilities incurred) to repurchase an equity award is charged to equity to the extent that the amount paid does not exceed the fair value of the equity instruments repurchased at the repurchase date. Any excess of the repurchase price over the fair value of the instruments repurchased is recognized as additional compensation cost.

> **NOTE**
>
> If an entity repurchases an award for which the requisite service has not been rendered has, in effect, modified the requisite service period to the period for which service already has been rendered. Therefore, the amount of compensation cost measured at the grant date but not yet recognized shall be recognized at the repurchase date.

## Cancellation and Replacement of Awards of Equity Instruments

Cancellation of an award accompanied by the concurrent grant of, or offer to grant, a replacement award or other valuable consideration is accounted for as a modification of the terms of the cancelled award using the following rules:

- Incremental compensation cost is measured as the excess of the fair value of the replacement award or other valuable consideration over the fair value of the cancelled award at the cancellation date; and
- Total compensation cost measured at the date of a cancellation and replacement is the portion of the grant-date fair value of the original award for which the requisite service is expected to be rendered (or has already been rendered) at that date plus the incremental cost resulting from the cancellation and replacement.

> **NOTE**
>
> An award cancellation that is not accompanied by a concurrent grant of, or offer to grant, a replacement award or other valuable consideration is accounted for as a repurchase for no consideration. Any previously unrecognized compensation cost is recognized at the cancellation date.

## STUDY QUESTIONS

**18.** In the recognition of compensation cost over the requisite service period, compensation cost for an award of share-based employee compensation classified as equity shall be recognized over the requisition service period, with a corresponding credit to equity (such as additional paid-in capital). ***True or False?***

**19.** With respect to modifications of awards of equity instruments, a modification of the terms or conditions of an equity award shall be treated as an exchange of the original award for a new award. **True or False?**

## ACCOUNTING FOR TAX EFFECTS OF SHARED-BASED COMPENSATION AWARDS

The amount of compensation cost differs for tax and financial statement purposes in terms of the amount and periods in which it is recognized. The cumulative amount of compensation cost recognized for instruments classified as equity or liabilities that ordinarily would result in a future tax deduction under existing tax law, shall be treated as a deductible temporary difference. The deductible temporary difference shall be based on the compensation cost recognized for financial reporting purposes. The change in the temporary difference is recognized in the income statement.

Recognition of compensation cost that does not result in tax deductions under existing tax law is not consolidated to result in a temporary difference. A future event that results in a tax deduction that ordinarily does not result in a tax deduction, is recognized only when it occurs.

---

**EXAMPLE**

An employee's disqualifying disposition of shares gives rise to a tax deduction that ordinarily does not result in a tax deduction.

---

Differences between the deductible temporary difference and the tax deduction that would result based on the current fair value of the entity's shares, is not considered in measuring the gross deferred tax asset or in determining the need for a valuation allowance for a deferred tax asset in accordance with FASB No. 109.

If a deduction reported on a tax return for an award exceeds the cumulative compensation cost recognized for financial reporting, any realized tax benefit that exceeds the previously recognized deferred tax asset for those instruments (the excess tax benefit) is recognized as additional paid-in capital. (The Statement notes that if only a portion of an award is exercised, determination of the excess tax benefits is based on the portion of the award that is exercised.)

Any excess of the realized tax benefit for an award over the deferred tax asset for that award is recognized in the income statement to the extent that the excess comes from a reason other than changes in the fair value of the entity's shares between the measurement date for accounting purposes and a later measurement date for tax purposes.

The amount deductible on the employer's tax return may be less than the cumulative compensation cost recognized for financial statement purposes. The write-off of the deferred tax asset related to the tax return and financial statement difference, net of the related valuation allowance, is first offset to the extent of any remaining additional paid-in capital from excess tax benefits from previous awards accounted for in accordance with the Statement.

The remaining balance of the write-off of a deferred tax asset related to a tax deficiency is to be recognized in the income statement.

An entity that continued to use APB No. 25's intrinsic method as authorized by FASB No. 123 shall calculate the amount available for offset as the net amount of excess tax benefits that would have qualified as such had it instead adopted FASB No. 123 for recognition purposes under FASB No. 123's original effective date and transition method. No distinction is made between excess tax benefits from different types of equity awards, such as restricted shares or share options.

An entity shall exclude the excess tax benefits from share-based payment arrangements that are outside the scope of the Statement. (Examples include employee share ownership plans and excess tax benefits that have not been realized under FASB No. 109.)

## STUDY QUESTION

**20.** In applying FASB No. 123R, the ultimate amount of compensation cost is the same for tax and financial statement purposes in terms of the amount and periods in which it is recognized. *True or False?*

## CONCLUSION

**The Financial Accounting Standards Board** issued FASB No. 123R to require the use of the fair value method (eliminate use of intrinsic value) to measure compensation cost. In addition, in so doing the FASB was following the IASB's initiative in requiring the use of the fair value (option) method, which was in line with the two boards' efforts toward convergence of international standards.

The Statement became effective for most companies beginning in 2006.

Requirements of the statement comprise general rules, plus rules pertaining to employee and nonemployee transactions, costs, and fair value measurement. For valuations, the Statement identifies two option-pricing model types: **close-form** and **lattice models**. A common closed-form model is **Black-Scholes-Merton**, and one common lattice model is the **Binomial Model**.

FASB No. 123R describes two exceptions to the requirement for use of the fair value method: one allowing the calculated value method to be used by nonpublic entities, the other allowing temporary estimation of fair value based on intrinsic value until a fair value estimation is possible.

The Statement provides rules for determining when ESPPs qualify as noncompensatory plans as well as how compensation cost should be recognized for awards accounted for as equity instruments. Finally, the Statement provides guidance on treatment of equity awards when their terms or conditions are modified.

Although the revision responds to the call by many in the world of finance to require companies to expense stock options, thus employing an external fair value method to value the options, others see the issuance as a death knell for the use of stock options as compensation incentives.

---

**CPE NOTE:** When you have completed your study and review of chapters 5 and 6 which comprise this Module, you may wish to take the Quizzer for this Module.

CPE instructions can be found on page 279.

The Module 3 Quizzer Questions begin on page 297. The Module 3 Answer Sheet can be found on pages 315 and 317. For your convenience, you can also take this Quizzer online at **www.cchtestingcenter.com**.

TOP ACCOUNTING ISSUES FOR 2007 CPE COURSE

# Answers to Study Questions

## MODULE 1 — CHAPTER 1

**1. a. Correct.** This is the correct answer, as this is not the correct percentage. The actual percentage is 90%.
**b. Incorrect.** This is not the correct response, as containing a bargain purchase option is indeed one of the criteria for a capital lease.
**c. Incorrect.** This is not the correct response, as a lease being substantially equal (75% or more) to the estimated useful life of the property is indeed one of the criteria for a capital lease.
**d. Incorrect.** This is not the correct response, as transfer of ownership to the lessee by the end of the lease term is indeed one of the criteria for a capital lease.

**2. a. Incorrect.** This is not the correct response, because there are other definitions for the inception date of the lease.
**b. Incorrect.** This is not the correct response, as the inception can be defined in other ways.
**c. Incorrect.** This is not the correct response, as a written commitment that does not contain all of the principal provisions of the lease does not establish the inception date.
**d. Correct.** This is the correct response, since the inception can be either of these dates.

**3. a. Incorrect.** This is not the correct response, since these costs do not qualify as initial direct costs.
**b. Incorrect.** This is not the correct response, as ancillary activities such as establishing and monitoring credit policies, supervision and administration are not classified as initial direct costs.
**c. Correct.** This is the correct response, since preparing and processing lease documents are initial direct costs.
**d. Incorrect.** This is not the correct response. Activities performed by the lessor for advertising do not qualify as initial indirect costs.

**4. a. Incorrect.** This is not the correct response, as such amounts are included in the normal minimum lease payments.
**b. Correct.** This is the correct answer, as such a guarantee is indeed excluded in determining minimum lease payments.
**c. Incorrect.** This is not the correct response, as the minimum rent called for during the lease term is included in the normal minimum lease payments.

**d. Incorrect.** This is not the correct response, as amounts stated to purchase the leased property are included in the normal minimum lease payments.

**5. a. Incorrect.** This is not the correct response. "Accelerated" implies a speeding up of a process, but it is not the correct term for this type of rental payment.
**b. Incorrect.** This is not the correct response. This type of rental payment is not avoidable. Although it can't be quantified until a future event occurs, it does represent an obligation to the firm.
**c. Incorrect.** This is not the correct response. "Deferred" is a term that is normally associated with revenue. It is not a rental payment that is based on future sales volume, interest rates, or machine hours.
**d. Correct.** Rental payments based on future sales volume, future machine hours, future interest rates, and future price indexes are examples or contingent rentals. Contingent rentals can either increase or decrease lease payments.

**6. a. Incorrect.** This is not the correct response, as the above statement is false. Direct financing is a form of capital leases.
**b. Correct.** This is the correct response, as direct financing leases do not create a manufacturer's or dealer's profit or loss.
**c. Incorrect.** This is not the correct response, as sales-type leases are indeed a form of capital leases.
**d. Incorrect.** This is not the correct response, as the occurrence of a manufacturer's or dealer's profit or loss is indeed generally present in a sales-type lease.

**7. a. Incorrect.** This is not the correct response, as "purported investment" does not accurately describe the above definition.
**b. Incorrect.** This is not the correct response, as "net investment" does not accurately match the above definition.
**c. Correct.** This is the correct response, as "gross investment" is the correct term for the above definition.
**d. Incorrect.** This is not the correct response, as the investment is not "contingent".

**8. a. Correct.** This is the correct response, as the above statement is false. Upward annual adjustments are not allowed.
**b. Incorrect.** This is not the correct response, as the above statement is true. These values should be reviewed at least annually.
**c. Incorrect.** This is not the correct response, since the above statement is true. The accounting for the transaction should be revised using the new estimate if a decline in estimated value is not temporary.

**d. Incorrect.** This is not the correct response, as the above statement is true. Under these conditions, the resulting loss should be recognized in the period that the change is made.

**9. a. Incorrect.** This is not the correct response, as FAS-98 deals with sale-leaseback transactions involving real estate, sales-type leases of real estate, and other issues, but not the above issue.
**b. Correct.** This is the correct response, as FAS-91 does indeed address this specific issue.
**c. Incorrect.** This is not the correct response, as this FAS deals with the inception of leases.
**d. Incorrect.** This is not the correct response, as FAS-28 deals with an accounting for sales with leasebacks and does not address the above issue.

**10. a. Incorrect.** This is not the correct response, as the statement is false. If the residual value is guaranteed, its transfer is indeed subject to the guidance of FAS-140.
**b. Incorrect.** This is not the correct response, as the statement is false. Sale or assignment of a sales-type of direct financing lease does not negate the original accounting treatment.
**c. Incorrect.** This is not the correct response, as the statement is false. Transfers of unguaranteed residual values are not subject to the guidance in FAS-140.
**d. Correct.** This is the correct response, as such transfers of minimum-lease payments are accounted for in accordance with FAS-140.

**11. a. Incorrect.** This is not the correct response, as FAS-94 has to do with Consolidation of All Majority-Owned Subsidiaries relating to the equity method.
**b. Incorrect.** This is not the correct response, as FAS-29 has to do with contingent rentals.
**c. Incorrect.** This is not the correct response, as FAS-145 concerns rescission and amendment of certain other FASB statements.
**d. Correct.** This is the correct response, as FAS-66 is the standard which discusses this issue.

**12. a. Incorrect.** This is not the correct response, as the criteria are not this stringent.
**b. Incorrect.** This is not the correct response, as this percentage is too low.
**c. Incorrect.** This is not the correct response, as this percentage is too high.
**d. Correct.** This is the correct response, as this is the correct percentage.

**13. a. Incorrect.** This is not the correct response, as the percentage is too low.
**b. Correct.** This is the correct response, as this is the correct percentage
**c. Incorrect.** This is not the correct response, as the percentage is too high.
**d. Incorrect.** This is not the correct response, as the percentage is far too high.

**14. a. Incorrect.** This is not the correct response. Equipment values, if material, should not be commingled with real estate values in leases.
**b. Incorrect.** This is not the correct response. Such payments should indeed be estimated appropriately and stated separately.
**c. Correct.** This is the correct response. Equipment values, if material, should not be commingled with real estate values in leases.
**d. Incorrect.** This is not the correct response, as FAS-13 does indeed address this issue.

**15. a. Correct.** This is the correct response, as the above statement is false. Under FAS-66, the purchaser's minimum initial investment does have to be made at or before time of sale.
**b. Incorrect.** This is not the correct response, as the above statement is true. A purchaser's note does not qualify for the minimum initial investment unless the above guarantees are in place.
**c. Incorrect.** This is not the correct response, as the above statement is true. Such loaned funds must be deducted from the purchaser's initial investment in determining whether the required minimum has been met.
**d. Incorrect.** This is not the correct response, as the above statement is true. To qualify for sale-leaseback accounting, the initial and continuing investment must indeed be adequate as prescribed by FAS-66.

## MODULE 1 — CHAPTER 2

**1. a. Incorrect.** Correct month and year but the day is wrong
**b. Correct.** June 30, 2001 is the date provided by SFAS No. 141.
**c. Incorrect.** The end of the accounting year is not adopted.
**d. Incorrect.** Beginning of the accounting year is not adopted.

**2. a. Incorrect.** The purchase method isn't superior or inferior.
**b. Incorrect.** The pooling method isn't superior or inferior.
**c. Correct.** All combinations will be accounted for identically thus providing improved comparability.
**d. Incorrect.** Neither pooling nor purchase methods have accuracy problems.

**3. True. Correct.** This is a combination of companies that qualifies as a business combination.

**False. *Incorrect.*** The transfer of all company assets to a new business qualifies as a business combination.

**4. True. *Correct.*** This is an exchange of a business for a business and qualifies as a business combination.

**False. *Incorrect.*** The exchange of a company's assets for the voting stock of a new company meets the required qualification of a business combination.

**5. True. *Incorrect.*** A not-for-profit entity cannot qualify as a business combination even though it is buying a for profit business.

**False. *Correct.*** Acquisition by a not-for-profit entity of a profit enterprise doesn't qualify as a business combination.

**6. True. *Incorrect.*** This is a minority (10%) interest of a subsidiary that does not meet the ownership threshold to qualify as a business combination.

**False. *Correct.*** 10% ownership is below the level required to be considered as an owner.

**7. a. *Incorrect.*** This is an example of a non-qualifying business combination and is specifically excluded from SFAS No. 141 treatment in the standard.

**b. *Incorrect.*** This is an example of a non-qualifying business combination and is specifically excluded from SFAS No. 141 treatment in the standard.

**c. *Incorrect.*** This is an example of a non-qualifying business combination and is specifically excluded from SFAS No. 141 treatment in the standard.

**d. *Correct.*** This is an example of a non-qualifying business combination but SFAS No. 141 specifically requires it to be treated as if it was.

**8. a. *Correct.*** December 1, 20x3 is the initiation date and does not qualify as an acquisition date.

**b. *Incorrect.*** The qualifying date can be one of two dates. It can be the date the transaction is consummated or another date if the end of the accounting period falls between the initiation and consummation date. December 31, 20x3 falls between the initiation date and the consummation date and is the end of an accounting period.

**c. *Incorrect.*** To qualify as an acquisition date it has to be the date the transaction is consummated or the end of an accounting period if it falls between the initiation and consummation date.

**9. a. *Correct.*** The assets and liabilities, including goodwill, are assigned to a reporting unit on the date of acquisition.

**b. *Incorrect.*** The end of the current accounting period is when statements are usually produced.

**c. *Incorrect.*** The day they are measurable usually occurs before the purchase day.

**10. a. Correct.** This is the fair market of consideration received. The liabilities have to be netted against the assets to get the net fair value which is $900,000.
**b. Incorrect.** This is the fair value of the assets received but it doesn't consider the $200,000 of the liabilities.
**c. Incorrect.** This is the fair market value of the stock given less the $200,000 of liabilities. This nets to $1,000,000. The liabilities are not a consideration of the fair market value of the stock given.

**11. a. Incorrect.** SFAS No. 142 provides that amortization of goodwill is no longer allowed.
**b. Incorrect.** Goodwill isn't expensed in the first year of acquisition. It is allocated pro rata to all acquired assets except financial assets, assets subject to sale, pension or postretirement prepaid assets, deferred tax assets, and other current assets.
**c. Correct.** Testing for impairment is a requirement for SFAS No. 142.

**12. a. Correct.** The fair market value is a factor in figuring goodwill. Goodwill is the difference between the amount paid and the fair market value of the assets bought.
**b. Incorrect.** Goodwill will not be a negative number since the total fair market value of the assets is greater than the purchase price.
**c. Incorrect.** Goodwill is determined by subtracting the fair market value from the amount paid for the net assets.

**13. a. Incorrect.** This is the amount of the fair value of the assets of the acquired company and the amount the acquiring company paid for the assets.
**b. Incorrect.** This is the net of the fair value of the assets less the liabilities.
**c. Correct.** The amount the acquiring company paid which is 100,000 shares @ $5 less the net fair value of the assets ($500,000-$25,000). $500,000-$475,000 = $25,000.
**d. Incorrect.** Since the amount given exceeds the net fair value of the assets and liabilities received, there has to be goodwill.

**14. a. Incorrect.** The amount of goodwill is allocated to both PPE & Franchises.
**b. Incorrect.** There is $160,000 of negative goodwill stated in the question; therefore $0 isn't a possible answer.
**c. Correct.** $120,000 ($160,000X$900/$1,200). The negative goodwill is allocated to the franchises and PPE only. Current Assets are initially recorded at fair value.

**d. Incorrect.** The amount of goodwill is allocated to both PPE & Franchises.

**15. a. Incorrect.** Pension prepaid assets are specifically excluded form allocation of negative goodwill.
**b. Incorrect.** Other current assets are specifically excluded from allocation of negative goodwill.
**c. Incorrect.** Deferred tax assets are specifically excluded from allocation of goodwill.
**d. Correct.** Negative goodwill is allocated pro rata to all assets acquired except for assets specifically excluded. Property, plant, & equipment and patents are not specifically excluded.

**16. a. Incorrect.** Since the amount given is less than the net fair value of the assets received there has to be negative goodwill.
**b. Correct.** The amount the acquiring company paid $800,000 less the net assets worth $950,000 = $150,000.
**c. Incorrect.** This is the amount the acquiring company paid less the book value of the assets.

**17. a. Incorrect.** The question states "what is the amount of the deferred liability" and not the amount of the deferred tax asset.
**b. Incorrect.** A deferred tax liability results when (book basis> tax basis).
**c. Correct.** A deferred tax liability of $200,000 results (40% X $500,000 difference).

**18. a. Incorrect.** The difference, in time is done away with so the difference is not permanent.
**b. Incorrect.** Whether immaterial or not the difference is always recognized and accounted for.
**c. Correct.** The difference is temporary and will disappear in future accounting periods.
**d. Incorrect.** It is not allowable to right of the difference as an expense.

**19. a. Incorrect.** This is the amount of the deferred tax liability that is attributable to the book basis of the assets exceeding the tax basis by $500,000. This omits the $300,000 difference between the fair value of $700,000 and the $1 million purchase price.
**b. Incorrect.** This is only the difference between fair value and the purchase price. It doesn't include the book basis of the assets exceeding the tax basis.
**c. Correct.** The deferred tax liability amount to $175,000 (35% of $500,000), which is added to the $300,000 difference between purchase price ($1,000,000) and net assets ($700,000).

**d. Incorrect.** This doesn't take in to fact that of the 35% tax rate or the difference between the purchase price and the fair value.

**20. a. Incorrect.** The contingency is uncertain so no estimate is needed.
**b. Incorrect.** The contingency is uncertain so no inclusion on the balance sheet is needed.
**c. Correct.** The contingency is uncertain and indeterminable so ignore it.

**21. a. Correct.** A preacquisition is recorded at its fair value.
**b. Incorrect.** Cost isn't what something is worth at the time of the acquisition. It may be worth more or less that the actual cost because of the time change or other developments.
**c. Incorrect.** Tax basis doesn't mean it is worth amount.
**d. Incorrect.** Present value may have already had depreciation or additional costs charged to it.

## MODULE 2 — CHAPTER 3

**1. a. Correct.** A company records the acquisition of identifiable intangible assets at fair market value. When the company purchases an identifiable intangible asset from a third party, the best estimate of fair market value is the cost of the asset.
**b. Incorrect.** The book value of the intangible asset on the books of the seller is not relevant to the amount recorded on the books of the buyer.
**c. Incorrect.** Liabilities incurred on the purchase of an intangible asset are a part of its cost. Therefore, liabilities incurred are relevant to the amount recorded on the books of the buyer for the purchase of an identifiable intangible asset.
**d. Incorrect.** Appraised value is less objective than other methods of determining fair market value on the purchase of an identifiable intangible asset. Therefore, appraised value is usually not the amount recorded on the books of the buyer for the purchase of an identifiable intangible asset.

**2. c. Correct.** A company records an impairment loss on the income statement as a loss from continuing operations. The loss is not considered an extraordinary item because losses from impairment are considered a normal and recurring part of ongoing business operations.
**a. Incorrect.** The impairment loss will affect the balance in retained earnings. However, the impairment loss is not reported as a prior period adjustment.
**b. Incorrect.** Impairment losses incurred during the period are generally not reported on the income statement as a change in accounting principle.
**d. Incorrect.** An impairment loss will reduce total stockholders' equity on the balance sheet. However, an impairment loss is not shown as a contra stockholders' equity amount on the balance sheet.

**3. b. *Correct.*** If a company must record an impairment loss for an intangible asset, the amount of the loss is the excess of the carrying value of the intangible asset over its fair value.

**a. *Incorrect.*** If the fair value of the intangible is higher than its carrying value, the company does not record an impairment loss.

**c. *Incorrect.*** If the carrying value of the intangible exceeds its total expected future net cash flows, the company must record an impairment loss. However, the amount of the loss is not the excess of the asset's carrying value over its total expected future net cash flows.

**d. *Incorrect.*** If the total expected net cash flows from the intangible exceed its carrying value, the company does not have to report an impairment loss.

**4. b. *Correct.*** An intangible asset with a finite useful life should be tested for impairment when the net cash flows related to the use and later disposition of the asset group are less than its book value.

**a. *Incorrect.*** When the book value of an intangible asset is less than the net cash flows related to its use and disposition, the company does not have to test it for impairment.

**c. *Incorrect.*** The fact that gross cash inflows to be derived from an intangible asset are greater than its book value has no effect on whether it should be tested for impairment.

**d. *Incorrect.*** Net cash flows, rather than gross cash flows, are involved in determining whether a company should test an intangible asset for impairment.

**5. d. *Correct.*** The legal life of a copyright is the life of the author plus 70 years. The holder of the copyright may not extend its life beyond that period.

**a. *Incorrect.*** The legal life of a copyright is longer than the life of the author.

**b. *Incorrect.*** The legal life of a copyright is longer than 20 years. The legal life of a utility or plant patent filed on or after June 8, 1995, is 20 years from the date of application.

**c. *Incorrect.*** The legal life of a copyright is not limited to 70 years.

**6. a. *Correct.*** The company does not have to disclose the method of determining the book value of the intangible asset. The book value of the intangible asset is its cost less its accumulated amortization.

**b. *Incorrect.*** When a company reports an impairment loss on an intangible asset, it must disclose the method of determining fair market value used to compute the loss.

**c. *Incorrect.*** When a company reports an impairment loss on an intangible asset, it must describe the intangible asset that has become impaired.

**d.** *Incorrect.* When a company reports an impairment loss on an intangible asset, it must disclose the situation causing the impairment.

**7. b.** *Correct.* Under the provisions of SFAS No. 2, a company must expense most research and development costs as incurred. Although some research and development costs will provide a company with future benefits, expensing research and development costs provides reliable information to users of a company's financial statements.
**a.** *Incorrect.* In most cases, a company may not capitalize research and development costs and amortize them over the useful lives of successful projects. Such a method of accounting for research and developments costs is too subjective to provide reliable financial information to users.
**c.** *Incorrect.* A company may not capitalize research and development costs and amortize them over five years. This could overstate the assets of the company, because there is no assurance that any of the research and development costs have any value.
**d.** *Incorrect.* In most cases, a company may not capitalize research and development costs and analyze them for impairment. Such a method would not provide reliable information to the users of the financial statements.

**8. a.** *Correct.* A product or process design modification is considered a research and development activity under SFAS No. 2.
**b.** *Incorrect.* Routine activities to improve an existing product are not considered a research and development activity. The costs of such activities are considered routine production costs.
**c.** *Incorrect.* Legal activities related to a patent application are not considered a research and development activity. The cost of such legal activities should be charged to the intangible asset Patents.
**d.** *Incorrect.* Activities during production such as testing and quality control are not considered research and development activities. The costs of such activities are considered routine production costs.

**9. d.** *Correct.* The design of tools and dies that relate to new technology is considered a research and development activity under SFAS No. 2. However, the routine design of tools and dies is not considered a research and development activity.
**a.** *Incorrect.* Discovery of new information through laboratory research is considered a research and development activity under SFAS No. 2.
**b.** *Incorrect.* Exploring for ways that the company can apply new research or knowledge is considered a research and development activity under SFAS No. 2.
**c.** *Incorrect.* Testing used to evaluate or search for alternative processes or products is considered a research and development activity under SFAS No. 2.

**10. b. *Correct.*** If the equipment has future use, the company capitalizes the cost of the equipment and charges the depreciation on the equipment to Research and Development Expense.
**a. *Incorrect.*** Whether or not the equipment has any future use is relevant to whether the company will capitalize the cost of the equipment.
**c. *Incorrect.*** Whether or not the equipment has any future use is relevant to whether the company will charge all of the cost of the equipment to Research and Development Expense.
**d. *Incorrect.*** The company may treat the cost of the equipment as Research and Development Expense under other conditions besides the worth of the equipment at the end of three years.

**11. c. *Correct.*** The company reduces its liability to the company that advanced the $500,000 by charging the $300,000 in research expenditures to the liability Advance Under Research and Development Arrangement.
**a. *Incorrect.*** Because the company spent the money provided by the other company in the research venture arrangement, it does not charge the research expenditures to Research and Development Expense.
**b. *Incorrect.*** The company may not capitalize research and development costs even if such costs are paid from money received as an advance from another company under a research venture arrangement.
**d. *Incorrect.*** In accounting for the research expenditures, the company would credit, not charge or debit, the Cash account.

**12. b. *Correct.*** A company must expense research and development costs related to the development of computer software as a company incurs such costs. See Software Products Developed Internally.
**a. *Incorrect.*** A company capitalizes and amortizes software production costs related to the development of computer software only after it achieves technological feasibility.
**c. *Incorrect.*** A company capitalizes software inventory costs when the software is ready for release to customers and charges such costs to Cost of Goods Sold when the company sells the software.
**d. *Incorrect.*** A company must charge the cost of marketing the software to expense when incurred, or when the company earns revenue, whichever occurs first.
**13. a. *Correct.*** The cost of achieving technological feasibility is a research and development cost. The company achieves technological feasibility for the software when the company completes all activities necessary to determine that it can produce the software product to meet all specifications.
**b. *Incorrect.*** The cost of testing after achieving technological feasibility is a production cost.
**c. *Incorrect.*** The cost of software documentation is an inventory cost.

**d. Incorrect.** The cost of software maintenance is a software cost and expensed as incurred.

**14. c. Correct.** The cost of developing software training materials is an inventory cost. Inventory costs occur after the software product is ready for sale. See Software Products Developed Internally.
**a. Incorrect.** The cost of detail program design is a research and development cost.
**b. Incorrect.** The cost of coding after achieving technological feasibility is a production cost.
**d. Incorrect.** The cost of software support is a software cost and expensed as incurred.

**15. d. Correct.** The cost of testing after achieving technological feasibility is a production cost. A company capitalizes and amortizes software production costs.
**a. Incorrect.** The cost of testing before achieving technological feasibility is a research and development cost.
**b. Incorrect.** The cost of duplicating software is an inventory cost.
**c. Incorrect.** The cost of software support is a software cost and expensed as incurred.

**16. a. Correct.** If the net realizable value is less than the unamortized production costs, the company must recognize a loss for the difference. The net realizable value then becomes the new basis for the production costs.
**b. Incorrect.** The accumulated amortization on the software production costs is not compared to the unamortized production costs because the unamortized production costs reflect the accumulated amortization.
**c. Incorrect.** The fair market value is the price that a willing buyer would pay a willing seller for an asset. However, it is not the value to which a company must compare its unamortized production costs.
**d. Incorrect.** A company does not have to discount the expected future cash flows from the software product to present value and compare them to the unamortized production costs.

**17. c. Correct.** Computer software expenses and related research and development costs are classified on the income statement as normal expenses under continuing operations. Such expenses are commonly incurred by companies that develop computer software.
**a. Incorrect.** Computer software expenses are not extraordinary items because they are not both unusual in nature and infrequent in occurrence.
**b. Incorrect.** Computer software expenses are not unusual for a company that develops computer software.

**d.** *Incorrect.* Computer software expenses are incurred often and on a regular basis by companies that develop computer software.

**18. d.** *Correct.* SFAS No. 142 specifies the accounting and reporting requirements for goodwill and other intangible assets. It supersedes APB Opinion No. 17.
**a.** *Incorrect.* APB Opinion No. 17 once governed the treatment of goodwill and other intangible assets. However, it has now been superseded.
**b.** *Incorrect.* SFAS No. 2 governs the treatment of research and development costs.
**c.** *Incorrect.* SFAS No. 68 governs venture arrangements for research and development.

**19. d.** *Correct.* Goodwill must be capitalized and analyzed for impairment at least annually. If the goodwill has become impaired, the company must record a loss and write down the carrying value of the goodwill.
**a.** *Incorrect.* Goodwill is an intangible asset. Therefore, it is not expensed in the year a company acquires it in a business acquisition.
**b.** *Incorrect.* Unlike other intangible assets with a finite life, goodwill is not amortized over its useful life.
**c.** *Incorrect.* Before SFAS No. 142, goodwill was amortized over its useful life, which could not exceed 40 years. Goodwill is no longer accounted for in such a manner.

**20. a.** *Correct.* A company may not record goodwill in the accounts unless the company purchased the goodwill in the acquisition of another company. A company may capitalize an internally generated intangible asset only if it has a determinable life. Goodwill has an indefinite life.
**b.** *Incorrect.* Internally generated good will is not capitalized and amortized over its useful life. Goodwill has an indefinite life.
**c.** *Incorrect.* Before SFAS No. 142, purchased goodwill was amortized over its useful life, which could not exceed 40 years. Purchased goodwill is no longer accounted for in such a manner. Internally generated goodwill has never been capitalized and amortized over 40 years.
**d.** *Incorrect.* Purchased goodwill is capitalized and analyzed for impairment. However, internally generated goodwill is not accounted for in that manner.

**21. d.** *Correct.* A company should test goodwill for impairment at least on an annual basis and earlier if evidence suggests that testing is warranted.
**a.** *Incorrect.* Goodwill does not have to be tested for impairment as frequently as monthly.
**b.** *Incorrect.* Goodwill does not have to be tested for impairment as frequently as quarterly. However, a company may test goodwill for impairment quarterly if evidence suggests that such testing is warranted.

**c. Incorrect.** Goodwill does not have to be tested for impairment as frequently as semiannually. However, a company may test goodwill for impairment quarterly or as often as evidence suggests that such testing is warranted.

**22. a. Correct.** The impairment loss for goodwill is equal to its carrying value over its implied fair value. A company uses implied fair value rather than fair value because the company cannot directly determine the fair value of goodwill.
**b. Incorrect.** If the implied fair value of goodwill exceeds its carrying value, no impairment of the goodwill has occurred.
**c. Incorrect.** Net realizable value is the estimated sales price minus the costs of disposal. A company cannot sell goodwill directly. Therefore, a company does not use net realizable value in computing an impairment loss for goodwill.
**d. Incorrect.** A company cannot directly determine the fair value of goodwill because a company cannot sell goodwill by itself.

**23. b. Correct.** The costs should be capitalized as a cost of the patent and amortized over the lesser of the patent's remaining useful life or legal life, whichever is less. The maximum legal life of a patent is 20 years.
**a. Incorrect.** The costs to defend a patent held by the company generally increase the value of the patent. Therefore, such costs should be capitalized rather than expensed.
**c. Incorrect.** Before SFAS No. 142 superseded APB Opinion No. 17, intangible assets were amortized over their useful life, which could not exceed 40 years. However, costs related to a patent have always been amortized over a shorter period because the legal life of a patent is less than 40 years.
**d. Incorrect.** The cost of defending a patent held by the company is not capitalized as a separate asset. The cost of defending a patent is related to the patent, and it does not create a separate asset.

**24. a. Correct.** Once a company has written down goodwill because of impairment, the company may not record any kind of gain if the value of the goodwill recovers in a subsequent period. See Goodwill.
**b. Incorrect.** A company may not record a gain from continuing operations if the implied fair value of the goodwill increases above its carrying value because of a reversal of an impairment loss. A company does not record gains for increases in the value of any intangible asset or any fixed asset if its fair value exceeds its carrying value.
**c. Incorrect.** The company may not report a reversal of a prior impairment loss as an extraordinary item. Extraordinary items must be unusual in nature and infrequent in occurrence.

**d.** *Incorrect.* A company may not show a reversal of prior impairment losses as a cumulative change in accounting principle. One reason is the company changed an accounting estimate, not an accounting principle.

**25. c.** *Correct.* Goodwill must be reported as a separate line item on the balance sheet. A company may not combine it with other intangible assets on the balance sheet and report an aggregate amount of intangible assets.
**a.** *Incorrect.* A company may include a patent with a class of similar intangible assets on the balance sheet.
**b.** *Incorrect.* A company may include a copyright with a class of similar intangible assets on the balance sheet.
**d.** *Incorrect.* A company may include a license with a class of similar intangible assets on the balance sheet.

# MODULE 2 — CHAPTER 4

**1. d.** *Correct.* The lumber, tobacco and distillery industries have an operating cycle that is longer than one year.
**a.** *Incorrect.* An operating cycle is defined as the average time elapsing between expending cash and receiving the cash back from the trade receivable, and therefore; this statement is true.
**b.** *Incorrect.* The operating cycle is used for segregating current assets when the operating cycle is longer than one year, making the statement true.
**c.** *Incorrect.* One year is indeed used as a basis for segregating current assets when more than one operating cycle occurs within a year, making the statement true.

**2. b.** *Correct.* This is the term used to describe this cycle.
**a.** *Incorrect.* The fiscal year is typically at fixed dates which do not coincide with natural business cycles.
**c.** *Incorrect.* The official business year is an inexact term which does not describe the relationship.
**d.** *Incorrect.* One of the other choices is the correct choice.

**3. a.** *Correct.* This revenue is classified as a liability for which repayment is expected to require the use of current assets during the operating cycle. It is therefore not a current asset.
**b.** *Incorrect.* Secondary cash resources are indeed current assets.
**c.** *Incorrect.* Inventories are indeed current assets.
**d.** *Incorrect.* Prepaid expenses are indeed current assets.

**4. d.** *Correct.* Prepaid expenses are current assets.
**a.** *Incorrect.* Payables from operations are classified as a liability for which payment is expected to require the use of current assets during the operating cycle.

**b. Incorrect.** This revenue is classified as a liability for which repayment is expected to require the use of current assets during the operating cycle. It is therefore not a current asset.

**c. Incorrect.** Debt maturities include amounts expected to be liquidated during the current operating cycle, such as short-term notes and the currently maturing portion of long-term debt.

**5. d. Correct.** The *current ratio*, or *working capital ratio*, is a measure of current position and is useful in analyzing short-term credit. The current ratio is computed by dividing the total current assets by the total current liabilities.

**a. Incorrect.** Working capital is the excess of current assets over current liabilities, and it is often used as a measure of the liquidity of an enterprise

**b. Incorrect.** The *acid-test ratio* (also called the quick ratio) is determined by dividing those assets typically closest to cash by total current liabilities. The assets used to calculate this ratio consist of only the most liquid assets, typically cash, receivables, and marketable securities.

**c. Incorrect.** The *acid-test ratio* (also called the quick ratio) is determined by dividing those assets typically closest to cash by total current liabilities. The assets used to calculate this ratio consist of only the most liquid assets, typically cash, receivables, and marketable securities.

**6. a. Correct.** Under the direct write-off method, bad debt expense is not matched with related sales.

**b. Incorrect.** An estimate of uncollectible accounts is not recorded each period under the direct write-off method.

**c. Incorrect.** Accounts receivable are overstated, because no attempt is made to account for the unknown bad debts included therein.

**d. Incorrect.** This is normally done under the allowance method.

**7. b. Correct.** Factoring is a process by which a company converts its receivables into immediate cash by assigning them to a factor.

**a. Incorrect.** Pledging is the process whereby the company uses existing accounts receivable as collateral for a loan.

**c. Incorrect.** The difference between the amount of cash received by the holder and the maturity value of the note is called the discount.

**d. Incorrect.** The account "discounted notes receivable" is a contra account, which is deducted from the related receivables for financial statement purposes.

**8. b. Correct.** An insurable interest in property insurance must exist at the time of the loss, unlike life insurance.

**a. Incorrect.** The increase in cash surrender value of a life insurance policy for a particular period is indeed considered an asset in the owner's statement of financial position.

**c. Incorrect.** If a policy owner intends such action, the cash surrender value is classified as a current asset in the statement of financial position.
**d. Incorrect.** An insurable interest in life insurance need only exist at the time the policy is issued.

**9. c. Correct.** The statement is false. FAS-43 concerns itself with compensated absences, not severance pay and postretirement benefits, which do not concern compensated absences.
**a. Incorrect.** The statement is true. FAS-43 is concerned with the proper accrual of the liability for compensated absences. It does not concern itself with the allocation of these costs to interim accounting periods.
**b. Incorrect.** The statement is true: FAS-43 does establish GAAP for employees' compensated absences.
**d. Incorrect.** The statement is true. FAS-43 does apply to such compensated absences.

**10. b. Correct.** Offsetting is the display of a recognized asset and a recognized liability as one net amount in a financial statement.
**a. Incorrect.** Pledging is the process whereby the company uses existing accounts receivable as collateral for a loan.
**c. Incorrect.** The difference between the amount of cash received by the holder and the maturity value of the note is called the discount.
**d. Incorrect.** The account "discounted notes receivable" is a contra account, which is deducted from the related receivables for financial statement purposes.

## MODULE 3 — CHAPTER 5

**1. True. Correct.** There is a presumption that a general partner controls a limited partnership unless certain rights are given to the limited partners that override that control. One category of such rights is substantive participating rights. Such rights are defined as limited partners' rights (whether granted by contract or by law) that would allow limited partners to effectively participate in the activities of the limited partnership should be considered substantive participating rights and would overcome the presumption that the general partners control the limited partnership.
**False. Incorrect.** The statement is not false because substantive participating rights do, in fact, override a general partner's control. Examples of actions that are considered substantive participating rights include, but are not limited to a) Selecting, terminating, and setting the compensation of management responsible for implement-ting the limited partnership's policies and procedures, b) Establishing operating and capital decisions of the limited partnership, including budgets, in the ordinary course of business, and, c) Any other actions where the limited partners are allowed to effectively participate in the decisions that occur as part of the ordinary

course of the limited partnership's business and that are significant factors in directing and carrying out the activities of the limited partnership.

**2. True. Correct.** The EITF defines the term "substantive" to mean the ability of the limited partners to approve or block actions proposed by the general partners. The general partners must have the limited partners' agreement to take actions outlined above in order for the rights to be substantive participating rights. Participation does not require the ability to initiate actions.

**False. Incorrect.** The statement is correct in that the ability to approve or block actions elevates the right to substantive under the EITF consensus opinion, thus making the statement true, and not false. Moreover, Limited partners' rights that appear to be participating rights but that by themselves are not substantive would not overcome the presumption of control by the general partners in the limited partnership. The likelihood that the veto right will be exercised by the limited partners should not be considered when assessing whether a limited partner's right is a substantive participating right.

**3. True. Correct.** One of the factors noted by EITF Issue 04-1 is the levels at which decisions are made as stated in the limited partnership agreement. Note further that any matters that can be put to a vote must be considered to determine if the limited partners have substantive participating rights by virtue of their ability to vote on matters submitted to a vote of the limited partnership. Determination of whether matters that can be put to a vote of the limited partners, or the vote of the limited partnership as a whole, are substantive should be based on a consideration of all relevant facts and circumstances.

**False. Incorrect.** Other factors noted by the EITF include 1) Relationships between the general and limited partners (other than investment in the common limited partnership) that are of a related-party nature (as defined in FASB No. 57) should be considered in determining if the participating rights of the limited partners are substantive, 2) The degree to which certain limited partners' rights that deal with operating or capital decisions are significant, and 3) Whether the general partners have a contractual right to buy out the interest of the limited partners (a call option).

**4. False. Correct.** All instruments that have embedded conversion features (such as contingently convertible debt, convertible preferred stock, and Instrument C in EITF Issue No. 90-19, with a market-based contingency) that are contingent on market conditions indexed to an issuer's share price should be included in diluted earnings per share computations (if dilutive) regardless of whether the market conditions have been met.

**True. *Incorrect.*** Although prior to EITF Issue No. 04-8, most issuers of Co-Cos excluded the potential dilutive effect of the conversion feature from diluted EPS until the market price contingency is met, EITF Issue No. 04-8 states that  All instruments that have embedded conversion features (such as contingently convertible debt, convertible preferred stock, and Instrument C in EITF Issue No. 90-19, with a market-based contingency) that are contingent on market conditions indexed to an issuer's share price should be included in diluted earnings per share computations (if dilutive) regardless of whether the market conditions have been met.

**5. True. *Correct.*** The EITF addresses the aggregation rules found in paragraph 19 of FASB No. 131. Thus the statement is true.
**False. *Incorrect.*** The EITF does deal with the paragraph 19 aggregation rules. FASB No. 131, Disclosures about Segments of an Enterprise and Related Information, requires that a public business enterprise report financial and descriptive information about its reportable operating segments. Operating segments are components of an enterprise about which separate financial information is available that is evaluated regularly by the chief operating decision maker in deciding how to allocate resources and in assessing performance. Typically, financial information is required to be reported on the basis that it is used internally for evaluating segment performance and deciding how to allocate resources to segments.

**6. True. *Correct.*** Unvested instruments issued as equity-based compensation (including options and nonvested stock) that provide the right to participate in dividends or dividend equivalents with common stock of the issuer are "participating securities" if the right to the dividends is contingent on factors other than employee service and the passage of time.
**False. *Incorrect.*** Under EITF issue 04-12, the EITF generally agreed that unvested instruments issued as equity-based compensation (including options and nonvested stock) are not participating securities if the right to dividends is contingent on factors other than employee service and the passage of time.

**7. False. *Correct.*** Because the transactions are made in contemplation of one another, they are linked and should be treated as one transaction. Thus the statement is false. Only if the transactions are entered into not in contemplation of one another should they be treated as two separate transactions. Also, the issuance of invoices and the exchange of offsetting cash payments is not a factor in determining whether two or more inventory transactions with the same counterparty should be considered as a single nonmonetary inventory transaction within the scope of APB No. 29.

**True. *Incorrect.*** The EITF states that such transactions should be combined and treated as a single exchange under APB No. 29 (carrying value used to record purchased goods). Moreover, in situations in which an inventory transaction is legally contingent upon the performance of another inventory transaction with the same counterparty, the two are in contemplation of one another and should be combined in applying APB No. 29.

**8. True. *Correct.*** The EITF 04-13 states that nonmonetary exchanges whereby finished goods inventory is transferred in exchange for the receipt of raw materials or work-in-progress (WIP) inventory within the same line of business should be recognized at fair value if fair value is determinable within reasonable limits and the transaction has commercial substance, as defined by FASB No. 153.

**False. *Incorrect.*** EITF Issue No. 04-13 states that nonmonetary exchanges whereby finished goods inventory is transferred in exchange for the receipt of raw materials or work-in-progress (WIP) inventory within the same line of business should be recognized at fair value if fair value is determinable within reasonable limits and the transaction has commercial substance, as defined by FASB No. 153. See example 2 under the EITF 04-13 subsection.

**9. True. *Correct.*** Under EITF Issue No. 05-5, the bonus feature and the additional contributions into the German government pension scheme under a Type II ATZ arrangement should be accounted for as a postemployment benefit under FASB No. 112. An entity should recognize the additional compensation over the period from the point at which the employee signs the ATZ contract until the end of the active service period.

**False. *Incorrect.*** EITF Issue No. 05-5 addresses specific features in the Altersteilzeit (ATZ) arrangements. The ATZ arrangement is an early retirement program in Germany designed to create an incentive for employees, within a certain age group, to transition from full or part-time employment into retirement before their legal retirement age. The consensus opinion was that the bonus feature and the additional contributions into the German government pension scheme under a Type II ATZ arrangement should be accounted for as a postemployment benefit under FASB No. 112. An entity should recognize the additional compensation over the period from the point at which the employee signs the ATZ contract until the end of the active service period.

**10. True. *Correct.*** The EITF states that such improvement should be amortized over the shorter of the useful life or the lease term, including reacquired lease periods and renewals. The EITF was issued because, in practice, questions have arisen as to whether the amortization period for leasehold improvements that are placed in service significantly after an not contemplated at or near the beginning of a lease can extend beyond the lease term that was determined at the lease inception.

**False. Incorrect.** The statement is correct. Moreover, leasehold improvements that are placed in service significantly after and not contemplated at or near the beginning of the lease term should be amortized over the shorter of the useful life of the assets or the term that includes reacquired lease periods and renewals that are deemed to be reasonably assured at the date the leasehold improvements are purchased.

**11. False. Correct.** The statement is false because it states an entity should not include the change when, in fact, the entity should include that change in the analysis. Previously, when an issuer modified previously issued convertible debt, there were differing views on whether to include the change in the fair value of an embedded conversion option in the analysis to determine whether a substantial modification had occurred under EITF Issue No. 96-19, *Debtor's Accounting for a Modification or Exchange of Debt Instruments.* This EITF clarifies the confusion. Further, because the determination of whether an extinguishment or modification has occurred focuses solely on a differential cash flow analysis, the EITF agreed to amend Issue 96-19 to include non-cash changes to the conversion terms under the consensus opinion.

**True. Incorrect.** The EITF specifically states that an entity should include the change in fair value in the analysis to determine whether a debt instrument has been extinguished. Moreover, the change in the fair value of an embedded conversion option should be calculated as the difference between the fair value of the embedded conversion option immediately before and after the modification and it should be included in the Issue 96-19 analysis because there is a direct correlation between the value of an embedded conversion option and the yields demanded on a convertible debt instrument.

**12. True. Correct.** The EITF was asked to opine as to whether the issuance of convertible debt with a beneficial conversion feature resulted in a basis difference for purposes of applying FASB No. 109, Accounting for Income Taxes. The EITF ruled that it did thus making the statement true.

**False. Incorrect.** The EITF did, in fact, conclude that the issuance of convertible debt with a beneficial conversion feature results in a basis difference under FASB No. 109.

**13. True. Correct.** A recent study indicates that companies are inconsistently accounting for the change in customer notes receivable as it relates to the statement of cash flows.   Many companies are including the change in notes receivable in the investing activities section of the statement of cash flows, instead of the operating activities section. In doing so, cash from operations may increase significantly.

**False. *Incorrect.*** See the example below.

### EXAMPLE

Assume the following:

| | |
|---|---:|
| Net sales | $10,000,000 |
| Operating expenses | 7,000,000 |
| Net income | $3,000,000 |

Of the $10,000,000 of sales, $6,000,000 is collected in cash and the remaining $4,000,000 remains in notes receivable.

**Scenario 1:** The $4,000,000 of change in notes receivable is presented in the operating activities section. The statement of cash flows is presented as follows:

| | |
|---|---:|
| Cash from operating activities | |
|    Net income | $3,000,000 |
|    Adjustments: | |
|       Change in notes receivable | (4,000,000) |
| Cash used in operating activities | $(1,000,000) |

**Scenario 2:** The $4,000,000 of change in notes receivable is presented in the investing activities section. The statement of cash flows is presented as follows:

| | |
|---|---:|
| Cash from operating activities | |
|    Net income | $3,000,000 |
|    Adjustments: | 0 |
|       Change in notes receivable | $3,000,000 |
| Cash used in operating activities | |
|    Change in notes receivable | (4,000,000) |

By presenting the change in notes receivable in the investing activities section, it appears that the company has generated $3,000,000 of operating cash flow and then invested it in investing activities.

**14. False. *Correct.*** Although FASB No. 95 addresses the collection of an installment sale, it does not specifically address the change in notes receivable. Instead, it does state that all cash collected from customers should be classified as operating cash flows, including notes receivable.

**True. *Incorrect.*** FASB No. 95, *Statement of Cash Flows*, is not clear as to whether customer notes receivable should be presented in the operating activities section, although FASB No. 95 deals with a similar situation related to installment sales by stating:

"A somewhat difficult classification issue arises for installment sales...for which...cash inflows....may occur several years after the date of transaction....The board agreed that all cash collected from customers should be classified as operating cash flows (paragraph 95 of FASB No. 95)."

**15. True. *Correct.*** The SEC requires the change in customer notes receivable to be classified in the operating activities section of the cash flow statement.

**False. *Incorrect.*** After The Georgia Institute of Technology published a report entitled Cash-Flow Reporting Practices for Customer-Related Receivables (the Study), the SEC sent a letter to the CFOs of the companies they believed may have presented the changes in customer-related notes receivable as investing cash flow. In the letter, the SEC noted that such a presentation was not in conformity with GAAP and called for the firms to change their reporting practices by reclassifying the changes in the operating activities section.

**16. True. *Correct.*** FASB No. 95, *Statement of Cash Flows*, requires that insurance proceeds received that are a direct result to investing activities, such as damage or destruction to equipment, should be recorded in the investing activities section of the statement of cash flows. The theory is that such proceeds are the same as a sale of assets.

**False. *Incorrect.*** More specifically, FASB No. 95 defines cash inflows from operating activities to include:

"All other cash receipts that do not stem from transactions defined as investing or financing activities, such as amounts received to settle lawsuits, proceeds of insurance settlements except for those that are directly related to investing or financing activities, such as from destruction of a building, and refunds from suppliers."

**17. False. *Correct.*** Some, but not all, insurance proceeds are included as part of operating activities, thereby making the statement false. In practice, insurance related to inventory, and business interruption insurance proceeds should be presented in the operating activities section of the Statement. But, other claims related to a combination of damage to equipment, inventory, as well as a portion of business interruption insurance, these proceeds should be split between operating and investing activities. Moreover, an inconsistency in cash flow reporting practices is the categorization of insurance proceeds related to property, plant and equipment. In practice, some companies report such proceeds as inflows in the operating activities section of the statement, which is incorrect and overstates cash flows from operating activities. FASB No. 95, *Statement of Cash Flows*, requires that insurance proceeds received that are a direct result to investing activities, such as damage or destruction to equipment, should be recorded in the investing activities section of the statement of cash flows. The theory is that such proceeds are the same as a sale of assets.

**True. Incorrect.** The FASB No. 95 definition states that insurance settlement proceeds are included in operating activities except for settlements related to the destruction of or damage to a building or equipment, which are included in investing activities. FASB No. 95, *Statement of Cash Flows*, requires that insurance proceeds received that are a direct result to investing activities, such as damage or destruction to equipment, should be recorded in the investing activities section of the statement of cash flows. The theory is that such proceeds are the same as a sale of assets. Thus, the statement is not true because not all insurance proceeds are included as part of operating activities.

**18. True. Correct.** The FASB statement does require recognition of an impairment loss thereby making the statement true. Moreover, FASB No. 144 applies to both personal and real property but does not apply to inventory.

**False. Incorrect.** The statement is correctly stated in that FASB No. 144 does, in fact, require a company to recognize an impairment loss. Specifically, FASB No. 144 states that an impairment loss exists when the carrying amount of real estate exceeds its fair value. Recently, there has been a softening in real estate values due to numerous factors including an overall building glut (supply exceeds demand) and a slight uptick in interest rates. The result is that for the first time since the issuance of FASB No. 144 in 2002, companies may start to have real estate that is impaired and need to be tested for that impairment. Rarely in the past decade has this issue been considered in most financial statement engagements.

**19. False. Correct.** Goodwill is not amortized but is tested for impairment at least annually. If it is impaired, goodwill is written down and an impairment loss is recorded.

**True. Incorrect.** Goodwill is not amortized but is tested for impairment at least annually. If it is impaired, goodwill is written down and an impairment loss is recorded. With respect to intangible assets other than goodwill, FASB No. 142 segregates such assets into two categories: intangibles with finite lives and intangibles with indefinite lives.

| Category | Accounting treatment |
|---|---|
| Intangible assets with finite lives | Amortized over their estimated useful lives |
| Intangible assets with indefinite lives | Not amortized until the lives become finite Are tested annually for impairment |

**20. True. Correct.** FASB No. 142 stipulates that an intangible asset that has an indefinite life is not amortized until the life is no longer indefinite.

If no legal, regulatory, contractual, competitive, economic, or other factors limit the useful life of an intangible asset, the useful life is considered indefinite. Note further that the term "indefinite" does not mean "infinite" or "indeterminate."

**False. Incorrect.** The statement is correctly stated as it relates to an indefinite lived intangible. An intangible asset is deemed to have an indefinite life if there is no legal, regulatory, contractual, competitive, economic, or other factors that limit the useful life of an intangible asset. That is, there is no limit placed on the end of the assets useful life to the reporting entity. Examples of intangible assets that might have indefinite lives include certain trademarks and tradenames, certain licenses such as liquor and broadcast licenses, taxi medallions, franchises, and airport routes

## MODULE 3 — CHAPTER 6

**1. True. Correct.** FASB No. 123 allowed companies to choose to measure and record compensation expense using either an external fair value model or an intrinsic method. If the intrinsic method was used, the company was required to provide the appropriate fair value information in the footnotes. Specifically, FASB No. 123 required the following: (1) The choice between two methods to account for stock options. Method 1 was to implement a fair value-based method for accounting for compensation for employee stock options. Options were valued at the grant date based on their fair value using an externally generated, option-pricing model such as Black-Scholes or binomial model. Compensation cost for the award of stock options to employees was recognized on a straight-line basis over the period(s) in which the related employee services were rendered by a charge to compensation cost and a corresponding credit to equity (APIC). Method 2 was to maintain the existing intrinsic value method used in APB No. 25. If the existing APB No. 25 intrinsic method was used, the entity had to disclose additional pro forma disclosures "as if" the entity had implemented the fair value based method: The pro forma information included pro forma net income, and earnings per share (if presented). Disclosures were also required, regardless of which method is used.

**False. Incorrect.** FASB No. 123 gave a choice between two methods to companies.

**2. True. Correct.** Because the FASB and IASB are trying to converge international accounting standards, the FASB was pressured to follow the IASB's action to change the accounting for stock options. The IASB had issued a new fair-value based standard in 2004. Other reasons for issuing the statement include: (1) the results of a FASB survey showed that 76 percent of investors responding being in favor of using an external fair value method to measure stock options even though 88 percent of responding companies were opposed to such a change; and (2) with the demise of Enron and its resulting devastation to its employees, members of Congress and others wanted to protect employees by changing the accounting and transparency for stock options.

**False. Incorrect.** One of the reasons for issuing FASB No. 123R was to follow the IASB's action.

**3. True. Correct.** FASB No. 123R makes several changes to FASB No. 123, one of which is that it requires that the cost resulting from all share-based payment transactions be recognized in the financial statements using the grant-date fair value as the measurement of cost. Other changes made by the Statement include: (1) the requirement for all entities to apply a fair-value-based measurement method in accounting for share-based payment transactions with employees (except for equity instruments held by ESOPs) and those in which an entity acquires goods or services from nonemployees in share-based payment transactions; (2) the provision that fair value is measured based on an observable value, then using an option model (such as the Black-Scholes Model); and (3) provision of certain exceptions to the measurement method if it is not possible to reasonably estimate the fair value of an award at the grant date.

**False. Incorrect.** The Statement does require that cost be recognized using a grant-date fair value. Fair value is generally measured using an observable value following use of an option model.

**4. False. Correct.** FASB No. 123R does not permit use of the intrinsic method for nonpublic entities for equity awards. It does allow nonpublic entities to elect to use the intrinsic method for awards classified as liabilities. Moreover, the Statement eliminates use of the minimum value method for nonpublic entities that assumed zero volatility in valuing its stock options under FASB No. 123.

**True. Incorrect.** The Statement eliminates use of the intrinsic value method for valuing equity awards that was permitted under FASB No. 123. Now all companies must value stock options using an externally generated fair value method.

**5. False. Correct.** The Statement does not apply to only certain types of share-based payment transactions. Such share-based transactions are in amounts based, at least in part, on the price of the entity's shares or other equity instruments or that require or may require settlement by issuing the entity's equity shares or other equity instruments. Moreover, the Statement applies to transactions with employees and nonemployees. The Statement does not apply to share-based payment transactions involving an employee share ownership plan (ESOP) that is subject to SOP 93-6, Employers' Accounting for Employee Stock Ownership Plans

**True. Incorrect.** FASB No. 123R applies to all types of share-based transactions in which an entity acquires goods or services by issuing (or offering to issue) its shares, share options, or other equity instruments or by incurring liabilities to an employee or other supplier.

**6. True. Correct.** The Statement requires that an entity must recognize the goods acquired or services received in a share-based payment transaction when it obtains the goods or as the services are received.

**False. Incorrect.** FASB No. 123R requires that the value of goods acquired or services received be recognized. Moreover, the entity shall recognize either a corresponding increase in equity or a liability, depending on whether the instruments granted satisfy the equity or liability classification criteria.

**7. True. Correct.** FASB No. 123R does apply to transactions with both employees and nonemployees. For transactions with nonemployees, the transaction should be measured and recorded at the fair value of the equity instruments issued or goods or services received, wherever is more determinable. With respect to transactions with employees (e.g., stock options), the transaction should be measured based on the fair value of the equity instruments issued.

**False. Incorrect.** The Statement does apply to transactions with both employees and nonemployees. Moreover, as the goods or services are disposed of or consumed, the entity shall recognize the corresponding cost. As it relates to transactions with employees, compensation cost related to a share-based award should be recognized over the period during which the employee is required to provide service in exchange for the award (the requisite service period, which is usually the vesting period).

**8. True. Correct.** The objective of accounting is to recognize in the financial statements the employee services received in exchange for equity instruments issued or liabilities incurred and the related cost to the entity as those services are consumed. An entity shall account for the compensation cost from share-based payment transactions with employees using a fair-value-based method. Further, the cost of services received from employees in exchange for awards of share-based compensation shall be measured based on the grant-date fair value of the equity instruments issued or at the fair value of the liabilities incurred. The portion of the fair value of an instrument attributed to employee service is net of any amount that an employee pays, or becomes obligated to pay, for that instrument when it is granted.

**False.** *Incorrect.* The objective of accounting for transactions under share-based payment arrangements with employees is to recognize in the financial statements the employee services received in exchange for equity instruments issued or liabilities incurred and the related cost to the entity as those services are consumed.

**9. False.** *Correct.* The exercise date is the date on which an employee may exercise his or her stock options; it is not the grant date. Moreover, awards that are subject to shareholder approval are not deemed to be granted until shareholder approval is obtained unless approval is essentially a formality, as in the case where management and the members of the board control enough votes to approve the arrangement. Finally, an individual must be an employee at the grant date. Thus, if an individual has been granted stock options but has not yet begun employment, the grant date is the date on which the individual begins employment.

**True.** *Incorrect.* The exercise date, not the grant date, is the date on which an employee may exercise his or her stock options. The grant date is the date at which an employer and an employee reach a mutual understanding of the key terms and conditions of a share-based payment award. The employer becomes contingently obligated on the grant date to issue equity instruments or transfer assets to an employee who renders the requisite service. On the grant date, an employee begins to benefit from, or to be adversely affected by, subsequent changes in the price of the employer's equity shares.

**10. True.** *Correct.* The statement is correctly stated in that the transaction is measured at the fair value on the grant date. The fair value of the goods and services received should be used if it is more reliably measurable than the fair value of the equity instruments issued.

**False.** *Incorrect.* The grant-date fair value is the date on which equity instrument transactions are measured. The estimate of fair value at the grant date of the equity instruments is based on the share price and other pertinent factors (such as expected volatility), and is not remeasured in subsequent periods under the fair value method. The restrictions and conditions inherent in equity instruments awarded to employees are treated differently depending on whether they continue in effect after the requisite service period. A restriction that continues in effect after an entity has issued instruments to employees, such as the inability to transfer vested equity share options to third parties or the liability to sell vested shares for a period of time, is considered in estimating the fair value of the instruments at the grant date.

**11. False. *Correct.*** The effect of both nontransferability and nonhedgeability are reflected in estimating fair value. Moreover, no compensation cost is recognized for instruments that employees forfeit because a service condition or a performance condition is not satisfied. Further, the effect of a market condition is reflected in the grant-date fair value of an award. Compensation cost is recognized for an award with a market condition provided the requisite service is rendered, regardless of when—if ever—the market condition is satisfied.

**True. *Incorrect.*** The effect of nontransferability and nonhedgeability are taken into account in estimating the fair value of the equity instrument. A restriction that stems from the forfeitability of instruments to which employees have not yet earned the right (such as the inability either to exercise a nonvested equity share option or to sell nonvested shares), is not reflected in the estimated fair value of the related instruments at the grant date. Those restrictions are taken into account by recognizing compensation cost only for awards for which employees render the requisite service.

**12. True. *Correct.*** Several factors are included in the measurement of fair value, whereas others are excluded. One that is included is restrictions that continue in effect after the entity has issued instruments to employees such as the inability to transfer vested equity share options to third parties and the inability to sell vested shares for a period of time.

**False. *Incorrect.*** Restrictions that continue after the entity has issued instruments to employees are included in the measurement of fair value. Factors excluded from the measurement of fair value include: (1) restrictions that stem from the forfeitability of instruments to which employees have not yet earned the right, such as the inability either to exercise a nonvested equity share option, and inability to sell nonvested shares; and (2) reload features, and contingent features that require an employee to transfer equity shares earned, or realized gains from the sale of equity instruments earned, to the issuing entity for consideration that is less than fair value on the date of transfer (including no consideration), such as a clawback feature.

**13. False. *Correct.*** Fair value is the measurement, not book value. Moreover, a restricted share awarded to an employee (e.g., a share that will be restricted after the employee has a vested right to it) shall be measured at its fair value, which is the same amount for which a similarly restricted share would be issued to third parties.

**True. *Incorrect.*** Under the rules for costs of FASB No. 123R, a nonvested equity share or nonvested equity share unit awarded to an employee is to be measured at its fair value as if it were vested and issued on the grant date.

**14. True.** *Correct.* FASB No. 123R states that awards classified as liabilities are measured at the fair value of the liability issued, as of the grant date. The treatment for liabilities is essentially the same as equity instruments, which are also measured at fair value.

**False.** *Incorrect.* Liabilities are measured at fair value. Unlike equity instruments, liabilities are subsequently remeasured to their fair values at the end of each reporting period until the liability is settled.

**15. True.** *Correct.* Observable market price is the means of measuring equity share options. A "similar instrument" is one whose fair value differs from its intrinsic value; for example, an instrument that has time value such as a SAR that requires net settlement in equity shares has time value, whereas an equity share does not.

**False.** *Incorrect.* Observable market price is the first means of determining fair value. Awards to employees of a public entity of shares of its common stock, subject only to a service or performance condition for vesting, should be measured based on the market price of otherwise identical (identical except for the vesting condition) common stock at the grant date. Absent an observable market price, the fair value of an equity share option or similar instrument shall be estimated using a valuation technique such as an option-pricing model. Further, an estimate of the amount at which similar instruments would be exchanged should factor in expectations of the probability that the service would be rendered and the instruments would vest (e.g., the performance or service conditions would be satisfied).

**16. True.** *Correct.* The Statement does not specify a preference for a specific valuation technique model provided the entity develops reasonable and supportable estimates for each assumption used in the model including the employee share option's expected term, taking into account the contractual term and the effects of employees' expected exercise and post-vesting employment termination behavior.

**False.** *Incorrect.* Although the exposure draft considered providing a preference for a specific valuation method, the final statement did not provide a preference. Moreover, an entity should change the valuation technique if it concludes that a different technique is likely to result in a better estimate of fair value. Types of option pricing models identified by the Statement include the lattice model, including types such as a binomial model, and the closed-form model: such as Black-Scholes-Merton model.

**17. False.** *Correct.* Typically, an ESPP is a noncompensatory plan. Other criteria that are required include: (1) substantially all employees that meet limited employment qualifications may participate on an equitable basis; and (2) the plan incorporates no option features, other than the employees are permitted a short period of time, not to exceed 31 days, after the purchase price has been fixed, to enroll in the plan, and the purchase price is based solely on the market price of the shares at the date of purchase, and employees are permitted to cancel participation before the purchase date and obtain a refund of amounts previously paid, such as those paid by payroll withholdings. The Statement indicates that if an entity justifies a purchase discount in excess of 5 percent, it is required to reassess that discount at least annually, and no later than the first share purchase offer during the fiscal year. If upon reassessment the discount is not considered justifiable, subsequent grants using the discount would be compensatory.

**True. *Incorrect.*** An ESPP that satisfies certain criteria does not recognize compensation cost and, thus, is a noncompensatory plan subject to the Statement. One criterion is that the plan satisfy at least one of the following: (1) The terms of the plan are no more favorable than those available to all holders of the same class of shares; and (2) any purchase discount from the market price does not exceed the per-share amount of share issuance costs that would have been incurred to raise a significant amount of capital by a public offering.

**18. True. *Correct.*** Compensation cost for an award of share-based employee compensation classified as equity shall be recognized over the requisition service period, with a corresponding credit to equity (such as additional paid-in capital). The requisite service period is the period during which an employee is required to provide service in exchange for an award, which is typically the vesting period, and is estimated based on an analysis of the terms of the share-based payment award.

**False. *Incorrect.*** Compensation cost is recognized over the requisite service period. The requisite service period may be explicit, implicit, or derived. An explicit service period is one that is stated based on the terms of the share-based payment award such as a stock option award states that shares vest after three-years of service. An implicit service period is one that may be inferred from an analysis of an award's terms, including other explicit service or performance conditions such as a stock option award vests only upon the completion of a new product design. The design is expected to be completed 18 months from the grant date. And, finally, a derived service period is one based on a market condition that is inferred from application of certain valuation techniques used to estimate fair value.

**19. True. *Correct.*** A modification of the terms or conditions of an equity award shall be treated as an exchange of the original award for a new award. The transaction is treated as if the entity repurchased the original instrument by issuing a new instrument of equal or greater value, incurring additional compensation cost for any incremental value.

**False. *Incorrect.*** A modification is treated as an exchange of the original award. Moreover, the effects of a modification are measured as follows: (1) Incremental compensation cost shall be measured as the excess of the fair value of the modified award over the fair value of the original award immediately before its terms are modified, measured based on the share price and other pertinent factors at that date; (2) Total recognized compensation cost for an equity award shall at least equal the fair value of the award at the grant date unless at the date of the modification the performance or service conditions of the original award are not expected to be satisfied. The total compensation cost measured at the date of a modification is to be based on the portion of the grant-date fair value of the original award for which the requisite service is expected to be rendered, or has already been rendered, at that date, plus the incremental cost resulting from the modification. Compensation cost shall be subsequently adjusted.

**20. False. *Correct.*** The ultimate amount of cost is not the same. The cumulative amount of compensation cost recognized for instruments classified as equity or liabilities that ordinarily would result in a future tax deduction under existing tax law shall be treated as a deductible temporary difference. Further, the deductible temporary difference shall be based on the compensation cost recognized for financial reporting purposes, with the change in the temporary difference recognized in the income statement.
**True. *Incorrect.*** Typically, the amount of compensation cost differs for tax and financial purposes. The amount of cost for financial statement purposes is based on fair value at the grant date. The amount of expense deductible for tax purposes is the difference between the fair value and exercise price at the exercise date. Thus, the two are not measured at the same date in time and are not ultimately the same.

TOP ACCOUNTING ISSUES FOR 2007 CPE COURSE

# Index

TOP ACCOUNTING ISSUES FOR 2007 CPE COURSE

# CPE Quizzer Instructions

The CPE Quizzer is divided into 3 Modules. There is a processing fee for each Quizzer Module submitted for grading. Successful completion of Module 1 is recommended for **6 CPE Credits.**\* Successful completion of Module 2 is recommended for **6 CPE Credits.**\* Successful completion of Module 3 is recommended for **7 CPE Credits.**\*You can complete and submit one Module at a time or all Modules at once for a total of **19 CPE Credits.**\*

To obtain CPE credit, return your completed Answer Sheet for each Quizzer Module to **CCH Continuing Education Department, 4025 W. Peterson Ave., Chicago, IL 60646**, or fax it to (773) 866-3084. Each Quizzer Answer Sheet will be graded and a CPE Certificate of Completion awarded for achieving a grade of 70 percent or greater. The Quizzer Answer Sheets are located after the Quizzer questions for this Course.

**Express Grading:** Processing time for your Answer Sheet is generally 8-12 business days. If you are trying to meet a reporting deadline, our Express Grading Service is available for an additional $19 per Module. To use this service, please check the "Express Grading" box on your Answer Sheet and provide your CCH account or credit card number **and your fax number.** CCH will fax your results and a Certificate of Completion (upon achieving a passing grade) to you by 5:00 p.m. the business day following our receipt of your Answer Sheet. **If you mail your Answer Sheet for Express Grading, please write "ATTN: CPE OVERNIGHT" on the envelope.** NOTE: CCH will not Federal Express Quizzer results under any circumstances.

---

**NEW ONLINE GRADING** gives you immediate 24/7 grading with instant results and no Express Grading Fee.

The **CCH Testing Center** website gives you and others in your firm easy, free access to CCH print Courses and allows you to complete your CPE Quizzers online for immediate results. Plus, the **My Courses** feature provides convenient storage for your CPE Course Certificates and completed Quizzers.

Go to **www.cchtestingcenter.com** to complete your Quizzer online.

---

\* Recommended CPE credit is based on a 50-minute hour. Participants earning credits for states that require self-study to be based on a 100-minute hour will receive ½ the CPE credits for successful completion of this course. Because CPE requirements vary from state to state and among different licensing agencies, please contact your CPE governing body for information on your CPE requirements and the applicability of a particular course for your requirements.

**Date of Completion:** The date of completion on your Certificate will be the date that you put on your Answer Sheet. However, you must submit your Answer Sheet to CCH for grading within two weeks of completing it.

**Expiration Date:** December 31, 2007

**Evaluation:** To help us provide you with the best possible products, please take a moment to fill out the Course Evaluation located at the back of this Course and return it with your Quizzer Answer Sheets.

CCH is registered with the National Association of State Boards of Accountancy (NASBA) as a sponsor of continuing professional education on the National Registry of CPE Sponsors. State boards of accountancy have final authority on the acceptance of individual courses for CPE credit. Complaints regarding registered sponsors may be addressed to the National Registry of CPE Sponsors, 150 Fourth Avenue North, Suite 700, Nashville, TN 37219-2417. Web site: www.nasba.org.

CCH is registered with the National Association of State Boards of Accountancy (NASBA) as a Quality Assurance Service (QAS) sponsor of continuing professional education. State boards of accountancy have final authority on the acceptance of individual courses for CPE credit. Complaints regarding registered sponsors may be addressed to NASBA, 150 Fourth Avenue North, Suite 700, Nashville, TN 37219-2417. Web site: www.nasba.org.

| | |
|---|---|
| **Recommended CPE:** | 6 hours for Module 1 |
| | 6 hours for Module 2 |
| | 7 hours for Module 3 |
| | 19 hours for all Modules |
| **Processing Fee:** | $60.00 for Module 1 |
| | $60.00 for Module 2 |
| | $70.00 for Module 3 |
| | $190.00 for all Modules |

One **complimentary copy** of this Course is provided with copies of selected CCH Accounting titles. Additional copies of this Course may be ordered for $27.50 each by calling 1-800-248-3248 (ask for product 0-0996-200).

# Quizzer Questions: Module 1

> Answer the True/False questions by marking a "T" or "F" on the Quizzer Answer Sheet. Answer Multiple Choice questions by indicating the appropriate letter on the Answer Sheet.

1.  Which of the following statements is **not** true?

    a. A leasc is an agreement that confers the right to use property, usually for a specified period.
    b. The term "lease" as used in promulgated GAAP includes agreements that concern the right to explore for or exploit natural resources such as oil and gas.
    c. Leases usually involve two parties.
    d. Leases have become an important alternative to the purchase of property through which lessees acquire the resources necessary to operate.

2.  The FAS that defines a lease and the terms "capital lease" and "operating lease" is _____.

    a. FAS-22
    b. FAS-27
    c. FAS-13
    d. FAS-14

3.  One of the possible criteria for a capital lease is that the lease term be _____ equal to the estimated useful life of the property.

    a. 75%
    b. 50%
    c. 95%
    d. 51%

4.  Which of the following statements is **false?**

    a. For a manufacturer or dealer, fair value is usually the normal selling price less trade or volume discounts.
    b. For others besides manufacturers or dealers, fair value is usually cost less trade or volume discounts.
    c. Fair value is the price for which leased property could be sold between unrelated parties in an arm's-length transaction.
    d. Fair value can never be less than cost.

5. The rate of interest that the lessee would have had to pay at the inception of the lease to borrow the funds, on similar terms, to purchase the leased property is called _____.

   a. the lessee's indexed borrowing rate
   b. the lessee's hypothetical borrowing rate
   c. the lessee's incremental borrowing rate
   d. the lessee's adjusted borrowing rate

6. In lease sale or assignment to third parties, agreements to reacquire the property or lease, or arrangements to substitute another existing lease agreement represent _____.

   a. substantial risk on the part of the seller
   b. substantial risk on the part of the buyer
   c. nonsubstantial risk on the part of the seller
   d. nonsubstantial risk on the part of the buyer

7. Which of the following is *false?*

   a. The lessor's income statement normally includes the expenses of the leased property unless it is a net lease.
   b. Leases that do not qualify as capital leases in accordance with the provisions of FAS-13 are classified as operating leases.
   c. The cost of property leased to the lessee is included in the lessor's balance sheet as property, plant and equipment.
   d. Material initial direct costs related to negotiation and consummation of an operating lease may not be deferred.

8. Under FAS-98, the seller-lessee may sublease a portion of the leased property, equal to _____ or less of the reasonable rental value for the entire leased property, and the lease will still qualify as a normal leaseback.

   a. 5%
   b. 10%
   c. 12.5%
   d. 25%

9. In a _____, a lessor leases equipment to a lessee and obtains nonrecourse financing from a financial institution using the leased receivable and the asset as collateral.

   a. wrap lease transaction
   b. package lease transaction
   c. related party lease
   d. none of the above

**10.** Which of the following is false?

**a.** A lease may be reclassified if as a result of a business combination, it is revised or modified to the extent that under FAS-13 it is considered a new agreement.

**b.** The acquiring company in a business combination accounts for a leveraged lease by assigning a fair value to the net investment in a leveraged lease based on the remaining future cash flows with appropriate recognition for any projected tax effects.

**c.** In a business combination in which an acquired lease has not been conformed to FAS-13, the acquirer classifies the lease to conform retroactively to FAS-13.

**d.** A business combination automatically affects the classification of a lease.

**11.** In a sublease, if the original lease was a capital lease for property other than real estate, if the original lessee remains secondarily liable, this guarantee obligation is recognized under the provisions of _____.

**a.** FAS-22
**b.** FAS-140
**c.** FAS-29
**d.** FAS-28

**12.** In a sublease, if the original lease was a capital lease for real estate, which of the following is true of the accounting for the termination of the lease agreement?

**a.** Any loss can be recognized at a later date.
**b.** The installment method of revenue recognition cannot be used.
**c.** The lease asset and liability should be removed from the books if the FAS-66 criteria for sale recognition are met.
**d.** The reduced-profit method of revenue recognition cannot be used.

**13.** Sale-leaseback transactions involving real estate are discussed under _____.

**a.** FAS-145
**b.** FAS-27
**c.** FAS-22
**d.** FAS-98

**14.** Which of the following statements is *false?*

   **a.** All non-real estate sale-leasebacks are covered by FAS-98.
   **b.** A sale-leaseback is a transaction in which an owner sells property and subsequently leases back part or all of it.
   **c.** The owner who sells the property and then leases it back in a sale-leaseback arrangement is called the seller-lessee.
   **d.** All sale-leaseback transactions involving real estate are addressed by FAS-98.

**15.** Which of the following is true?

   **a.** FAS-28 defines "reasonable rental" but not "fair value."
   **b.** FAS-13 does not define "fair value" or "fair rental."
   **c.** FAS-28 does not define "reasonable rental or "fair value."
   **d.** FAS-28 defines "fair value" but not "reasonable rental."

**16.** What is the earliest date that can be selected for the company's acquisition date?

   **a.** The date the transaction is initiated
   **b.** The date of the first payment
   **c.** The end of the accounting period
   **d.** The date of the final payment, when assets and liabilities are transferred from the acquired company

**17.** What FASB pronouncement resulted in elimination of the pooling method of accounting for business combinations?

   **a.** APB Opinion No. 16
   **b.** SFAS No. 141
   **c.** ARB No. 51
   **d.** SFAS No. 94

**18.** What is the fair market value of the consideration that is first used when the acquiring company exchanges 10,000 shares of its $10 par, $90 market value stock for assets with a fair value of $1,000,000 and liabilities of $200,000?

   **a.** $800,000
   **b.** $900,000
   **c.** $1,200,000
   **d.** Cannot be determined

**19.** Which is not the correct amount at which to value each of the following assets?

   **a.** Receivables at present value less collection costs
   **b.** Long-term investments at realizable value
   **c.** Property, plant, and equipment at book value
   **d.** Intangibles at fair market value

**20.** Over what period is goodwill amortized?

   **a.** 40 years
   **b.** Lesser of 40 years or estimated useful life
   **c.** Goodwill is never reduced
   **d.** Goodwill is not amortized but rather reduced when impaired

**21.** Under what minimum circumstances does the acquiring company control the acquired company?

   **a.** 50% or more
   **b.** 80%
   **c.** More than 80%

**22.** Find goodwill for the acquiring company given a purchase price of $1,300,000 in exchange for current assets $200,000, plant and equipment $800,000, intangibles of $300,000, and liabilities of $150,000.

   **a.** $150,000
   **b.** $0
   **c.** $450,000

**23.** Negative goodwill is allocated to which of the following assets?

   **a.** Current assets
   **b.** Deferred taxes
   **c.** Financial assets
   **d.** Patent

**24.** Two calendar-year entities, Sigma and Delta, enter into an arrangement on April 1, 20X1 for Sigma to purchase the net assets of Delta on March 31, 20X2. Which of the following is not an acceptable date to utilize for the acquisition date?

   **a.** December 31, 20X1
   **b.** April 1, 20X1
   **c.** March 31, 20X2

**25.** Assume a 40-percent corporate tax rate and the book basis of the assets exceeds the tax basis by $500,000. If the deferred tax item is included as a liability in the acquisition, what is the amount of goodwill reported when the fair value of other net assets is $800,000 and the purchase price is $1 million?

**a.** $200,000
**b.** $280,000
**c.** $300,000
**d.** $400,000

**26.** What is an example of an exception of the excess of purchase price over fair value constituting goodwill?

**a.** In banking, when loans and deposits are involved
**b.** When the tax basis differs from the book value
**c.** When the fair value differs from the tax basis

**27.** If the acquiring company pays $6 per share for 100,000 shares of acquired company voting stock in exchange for assets with a fair value of $500,000 and liabilities of $100,000, what is the amount of goodwill recorded by the acquiring company?

**a.** $0
**b.** $100,000
**c.** $200,000
**d.** $500,000

**28.** Assume that negative goodwill amounts to $200,000 and the purchase price is $550,000. The total amount allocated to PPE and Identifiable Intangibles is 600,000 when presented with the following partial balance sheet at fair value.

| Current Assets | $200,000 |
|---|---|
| PPE | $500,000 |
| Intangibles | $300,000 |
| Liabilities | $250,000 |
| Net Assets | $750,000 |

Allocate the remaining purchase price to PPE and intangibles.

**a.** PPE $375,000 and intangibles $125,000
**b.** PPE $375,000 and intangibles $225,000
**c.** PPE $500,000 and intangibles $300,000
**d.** PPE $500,000 and intangibles $250,000

**29.** Which of the following does not qualify as a business combination and does **not** require use of accounting methods under SFAS No. 141?

   **a.** Acquisition of not-for-profit entity by for-profit company
   **b.** Acquisition of minority (noncontrolling) interest of a subsidiary
   **c.** Transfer of equity interest or net assets between entities under common control
   **d.** Formation of a joint venture

**30.** How is comparability across companies enhanced by the provisions in SFAS No. 141?

   **a.** Disclosure is substantially increased
   **b.** The pooling method requires adequate disclosure
   **c.** Only the purchase method is used to account for combinations
   **d.** All acquisitions of minority interests now require full disclosure

**31.** Which one of the following statements is correct?

   **a.** Book basis of the assets < the tax basis, a deferred tax liability is reported.
   **b.** Tax basis of the assets > the book basis, a deferred tax asset is reported.
   **c.** There is always a difference between book basis and tax basis in a combination.
   **d.** Deferred taxes do not include differences attributable to goodwill & negative goodwill.

**32.** A business combination occurs on June 15, 2001. Is it acceptable to use the pooling-of-interests accounting method?

   **a.** Yes
   **b.** No
   **c.** Yes if the combining business meet certain criteria
   **d.** Pooling-of-interests is not an acceptable method for reporting business combinations.

**33.** Which of the following does **not** qualify for SFAS No. 141 treatment.

   **a.** Jones Inc. acquires Smith Company with 500 shares of its preferred stock.
   **b.** Red Cross merges with the Salvation Army and is called the Red Army.
   **c.** Ruger Inc. trades 100% of their stock for 80% of Winchester Inc.
   **d.** Hale Inc. acquired 10% interest in Bingham Company for cash.

**34.** Mr. Burns and Mr. Adams each put up $1,000,000 in cash and assets to form a joint venture. They account for their business combination accordingly to SFAS No. 141. Which of the following statements is true?

   **a.** This is a joint venture so they need to use the pooling-of-assets method.
   **b.** This is a joint venture and not a business combination so they don't use SFAS No.141.
   **c.** This will be considered a partnership and no special reporting treatment is required.
   **d.** This is a joint venture and not a business combination but they are still required to meet SFAS No. 141 requirements.

**35.** When the fair value of the acquired assets exceeds the acquisition cost this is an example of:

   **a.** Goodwill
   **b.** Negative goodwill

# Quizzer Questions: Module 2

**36.** Intangible assets with indefinite lives must be tested for impairment under the provisions of:

   **a.** APB Opinion No. 17
   **b.** SFAS No. 2
   **c.** SFAS No. 69
   **d.** SFAS No. 142

**37.** If a company purchases intangible assets in a basket purchase, the total cost should be allocated to the different assets based on their relative:

   **a.** Book values on the books of the seller
   **b.** Fair market values
   **c.** Asking prices
   **d.** Original cost on the books of the seller

**38.** Intangible assets generally:

   **a.** Are classified as current assets
   **b.** Confer legal rights or contractual obligations
   **c.** Have physical substance
   **d.** Include accounts receivable

**39.** At disposition, the difference between the selling price of an intangible asset and its book value represents:

   **a.** Accumulated amortization
   **b.** Impairment loss
   **c.** Gain or loss on disposal
   **d.** Fair value

**40.** When a company reports an impairment loss in its financial statements, which of the following does the company not have to disclose?

   **a.** The description of the asset
   **b.** The situation causing impairment
   **c.** Business segment affected by the loss
   **d.** Name of the person or company from whom the company acquired the asset

**41.** If a company determines that the carrying value of an intangible asset is not totally recoverable, then the company must:

    **a.** Write off the carrying value of the intangible asset as a loss from continuing operations

    **b.** Write off the carrying value of the intangible asset as an extraordinary loss

    **c.** Test the asset for possible impairment

    **d.** Double the annual amortization expense of the asset

**42.** An impairment loss is usually reported on the income statement as a(n):

    **a.** Extraordinary loss

    **b.** Loss from continuing operations

    **c.** Loss from discontinued operations

    **d.** Cumulative change in accounting principle

**43.** Which of the following activities is considered a research and development activity?

    **a.** A product or process design modification

    **b.** Routine activities to improve an existing product

    **c.** Activities during production such as routine testing and quality control

    **d.** Legal activities related to a patent application

**44.** Which of the following activities is considered a research and development activity?

    **a.** Changes in design of existing products that are considered periodic or seasonal

    **b.** Design of items such as tools and dies that are routine in nature

    **c.** Discovery of new information through laboratory research

    **d.** Legal activities related to a patent application

**45.** In general, research and development costs must be:

    **a.** Capitalized and amortized over the useful life of successful products

    **b.** Capitalized and amortized over five years

    **c.** Capitalized and analyzed for impairment

    **d.** Expensed as incurred

**46.** A company advances money to another company as a part of a venture arrangement for research and development. The other company does not have to repay any of the money unless the project is successful. At the time the company advances the money to the other company, the company advancing the money should charge the amount to:

**a.** Accounts Receivable
**b.** The asset Advance Under Research and Development Arrangement
**c.** Research and Development Expense
**d.** Goodwill

**47.** A company receives money from another company as a part of a venture arrangement for research and development. The company does not have to repay the money unless the project is successful. As the company spends the money it received from the other company on research and development activities, it charges the expenditures to:

**a.** Accounts Payable
**b.** The liability Advance Under Research and Development Arrangement
**c.** The asset Advance Under Research and Development Arrangement
**d.** Research and Development Expense

**48.** Indirect costs that are clearly related to research and development activities should be:

**a.** Expensed as incurred
**b.** Charged to the Manufacturing Overhead account
**c.** Capitalized and analyzed for impairment
**d.** Capitalized and amortized over their useful life

**49.** The cost of duplicating software is a(n):

**a.** Research and development cost
**b.** Production cost
**c.** Inventory cost
**d.** Other software cost

**50.** The cost of software maintenance is a(n):

**a.** Research and development cost
**b.** Production cost
**c.** Inventory cost
**d.** Other software cost

**51.** The cost of achieving technological feasibility is a(n):

   **a.** Research and development cost
   **b.** Production cost
   **c.** Inventory cost
   **d.** Other software cost

**52.** The cost of testing after achieving technological feasibility is a(n):

   **a.** Research and development cost
   **b.** Production cost
   **c.** Inventory cost
   **d.** Other software cost

**53.** Software research and development costs should be:

   **a.** Expensed as incurred
   **b.** Charged to the Manufacturing Overhead account
   **c.** Capitalized and amortized over the useful life of the software
   **d.** Capitalized as inventory costs and charged to Cost of Goods Sold when the company sells the software

**54.** Once a company achieves technological feasibility for a software product, its software production costs are:

   **a.** Expensed as incurred
   **b.** Capitalized and amortized over the software's useful life.
   **c.** Capitalized and amortized over 40 years
   **d.** Capitalized and charged to Cost of Goods Sold on a sale of the software

**55.** Which accounting standard governs the costs of software developed internally?

   **a.** APB Opinion No. 17
   **b.** SFAS No. 2
   **c.** SFAS No. 86
   **d.** SFAS No. 142

**56.** A company must recognize a loss if its unamortized production costs are greater than the software product's:

   **a.** Fair market value
   **b.** Implied fair market value
   **c.** Expected revenue
   **d.** Net realizable value

**57.** The inventory costs related to internally developed computer software are classified on the balance sheet as:

    **a.** Current assets
    **b.** Long-term assets
    **c.** Intangible assets
    **d.** Other assets

**58.** Internally generated goodwill is:

    **a.** Capitalized and amortized over its useful life
    **b.** Capitalized and amortized over 40 years
    **c.** Capitalized and analyzed for impairment
    **d.** Not recorded in the accounts

**59.** Goodwill purchased in the acquisition of another company is:

    **a.** Capitalized and amortized over its useful life
    **b.** Capitalized and amortized over 40 years
    **c.** Capitalized and analyzed for impairment
    **d.** Not recorded in the accounts

**60.** The costs to defend a patent held by the company should be charged to:

    **a.** Legal Fees Expense
    **b.** Research and Development Expense
    **c.** Goodwill
    **d.** Patent

**61.** Which of the following is *false?*

    **a.** Current assets are resources expected to be realized in cash, sold or consumed during the next year or longer operating cycle.
    **b.** Current assets are sometimes called circulating assets.
    **c.** Cash that is restricted as to its withdrawal or use for other than current operations is still classified as a current asset.
    **d.** Current assets are sometimes called working assets.

**62.** Short-term, highly liquid investments that are readily convertible to known amounts of cash and so near their maturities that they present insignificant interest rate risk are called _____.

    **a.** Cash
    **b.** secondary cash resources
    **c.** non-cash resources
    **d.** cash equivalents

**63.** _____ is the excess of current assets over current liabilities.

   **a.** Working capital
   **b.** Debt-to-equity ratio
   **c.** Acid-test ratio
   **d.** Quick ratio

**64.** Which of the following is *false?*

   **a.** The direct write-off method recognizes a bad debt expense only when a specific account is identified as uncollectible.
   **b.** The direct write-off method is normally considered GAAP.
   **c.** Under the direct write-off method, bad debt expense is not matched with sales.
   **d.** Accounts receivable are generally overstated in the direct write-off method.

**65.** _____ is the process whereby a company uses existing accounts receivable as collateral for a loan.

   **a.** Factoring
   **b.** Defactoring
   **c.** Kiting
   **d.** Pledging

**66.** The difference between the amount of cash received by the holder and the maturity value of the note is called the:

   **a.** Factor
   **b.** Discount
   **c.** Kiting
   **d.** Pledge

**67.** The account "discounted notes receivable" is a(n):

   **a.** Income account
   **b.** Expense account
   **c.** Equity account
   **d.** Contra account

**68.** The cash surrender value of a life insurance policy is classified either as a current or noncurrent asset in the policy owner's statement of financial position, depending upon:

**a.** The age of the insured
**b.** The materiality of its surrender value
**c.** The intentions of the policy holder
**d.** The term of the policy

**69.** A short-term obligation can be excluded from current liabilities if the company intends to refinance it on a long-term basis and the intent is supported by the ability to refinance that is demonstrated in one of the following ways as detailed under FAS-6, pars. 9–11. *True or False?*

**70.** FAS-150 requires an issuer to classify a financial instrument issued in the form of shares that is mandatorily redeemable in that it embodies an unconditional obligation that requires the issuer to redeem the shares by transferring the entity's assets at a specified or determinable date(s) or upon an event that is certain to occur as equity. *True or False?*

TOP ACCOUNTING ISSUES FOR 2007 CPE COURSE

# Quizzer Questions: Module 3

Answer the True/False questions by marking a "T" or "F" on the Quizzer Answer Sheet. Answer Multiple Choice questions by indicating the appropriate letter on the Answer Sheet.

**71.** In EITF Issue No. 04-5, the issue does not apply to a general partner that, under GAAP, carries its investment in the limited partnership at fair value with changes in the fair value reported in a statement of operations or financial performance. *True or False?*

**72.** EITF Issue No. 04-5 states that a general partner that controls a limited partnership should _____.

   **a.** Use the equity method
   **b.** Consolidate the partnership into its financial statements
   **c.** Record the investment at cost
   **d.** None of the above

**73.** In EITF Issue No. 04-5, the presumption that general partners control a partnership is overcome (the general partners *do not control* the limited partnership) if the limited partners have:

   **a.** Substantive kick-out rights
   **b.** Substantive protective rights
   **c.** Substantive liquidation rights
   **d.** None of the above

**74.** Under EITF Issue No. 04-5, rights that would allow the limited partners to block specific partnership actions would be considered _____.

   **a.** Protective rights
   **b.** Participating rights
   **c.** Conversion rights
   **d.** None of the above

**75.** Under EITF Issue No. 04-5, the assessment of limited partners' rights should be made when an investor(s) becomes a general partner(s) and should be reassessed if any one of the following occurs *except:*

   **a.** There is a change to the terms or in the exercisability of the right of the limited partners or general partners
   **b.** There is a change in the general partner's fees or compensation associated with the limited partnership
   **c.** The general partners increase or decrease their ownership of limited partnership interests
   **d.** There is an increase or decrease in the number of outstanding limited partnership interests

**76.** Under EITF Issue No. 04-8, all instruments that have embedded conversion features (such as contingently convertible debt, convertible preferred stock, and Instrument C in EITF Issue No. 90-19, with a market-based contingency) that are contingent on market conditions indexed to an issuer's share price should be:

   **a.** Excluded from diluted EPS except for any impairment value
   **b.** Excluded from diluted EPS until the market price contingency is met.
   **c.** Included in diluted earnings per share computations (if dilutive) regardless of whether the market conditions have been met
   **d.** Included in diluted earnings per share computations (if dilutive) only if the market conditions have been met.

**77.** Debt instruments, commonly referred to as "Co-Cos," that have embedded conversion features with a market-based contingency would include which of the following?

   **a.** Contingently convertible debt
   **b.** Common stock
   **c.** Treasury stock
   **d.** All of the above

**78.** Under EITF Issue No. 04-10, operating segments that do not meet the quantitative thresholds can be aggregated into a single operating segment only if which of the following conditions are met:

**a.** Aggregation is consistent with the objective and basic principles of FASB No. 131
**b.** The segments have similar economic characteristics
**c.** The segments share a majority of the aggregation criteria in sections (a) through (e) of paragraph 17 of FASB No. 131
**d.** All of the above

**79.** Under EITF Issue No. 04-12, unvested instruments issued as equity-based compensation (including options and nonvested stock) are *not* participating securities if the right to dividends is contingent on which of the following?

**a.** Employee service
**b.** Passage of time
**c.** Both (a.) and (b.) above
**d.** None of the above

**80.** Under EITF Issue No. 04-13, inventory purchase and sales transactions with the same counterparty that are entered into _____ _____ should be combined and treated as a single exchange under APB No. 29.

**a.** In contemplation of one another
**b.** In a joint cross sales agreement
**c.** As part of a business combination
**d.** None of the above

**81.** Under EITF Issue No. 04-13, factors indicating two transactions were entered into in contemplation of each other include all of the following *except:*

**a.** Inventory purchase and sales transactions with the same counterparty are entered into simultaneously
**b.** Inventory purchase and sales transactions were at off-market terms
**c.** There is relative certainty that reciprocal inventory transactions with the same counterparty will occur
**d.** Finished goods are transferred for finished goods

**82.** Under EITF Issue No. 04-13, nonmonetary exchanges whereby finished goods inventory is transferred in exchange for the receipt of raw materials or work-in-progress (WIP) inventory within the same line of business should be recognized at fair value if:

   **a.** Fair value is determinable within reasonable limits

   **b.** The transaction has commercial substance, as defined by FASB No. 153

   **c.** Both (a.) and (b.) above

   **d.** None of the above

**83.** Under EITF Issue No. 05-5, how should an entity account for the bonus feature and additional contributions into the German governmental pension scheme under a Type II ATZ arrangement?

   **a.** Report as a change in accounting estimate

   **b.** Report as a postemployment benefit under FASB No. 112

   **c.** Report as a change in accounting principle under FASB No. 154

   **d.** Do not report on the additional compensation until the end of the active service period

**84.** Under EITF Issue No. 05-6, the issue does not apply to preexisting leasehold improvements. *True or False?*

**85.** Under EITF Issue No. 05-6, leasehold improvements acquired in a business combination should be amortized over the longer of the useful life of the assets or the term that includes reacquired lease periods and renewals that are deemed to be reasonably assured at the date of acquisition. *True or False?*

**86.** Intangible assets with finite lives are _____.

   **a.** Amortized over their estimated useful lives

   **b.** Not amortized until the lives become indefinite

   **c.** Capitalized and tested for impairment on an annual basis

   **d.** None of the above

**87.** A life of an intangible asset is considered to be which of the following if it extends beyond the foreseeable horizon (e.g., there is no foreseeable limit on the period of time over which it is expected to contribute to cash flows of the reporting entity)?

   **a.** Immeasurable

   **b.** Indeterminable

   **c.** Infinite

   **d.** Indefinite

**88.** Examples of intangible assets that might have indefinite lives include all of the following *except*:

a. Certain trademarks and tradenames
b. Agreements not to compete
c. Taxi medallions
d. Franchises

**89.** In accordance with FASB No. 144, *Accounting for the Impairment or Disposal of Long-Lived Assets*, examples of events and changes in circumstances that might warrant a test of real estate for impairment include all of the following *except:*

a. Significant decline in the market price of the real estate or similar real estate
b. Continued decline in rental rates and vacancies
c. Known environmental contamination
d. Conversion of property to a condominium or cooperative

**90.** Company X purchases a broadcast license for $1,000,000 which is renewable after three years. At the time of renewal, X is in compliance with all laws and regulations that provide for renewal and such renewal can be made by paying a nominal licensing fee. Unless the Company violates FCC laws and regulations, the company believes the license is renewable indefinitely. How should the asset be accounted for on Company X's books?

a. The asset has a finite life and is amortized.
b. The asset has a indefinite life and is amortized.
c. The asset has a finite life and is not amortized. Instead, it should be tested annually for impairment.
d. The asset has an indefinite life and is not amortized. Instead, it should be tested annually for impairment.

**91.** FASB No. 123R requires that the cost resulting from all share-based payment transactions be recognized in the financial statements using the _____ as the measurement of cost.

a. Exercise date book value
b. Grant-date fair value
c. Adoption date fair value
d. Measurement date intrinsic value

**92.** FASB No. 123R provides that fair value be measured based on a (an):

    **a.** Observable value
    **b.** Intrinsic value
    **c.** Book value
    **d.** None of the above

**93.** FASB No. 123R eliminates FASB No. 123's use of the _____ _____for valuing equity awards that was permitted under FASB No. 123.

    **a.** Intrinsic value method
    **b.** Fair value method
    **c.** Current value method
    **d.** None of the above

**94.** FASB No. 123R applies to:

    **a.** Transactions with employees and nonemployees
    **b.** Transactions with employees only
    **c.** Transactions with nonemployees only
    **d.** None of the above

**95.** FASB No. 123R does not apply to share-based payment transactions involving an employee share ownership plan (ESOP) that is subject to SOP 93-6, Employers' Accounting for Employee Stock Ownership Plans. ***True or False?***

**96.** Under FASB No. 123R, with respect to transactions with employees (e.g., stock options), the transaction should be measured based on the

    _____.

    **a.** Fair value of the equity instruments issued
    **b.** Fair value of the goods or services received
    **c.** Intrinsic value of the goods or services received
    **d.** Intrinsic value of the equity instruments issued

**97.** The grant date is the date at which:

    **a.** Share options are exercisable
    **b.** An employer and an employee reach a mutual understanding of the key terms and conditions of a share-based payment award
    **c.** An employer receives a federal government grant for funding of a stock option program
    **d.** None of the above

**98.** For equity instruments awarded to employees, the estimate of fair value at the grant date of the equity instruments is based on the share price and other pertinent factors (such as expected volatility), and is _____in subsequent periods under the fair value method.

   **a.** Measured
   **b.** Not remeasured
   **c.** Partially measured
   **d.** None of the above

**99.** With respect to FASB No. 123R, the Statement:

   **a.** Does not specify a preference for a particular valuation technique or model in estimating the fair value of employee share options and similar instruments
   **b.** Prefers use of any one of three particular methods as the valuation techniques of choice
   **c.** Requires an entity to use the expected cash flows method as defined by Concept Statement No. 7
   **d.** None of the above

**100.** An example of a type of option pricing model identified by FASB No. 123R is:

   **a.** Lattice Model
   **b.** Observable model
   **c.** Net present value model
   **d.** Internal rate of return model

**101.** A closed-form model (Black-Scholes-Merton Model) assumes the option exercise occurs:

   **a.** At the end of the option's contractual term
   **b.** At the beginning of the option's contractual term
   **c.** Evenly over the option's contractual term
   **d.** None of the above

**102.** A lattice model (Binomial Model) more fully reflects the substantive characteristics of a particular employee share option or similar instrument. *True of False?*

**103.** At a minimum, an option model must include all of the following requirements except:

  **a.** Exercise price of the option
  **b.** Current price of the underlying share
  **c.** Risk-free interest rate for the expected term of the option
  **d.** Age of each employee likely to exercise stock options

**104.** FASB No. 123R provides two exceptions from the use of the fair value method to value stock options. One exception is use of the _____ _____ by a nonpublic entity.

  **a.** Intrinsic value method
  **b.** Current value method
  **c.** Fair value method
  **d.** None of the above

**105.** Under Exception 2 to use of the fair value method, an equity instrument for which it is not possible to reasonably estimate fair value at the grant date shall be accounted for based on its _____ remeasured at each reporting date through the date of exercise or other settlement, until it can reasonably estimate fair value.

  **a.** Intrinsic value
  **b.** Current value
  **c.** Remeasured value
  **d.** None of the above

**106.** Compensation cost for an award of share-based employee compensation classified as equity shall be recognized over the _____ with a corresponding credit to equity (such as additional paid-in capital).

  **a.** Requisite service period
  **b.** Actuarial life of each employee
  **c.** Average age of each applicable employee
  **d.** None of the above

**107.** The requisite service period may be all of the following except:

  **a.** Explicit
  **b.** Implicit
  **c.** Derived
  **d.** Implied

**108.** The service inception date is the beginning of the requisite service period and is usually the _____.

   **a.** Measurement date
   **b.** Grant date
   **c.** Exercise date
   **d.** None of the above

**109.** If vesting of an award is based on satisfying both a market condition and a performance or service condition, and it is probable that the performance or service condition will be satisfied, the estimate of the requisite service period is the _____ of the explicit, implicit, or derived service periods.

   **a.** Longest
   **b.** Shortest
   **c.** Average
   **d.** None of the above

**110.** The explicit service period is:

   **a.** One that is stated based on the terms of the share-based payment award
   **b.** One that may be inferred from an analysis of an award's terms, including other explicit service or performance conditions
   **c.** One based on a market condition that is inferred from application of certain valuation techniques used to estimate fair value
   **d.** None of the above

TOP ACCOUNTING ISSUES FOR 2007 CPE COURSE          (0794-2)

# Module 1: Answer Sheet

NAME _____

COMPANY NAME _____

STREET _____

CITY, STATE, & ZIP CODE _____

BUSINESS PHONE NUMBER _____

E-MAIL ADDRESS _____

DATE OF COMPLETION _____

CFP REGISTRANT ID (for Certified Financial Planners) _____

On the next page, please answer the Multiple Choice questions by indicating the appropriate letter next to the corresponding number. Please answer the True/False questions by marking "T" or "F" next to the corresponding number.

A $60.00 processing fee wil be charged for each user submitting Module 1 for grading.

Please remove both pages of the Answer Sheet from this book and return them with your completed Evaluation Form to CCH at the address below. You may also fax your Answer Sheet to CCH at 773-866-3084.

You may also go to **www.cchtestingcenter.com** to complete your Quizzer online.

**METHOD OF PAYMENT:**

☐ Check Enclosed     ☐ Visa     ☐ Master Card     ☐ AmEx

☐ Discover     ☐ CCH Account* _____

Card No. _____ Exp. Date _____

Signature _____

* Must provide CCH account number for this payment option

---

**EXPRESS GRADING:** Please fax my Course results to me by 5:00 p.m. the business day following your receipt of this Answer Sheet. By checking this box I authorize CCH to charge $19.00 for this service.

☐ Express Grading $19.00     Fax No. _____

a Wolters Kluwer business

**Mail or fax to:**
CCH Continuing Education Department
4025 W. Peterson Ave.
Chicago, IL 60646-6085
1-800-248-3248
Fax: 773-866-3084

PAGE 1 OF 2

TOP ACCOUNTING ISSUES FOR 2007 CPE COURSE     (0794-2)

# Module 1: Answer Sheet

Please answer the Multiple Choice questions by indicating the appropriate letter next to the corresponding number. Please answer the True/False questions by marking "T" or "F" next to the corresponding number.

| | | | |
|---|---|---|---|
| 1. ___ | 10. ___ | 19. ___ | 28. ___ |
| 2. ___ | 11. ___ | 20. ___ | 29. ___ |
| 3. ___ | 12. ___ | 21. ___ | 30. ___ |
| 4. ___ | 13. ___ | 22. ___ | 31. ___ |
| 5. ___ | 14. ___ | 23. ___ | 32. ___ |
| 6. ___ | 15. ___ | 24. ___ | 33. ___ |
| 7. ___ | 16. ___ | 25. ___ | 34. ___ |
| 8. ___ | 17. ___ | 26. ___ | 35. ___ |
| 9. ___ | 18. ___ | 27. ___ | |

**Please complete the Evaluation Form (located after the Module 3 Answer Sheet) and return it with this Quizzer Answer Sheet to CCH at the address on the previous page. Thank you.**

TOP ACCOUNTING ISSUES FOR 2007 CPE COURSE     (0795-2)

# Module 2: Answer Sheet

NAME _____

COMPANY NAME _____

STREET _____

CITY, STATE, & ZIP CODE _____

BUSINESS PHONE NUMBER _____

E-MAIL ADDRESS _____

DATE OF COMPLETION _____

CFP REGISTRANT ID (for Certified Financial Planners) _____

On the next page, please answer the Multiple Choice questions by indicating the appropriate letter next to the corresponding number. Please answer the True/False questions by marking "T" or "F" next to the corresponding number.

A $60.00 processing fee wil be charged for each user submitting Module 2 for grading.

Please remove both pages of the Answer Sheet from this book and return them with your completed Evaluation Form to CCH at the address below. You may also fax your Answer Sheet to CCH at 773-866-3084.

You may also go to **www.cchtestingcenter.com** to complete your Quizzer online.

**METHOD OF PAYMENT:**

☐ Check Enclosed   ☐ Visa   ☐ Master Card   ☐ AmEx

☐ Discover   ☐ CCH Account* _____

Card No. _____ Exp. Date _____

Signature _____

* Must provide CCH account number for this payment option

**EXPRESS GRADING:** Please fax my Course results to me by 5:00 p.m. the business day following your receipt of this Answer Sheet. By checking this box I authorize CCH to charge $19.00 for this service.

☐ Express Grading $19.00   Fax No. _____

**Mail or fax to:**

CCH Continuing Education Department
4025 W. Peterson Ave.
Chicago, IL 60646-6085
1-800-248-3248
Fax: 773-866-3084

PAGE 1 OF 2

TOP ACCOUNTING ISSUES FOR 2007 CPE COURSE          (0795-2)

# Module 2: Answer Sheet

Please answer the Multiple Choice questions by indicating the appropriate letter next to the corresponding number. Please answer the True/False questions by marking "T" or "F" next to the corresponding number.

| | | |
|---|---|---|
| 36. ⎯ | 48. ⎯ | 60. ⎯ |
| 37. ⎯ | 49. ⎯ | 61. ⎯ |
| 38. ⎯ | 50. ⎯ | 62. ⎯ |
| 39. ⎯ | 51. ⎯ | 63. ⎯ |
| 40. ⎯ | 52. ⎯ | 64. ⎯ |
| 41. ⎯ | 53. ⎯ | 65. ⎯ |
| 42. ⎯ | 54. ⎯ | 66. ⎯ |
| 43. ⎯ | 55. ⎯ | 67. ⎯ |
| 44. ⎯ | 56. ⎯ | 68. ⎯ |
| 45. ⎯ | 57. ⎯ | 69. ⎯ |
| 46. ⎯ | 58. ⎯ | 70. ⎯ |
| 47. ⎯ | 59. ⎯ | |

**Please complete the Evaluation Form (located after the Module 3 Answer Sheet) and return it with this Quizzer Answer Sheet to CCH at the address on the previous page. Thank you.**

TOP ACCOUNTING ISSUES FOR 2007 CPE COURSE     (0796-2)

# Module 3: Answer Sheet

NAME _____

COMPANY NAME _____

STREET _____

CITY, STATE, & ZIP CODE _____

BUSINESS PHONE NUMBER _____

E-MAIL ADDRESS _____

DATE OF COMPLETION _____

CFP REGISTRANT ID (for Certified Financial Planners) _____

On the next page, please answer the Multiple Choice questions by indicating the appropriate letter next to the corresponding number. Please answer the True/False questions by marking "T" or "F" next to the corresponding number.

A $70.00 processing fee wil be charged for each user submitting Module 3 for grading.

Please remove both pages of the Answer Sheet from this book and return them with your completed Evaluation Form to CCH at the address below. You may also fax your Answer Sheet to CCH at 773-866-3084.

You may also go to **www.cchtestingcenter.com** to complete your Quizzer online.

**METHOD OF PAYMENT:**

☐ Check Enclosed   ☐ Visa   ☐ Master Card   ☐ AmEx

☐ Discover   ☐ CCH Account* _____

Card No. _____ Exp. Date _____

Signature _____

* Must provide CCH account number for this payment option

**EXPRESS GRADING:** Please fax my Course results to me by 5:00 p.m. the business day following your receipt of this Answer Sheet. By checking this box I authorize CCH to charge $19.00 for this service.

☐ Express Grading $19.00   Fax No. _____

**CCH**
a Wolters Kluwer business

**Mail or fax to:**
CCH Continuing Education Department
4025 W. Peterson Ave.
Chicago, IL 60646-6085
1-800-248-3248
Fax: 773-866-3084

TOP ACCOUNTING ISSUES FOR 2007 CPE COURSE          (0796-2)

# Module 3: Answer Sheet

Please answer the Multiple Choice questions by indicating the appropriate letter next to the corresponding number. Please answer the True/False questions by marking "T" or "F" next to the corresponding number.

| | | |
|---|---|---|
| 71. —— | 85. —— | 99. —— |
| 72. —— | 86. —— | 100. —— |
| 73. —— | 87. —— | 101. —— |
| 74. —— | 88. —— | 102. —— |
| 75. —— | 89. —— | 103. —— |
| 76. —— | 90. —— | 104. —— |
| 77. —— | 91. —— | 105. —— |
| 78. —— | 92. —— | 106. —— |
| 79. —— | 93. —— | 107. —— |
| 80. —— | 94. —— | 108. —— |
| 81. —— | 95. —— | 109. —— |
| 82. —— | 96. —— | 110. —— |
| 83. —— | 97. —— | |
| 84. —— | 98. —— | |

**Please complete the Evaluation Form (located after the Module 3 Answer Sheet) and return it with this Quizzer Answer Sheet to CCH at the address on the previous page. Thank you.**

TOP ACCOUNTING ISSUES FOR 2007 CPE COURSE          (0996-2)

# Evaluation Form

Please take a few moments to fill out and mail or fax this evaluation to CCH so that we can better provide you with the type of self-study programs you want and need. Thank you.

## About This Program

1. Please circle the number that best reflects the extent of your agreement with the following statements:

|  | Strongly Agree | | | | Strongly Disagree |
|---|---|---|---|---|---|
| a. The Course objectives were met. | 5 | 4 | 3 | 2 | 1 |
| b. This Course was comprehensive and organized. | 5 | 4 | 3 | 2 | 1 |
| c. The content was current and technically accurate. | 5 | 4 | 3 | 2 | 1 |
| d. This Course was timely and relevant. | 5 | 4 | 3 | 2 | 1 |
| e. The prerequisite requirements were appropriate. | 5 | 4 | 3 | 2 | 1 |
| f. This Course was a valuable learning experience. | 5 | 4 | 3 | 2 | 1 |
| g. The Course completion time was appropriate. | 5 | 4 | 3 | 2 | 1 |

2. This Course was most valuable to me because of:

____ Continuing Education credit         ____ Convenience of format
____ Relevance to my practice/           ____ Timeliness of subject matter
     employment                          ____ Reputation of author
____ Price
____ Other (please specify) _____

3. How long did it take to complete this Course? (Please include the total time spent reading or studying reference materials and completing CPE Quizzer).

Module 1 ____          Module 2 ____          Module 3 ____

4. What do you consider to be the strong points of this Course?

5. What improvements can we make to this Course?

TOP ACCOUNTING ISSUES FOR 2007 CPE COURSE        (0996-2)

# Evaluation Form *cont'd*

## General Interests

1. Preferred method of self-study instruction:
   _____ Text   _____ Audio   _____ Computer-based/Multimedia   _____ Video

2. What specific topics would you like CCH to develop as self-study CPE programs?
   _____
   _____
   _____

3. Please list other topics of interest to you _____
   _____
   _____

## About You

1. Your profession:

   _____ CPA                    _____ Enrolled Agent
   _____ Attorney               _____ Tax Preparer
   _____ Financial Planner      _____ Other (please specify)
                                _____

2. Your employment:

   _____ Self-employed          _____ Public Accounting Firm
   _____ Service Industry       _____ Non-Service Industry
   _____ Banking/Finance        _____ Government
   _____ Education              _____ Other _____

3. Size of firm/corporation:

   _____ 1   _____ 2-5   _____ 6-10   _____ 11-20   _____ 21-50   _____ 51+

4. Your Name _____
   Firm/Company Name _____
   Address _____
   City, State, Zip Code _____
   E-mail Address _____

**THANK YOU FOR TAKING THE TIME TO COMPLETE THIS SURVEY!**

**NOTES**

# NOTES

# NOTES

# NOTES

**NOTES**

**NOTES**